Creating Colonial Williamsburg

Creating
COLONIAL
WILLIAMSBURG

ANDERS GREENSPAN

SMITHSONIAN INSTITUTION PRESS • Washington and London

EDITOR: Ruth G. Thomson
DESIGNER: Janice Wheeler

Library of Congress Cataloging-in-Publication Data
Greenspan, Anders.
   Creating Colonial Williamsburg / Anders Greenspan.
      p.   cm.
   Includes bibliographical references and index.
   ISBN 1-58834-026-0 (cloth : alk. paper) — ISBN 1-58834-001-5 (pbk. : alk. paper)
      1. Historic sites—Conservation and restoration—Virginia—Williamsburg—History.
      2. Historic buildings—Conservation and restoration—Virginia—Williamsburg—History.
      3. Architecture—Conservation and restoration—Virginia—Williamsburg—History.
      4. Williamsburg (Va.)—Buildings, structures, etc.   5. Williamsburg (Va.)—Antiquities.
      6. Williamsburg (Va.)—History.   7. Public history—Virginia—Williamsburg.   8. Colonial
      Williamsburg Foundation—History.   I. Title.
      F234.W7 G74   2002
      945.5'4252—dc21   2001034174

British Library Cataloging-in-Publication Data available

Manufactured in the United States of America
09 08 07 06 05 04 03 02   5 4 3 2 1

∞ The paper used in this publication meets the minimum requirements of the American
National Standard for Information Sciences—Permanence of Paper for Printed Library
Materials ANSI Z39.48-1984.

For permission to reproduce illustrations appearing in this book, please correspond directly
with the owners of the works, as listed in the individual captions. The Smithsonian
Institution Press does not retain reproduction rights for these illustrations individually or
maintain a file of addresses for photo sources.

To my parents

Contents

Acknowledgments

Any major project such as this one inevitably requires the assistance of many people. I greatly appreciate the wisdom and counsel of a number of individuals who helped in the completion of this task. Primary among those is John Bodnar, whose continued encouragement was an invaluable asset. Other historians who helped at various stages of this project were Casey Blake, D'Ann Campbell, Larry Friedman, Barry Karl, Michael McGerr, Bernard W. Sheehan, and Steven Stowe. Many who have written extensively on the Williamsburg restoration were instrumental in shaping my ideas, including Charles Hosmer, Mary Hoffschwelle, Michael Wallace, and Carroll Van West. My friends in Bloomington were excellent advisors, companions, and critics. Special thanks go to George Boudreau, Allis Bennett, Derek Johnson, and Greg Sumner. My teaching colleagues in Brookville were also important suppliers of advice and friendship, and many thanks are due to all, especially Carol Bauer and Fred Black.

I also received generous financial assistance from the Indiana University Center on Philanthropy through the Project on Governance of Nonprofit Organizations fellowship program. In addition, timely grants-in-aid from the Rockefeller Archive Center of Rockefeller University, the history department and graduate school of Indiana University, Bloomington, and a reduced teaching load and financial assistance from the Research Committee and the Dean of the Liberal Arts and Sciences at the C. W. Post Campus of Long Island University aided in the completion of this work.

The friendly and helpful staff at the Rockefeller Archive Center in Sleepy Hollow, New York, and the Archives and Records Department of the Colonial Williamsburg Foundation in Williamsburg, Virginia, were indispensable in acquiring the manuscript sources needed for this project. Thanks go especially to Emily Oakhill in Sleepy Hollow and Donna Cook, Steve Haller, and Cathy Grosfils in Williamsburg, whose ready assistance made my research faster and more pleasurable.

I am also indebted to the editorial staff at Smithsonian Institution Press, especially Mark Hirsch, Ruth Thomson, and Mary DeYoung, who were always ready to answer questions and to offer valuable advice. In addition, the press's anonymous readers provided many useful comments that helped to improve the manuscript.

Last, but not least, I must acknowledge the continuing debt I owe my father and mother, who have always encouraged me to do my best. Although my father did not live to see this work completed, I can still feel his presence encouraging me to pursue every avenue of inquiry and to learn all I can.

Introduction

For many Americans today, Colonial Williamsburg has become synonymous with television commercials that herald the sights and sounds of the restored colonial capital of Virginia. From cannons firing, to interpreters dressed in colonial costume, many visitors see Colonial Williamsburg as a quaint trip back to an earlier and "simpler" time. Strolling down the streets of the restored capital, tourists may believe that they are traveling back in time to the eighteenth century. Yet the reality of the colonial era was more complex, as is the story behind the re-creation of this eighteenth-century village. Many visitors to the restoration's social history museum may believe that this presentation has been Williamsburg's mission since its founding. This is not the case, however, as Colonial Williamsburg has gone through several manifestations in the last seventy-five years. From the dreams of its founders, to the work of the present-day historians who design its interpretative programs, Colonial Williamsburg has been many things to many people. This book will explain the transformation of Williamsburg, Virginia, from a small, neglected town in the 1920s to its present status of one of the United States's premier social history museums and tourist destinations. Along the way, Colonial Williamsburg was forced to change its presentation of the colonial era and to develop a greater understanding of the lives of the men and women who inhabited the southeastern part of Virginia in the eighteenth century.

In 1607 English settlers established the first permanent colony at Jamestown, Virginia, which was also the Virginia colony's first capital. The

settlement survived hard times and, following the harvesting of the first tobacco crop in 1617, grew with increasing prosperity. Many early Virginians
were white indentured servants who after their release moved northwest
and settled the area between the York and James Rivers, which was first
known as Middle Plantation. The burning of the statehouse in Jamestown
in 1698 forced the capital to move to this area, which was renamed Williamsburg after King William III. Much of the town was designed by a royal governor, Francis Nicholson, who took the liberty of naming two of the town's
major thoroughfares after himself. From 1699 until 1780, when the capital
was moved to Richmond, the town of Williamsburg was the most powerful
in Virginia. The Old Dominion, as it was commonly known, was the most
populous of the thirteen colonies, containing 230,000 residents by 1750,
more than 40 percent of whom were enslaved. By the time of the American
Revolution, Virginia held one-fifth of the total colonial population.[1]

Williamsburg was also the home of the College of William and Mary,
founded in 1693. The college, which was the colonies' second oldest institution of higher learning after Harvard College, attracted young men from
across Virginia. Although a college education was a rarity in colonial times,
young men of sufficient means who wished to practice law, the ministry, or
pedagogy made the trip to Williamsburg to attend the college. The Phi Beta
Kappa honor society was founded at William and Mary in 1776, a fact that
would play an important role in the area's twentieth-century restoration. Although Williamsburg's permanent population, about two thousand residents
throughout the eighteenth century, was divided among approximately 230
houses that made up the town's residences, the actual population varied
with the political season. It grew dramatically when the House of Burgesses,
the colony's lower legislative body, was in session. Because of this variation,
there were actually two Williamsburgs: a bustling capital during the legislative period, known as the "publick" time, and a less populated and quieter town during the rest of the year. Slaves composed about 50 percent of
the permanent population of the town, with relatively few free blacks in
residence. Williamsburg was, therefore, a relatively close-knit community
where most townspeople knew each other's businesses, families, and slaves.
This community included many who would later be idolized as the country's Founding Fathers. George Washington, Thomas Jefferson, Patrick
Henry, and George Wythe all lived in Williamsburg at one time or another;
perhaps the best-known relationship among these men is the teacher and
student bond between Wythe and Jefferson.[2]

Williamsburg in the eighteenth century took its direction from similar towns in Great Britain. The town's residents sought to emulate the styles and fashions of their British counterparts. Such professions as the wig maker and the silversmith demonstrated the desire for English finery and the ties the colonists had with the mother country. Slaves who served as house servants often dressed in livery, which was a rarity in the rest of the colony. Thus the town attempted to project an air of refinement not present anywhere else in Virginia. Williamsburg was a fully functioning community, but one that was constantly reliant on the outside world. Well into the 1760s, Virginians thought of themselves primarily as English men and women and loyal subjects of the king. Legislatively, however, most colonists resisted the control of the British Parliament, where they had no representation. Colonists felt that they were represented by their local colonial governments and were subjects of the king.

The presence of the royal governor in Williamsburg was a clear link with Britain and the king, who was responsible for appointing the colony's chief executive. Prominent colonists eagerly sought invitations to the numerous social gatherings hosted by the king's representative in Virginia. The governor could make all civil and military appointments, as well as religious ones. He could grant pardons and was also the commander-in-chief of the military forces in the colony. The House of Burgesses moved by 1750 to limit some of these powers, but the governor still held the right to dissolve the legislature if he so chose.[3]

Naturally, Williamsburg was also home to individuals who were not so prominent. Many people, both white and black, worked to provide the housing, clothing, food, and labor for those who could spend their time concentrating on education, social engagements, and political life. These workers, free and enslaved, were the unheralded members of the community—yet without them the town would not have been able to function. Through their efforts, Williamsburg grew and flourished. They worked in a variety of occupations, from menial labor to skilled crafts, and provided the town with everything from fine household wares to basic items such as barrels, harnesses, candles, soap, and clothing. They were the lifeblood of the economy and played vital roles in assuring the colony's survival.

Williamsburg was, therefore, a complex community with people at all strata from the royal governor all the way down to slaves. These individuals formed a living town full of gaiety and wealth, poverty and sadness. Their livelihoods were inextricably linked to each other. This dependency was rarely acknowledged by the privileged groups but was certainly understood by those further down on the socioeconomic ladder. In addition, the rigidity of society made it difficult for one to rise significantly above one's station. Slaves were almost always chattel for life, women were considered inferior to men, and most men of the laboring class found it almost impossible to move into the realm of the educated elite. Commonly held perceptions of America as the land of opportunity were borne out less often than many would like to believe. Although class lines were generally not as rigid as they were in Britain, and the availability of land offered the possibility of financial gain, there was no guarantee of success.

Although later generations would focus strongly on Williamsburg's political heritage, in the eighteenth century politics was only one part of town life. Most residents did not participate in the colony's political process and therefore were necessarily outsiders in legislative matters. Life was repetitive and monotonous for most of the town's residents, who were consumed by duties and chores and had scant opportunities for recreation, although Williamsburg did possess a race track, and dramatic presentations attracted large audiences. Both white and black residents attended these plays, but African Americans were forbidden from occupying box seats and were forced to content themselves with the pit, which also accommodated less prosperous whites. As was common in the eighteenth century, the audience often spoke back to the actors, removing the imaginary fourth wall that prevents modern-day viewers from communicating with the actors on stage.[4]

Taverns, such as the Raleigh and Wetherburn, were also places of recreation, bringing together men of different classes, although there was generally a division between "gentlemen" and others who might partake in food, drink, and merriment. Catering to a strictly male clientele, these inns were particularly attractive for single men or those looking for an evening away from home, as well as travelers who needed overnight accommodations. As one of the few places available where one could privately assemble a large group, taverns were also common meeting places in colonial times. Few other private eighteenth-century buildings were large enough for this purpose. In fact, the members of the House of Burgesses adjourned to the Raleigh Tavern when they were unexpectedly dissolved by the royal governor, Lord Botetourt, in 1769.[5]

News came to the residents through the town newspaper, the *Virginia Gazette*. The paper was established by William Parks in 1736 and provided information about local events such as runaway slaves, slave auctions, newly acquired items in the local shops, and events from the town, colony, and world. English newspapers, weeks or months old, were also available in town, but their circulation was quite limited. A large number of town residents, including most slaves and many women, were probably illiterate, so information also traveled by word of mouth. Since news from Europe commonly took six weeks to reach the New World in colonial times, the information that the colonists received about events in London and Britain was often outdated, as was the information that the British received from the colonies.[6]

When the British Parliament began to enact laws such as the Stamp Act of 1765, necessitated by the large expenditures of the Seven Years War and the high cost of maintaining British troops in the thirteen colonies, colonists were forced to pay taxes to Britain every time they purchased certain paper goods, including newspapers and playing cards. This taxation caused many colonists to feel that their liberties were being circumscribed. As the control of the British grew stronger, American resistance did as well. Williamsburg, as the capital of the largest colony, received a good deal of attention from those who wanted to gauge colonial reaction to the imposition of these new taxes. Patrick Henry delivered his famous Caesar-Brutus speech in the House of Burgesses, warning King George III to pay attention to the desires of his subjects or to face the consequences. The Stamp Act was repealed shortly thereafter, only to be replaced by the Townshend Acts of 1767, which placed an import tariff on products such as paint, glass, and tea. Virginians demonstrated their disaffection with their mother country by refusing to purchase products supplied by Britain, resorting instead to less refined domestically produced products or items smuggled in from other countries.[7]

The British reacted by withdrawing all such duties except the tax on tea. The implementation of the Tea Act in 1773, which essentially forced the colonists to purchase the tea of the British East India Company, led to the Boston Tea Party and eventually to the closing of the port of Boston and the imposition of the Intolerable Acts in 1774. When word arrived in Virginia of this act, the House of Burgesses set aside a day for fasting, humiliation, and prayer in solidarity with the people of Massachusetts. This move angered the king's representative, Lord Dunmore, who like Lord Botetourt five years before, dissolved the legislature. Tensions grew higher throughout most of the colonies as the British government insisted on its right to tax the colonists. Fueled by a growing animosity toward the British in Massachusetts, the colonies went to war in April 1775 to protect their rights as Englishmen turned Americans. George Washington, a Virginian and former Williamsburg resident during his time in the House of Burgesses, was chosen to be the commander-in-chief of the Continental Army. Shortly over a year later, Thomas Jefferson was chosen to be the primary author of the Declaration of Independence. Williamsburg, therefore, could lay claim to two of the most important men who worked to gain American freedom. But in 1780 Governor Thomas Jefferson, with the consent of the state assembly, moved the capital west to Richmond. This was done to help preserve the capital from British attack, to give it a more central location, and to bring it closer to Jefferson's home, Monticello, which was outside Charlottesville.[8]

Williamsburg then began 146 years of anonymity, a former capital that modern times had left behind. Military campaigns were fought in the area during the Civil War, including the Battle of Williamsburg in 1862, but aside from that, little attention was paid to the small town. In the early twentieth century, Williamsburg was often described as a backwater. It possessed inadequate sewage and electricity, as well as large holes in some streets that made them impassable for automobiles. Although most residents were familiar with their town's historical importance, many Americans were unaware of Williamsburg's past. Many of the original buildings from colonial days were still standing; the Public Magazine, the Courthouse, and George Wythe's home were the most notable of these. But a large number of colonial-era structures were in disrepair or had been modified from their original form during the nineteenth century to reflect Victorian architectural tastes. Some, like the Capitol and the Governor's Palace, only had their foundations remaining. Newer buildings had also sprung up, as well as gas stations and telephone poles, destroying the colonial ambiance of the town and creating an odd setting in which older buildings stood alongside modern ones. Thus modernity masked the town's colonial character to such a degree that a passerby would not necessarily notice its rich heritage.

As remote as the eighteenth century was, however, the past was easier to reinvigorate in Williamsburg than in most of the other colonial capitals, which had been greatly developed in the intervening years. Boston and Philadelphia, for example, had changed far too much to permit them to be returned to their eighteenth-century appearance. That task would therefore fall to Williamsburg and the men who wished to rejuvenate its history. They would have many remaining buildings to work with—eighty-eight in all. But other major structures would have to be rebuilt, the Governor's Palace, Raleigh Tavern, and the Capitol among them. The challenge would rest not only in re-creating the town's physical presence but also in promoting a sense of the eighteenth-century community of Williamsburg.

This second task would prove even more daunting than the first because it required the ability to capture the feeling of life from a period that was long gone. To a certain extent this re-creation of an eighteenth-century community could be accomplished through the use of working businesses that demonstrated trades such as carpentry, silversmithing, and wig making. In addition, the use of guides, and in later years costumed interpreters, would enhance the verisimilitude of the town. Yet problems would inevitably exist because re-creating the past is difficult. The greatest challenge would be the portrayal and discussion of slavery. This "peculiar institution" would be a thorn in the restoration's side for most of its first half century. Although slavery was virtually ignored at first, by the 1950s and 1960s many visitors began to notice the lack of discussion of African Americans. By the 1970s, Williamsburg was assailed on all sides for failing to do an adequate job in explaining the lives of half of the town's colonial population. Why it failed to adequately present the lives of slaves, along with working-class people and, to a large extent, women, is one of the questions this study seeks to answer.

To better understand the restoration's presentation of the past, it is necessary to comprehend those individuals whose vision created Colonial Williamsburg. Men such as John D. Rockefeller Jr. (JDR Jr.) and Rev. W. A. R. Goodwin dreamed of creating a wholly peaceful world that stressed the rights of the individual and the importance of representative government. JDR Jr. assumed that a democratically led nation would be far less belligerent than one that was controlled by one individual or a select group. He also favored the promotion of the beauty of the past and to this end helped to restore Louis XIV's palace at Versailles. He also supported the Sleepy Hollow restorations in upstate New York and the building of the Cloisters, a branch of the Metropolitan Museum of Art in upper Manhattan. With his almost unlimited financial resources JDR Jr. could easily make his dreams a reality. Throughout the 1920s, along with other philanthropists such as Henry Ford and Edward Harkness, JDR Jr. pursued an ambitious program to help re-create a lost world that he believed needed to be better appreciated and understood.[9]

Rev. W. A. R. Goodwin served as rector of Bruton Parish Church during the early years of the twentieth century. He was born in Richmond in 1869 and grew up on a farm in Nelson County, Virginia. Goodwin was educated at Roanoke College in Salem, Virginia, and entered the Virginia Theological Seminary in 1890. His first ecclesiastical assignment was in Petersburg, Virginia, and he accepted the rectorship of Bruton Parish Church in Williamsburg in 1903 on the condition that the interior of the building be returned to its colonial form. He oversaw the initial restoration of the church starting in 1905 and had dreams of rebuilding the whole town along those lines at a later date. Upon returning to Williamsburg from Rochester, New York, in 1923, Goodwin noted with sadness the growing decay of the once glorious colonial city. The notion that Williamsburg should be nothing more than a run-down village troubled him greatly. He dreamed that Williamsburg's past glory could be restored and that people could once again see the beautiful town of the eighteenth century instead of the dilapidated one of the twentieth. He also thought that a restored Williamsburg would serve as an introduction to the history of colonial Virginia and colonial North America. This introduction would provide Americans with an appreciation of the trials of the eighteenth century, as well as helping to imbue the modern era with a renewed sense of Americanism. Such an understanding was important because, in Goodwin's opinion, the divisions in American society emanated from the country's heterogeneous heritage. He believed that if all Americans felt that they had a common background and a united national purpose, there would be a stronger sense of national community and less of a likelihood that socialists or anarchists could destroy the country's economic and political framework.[10]

The plan that Goodwin envisioned, an accurate reconstruction of a whole colonial town, would require huge financial backing. The prominent philanthropists of the day, Henry Ford and JDR Jr., both possessed the capital to fund such a venture, but did they wish to spend the funds necessary to complete such a project? Since Goodwin felt that much of the modernization of Williamsburg was due to the automobile, he decided to ask help from the person who had benefited the most from its invention: Henry Ford. Instead of contacting Goodwin directly, however, Ford had his office send a note indicating that he was not sufficiently interested in Goodwin's proposal. A similar proposition to Ford's brother, William, also met with failure, forcing Goodwin to think more seriously about Rockefeller. Ford's reluctance to relinquish his Greenfield Village project, the primary reason why he turned down Goodwin's proposal, turned out to be a stroke of good luck for the restoration. Ford had a limited view of the past, which centered primarily on the history of industrialization. As he commented, "[H]istory is bunk. . . . I'm going to start up a museum and give people a *true* [emphasis in original] picture of the development of our country. . . . We're going to build a museum that's going to show industrial history, and it won't be bunk."[11]

Although his fortune was made from oil, JDR Jr. was not interested in industrial history. Rather, he preferred to return to the pre-industrial past, feeling that it possessed superior attributes to the present day. He was also a perfectionist of the highest order and took the greatest care in most things, even down to the signing of his name. For JDR Jr., if something was to be done, it had to be done properly or not at all. This insistence on accuracy, authenticity, and precision was a quality that had served him well throughout his life. Able to afford virtually anything in the world he desired, he insisted on high quality. He combined this need for perfection with a desire to better his family's reputation. He viewed the chance to raise the standing of the Rockefeller name as one of his primary missions in life and sought to do so through a string of generous philanthropic endeavors.[12]

Born in 1874, the only son of John D. and Laura Spelman Rockefeller and the youngest of four children, JDR Jr. had been groomed to take over his father's position at the head of Standard Oil. As a youngster, however, he did not seem to possess his father's drive to acquire wealth and power—perhaps because his family already had all the wealth and power one could desire. Cloistered at home with his mother and three older sisters, JDR Jr. became more proficient at traditional feminine tasks, such as sewing, than masculine ones. He emerged as a sensitive and sheltered young man who was introspective and moral.[13]

Later in life, he and his wife, Abby Aldrich Rockefeller, would donate millions to the Museum of Modern Art and contribute substantial amounts to promote Native American and folk art. The artistic aspect of Williamsburg attracted Rockefeller, as well as the possibility of establishing a positive family legacy. Over the years, from the start of the project in 1926 to his death in 1960, Williamsburg became an important part of his schedule; he usually spent one month there in the spring and again in the fall. These trips gave him the chance to survey the progress of the work and to get a feel for the town he was so instrumental in re-creating. JDR Jr. was deeply interested in the progress of the restoration and often consulted with officials and architects on the scene as to the growth and presentation of the restored village. He saw Colonial Williamsburg as his most important project, greater than Rockefeller Center or any of his other philanthropic works. This view gave him an affinity with the town and the people that he and the residents of Williamsburg found mutually beneficial.[14]

Williamsburg served to portray JDR Jr.'s ideal of the past and to repudiate the society that his father had wrought. While Rockefeller Center expressed his role as the heir of one of the country's great industrial fortunes, Williamsburg demonstrated his personal ideals. By restoring a colonial town, and with it an appreciation of traditional values, JDR Jr. sought to distance himself from his father's world of industrial might. He preferred his legacy to be one of quaint manners, cobblestone streets, and a tribute to those individuals who had created a nation based on liberty, democracy, and the worth of the individual. The senior Rockefeller, however, never discussed the work at Williamsburg with his son and apparently took little interest in this particular philanthropic project.[15]

Even before the 1920s and 1930s, however, the idea of the greatness of early America was demonstrated in the colonial revival of the late nineteenth century. At the end of the 1800s, a fascination with the American past promoted a type of "Americanism," the elements of which were a recognition and glorification of the Revolutionary period. In addition, Americans began to focus on American art and furniture, including armchairs, sofas, and desks. As far back as the early nineteenth century, novels and plays glorified the Revolution and the Founding Fathers. Fourth of July orations in the Jacksonian era not only spoke reverently of the founders but also expressed concern for the future of the republic.[16]

A lingering fear of failure of the noble experiment of American republicanism prompted many to attempt to keep the glory of the Revolution alive and well. When the Civil War threatened to wrench a growing nation apart, Abraham Lincoln evoked the memory of the Revolution in the Gettysburg Address, hoping that this great conflict would see a "new birth of freedom." After American ideals survived the carnage of the war, waves of immigrants and economic depressions helped cast doubt on the cultural integrity of the country and the future of the American cause. In such an atmosphere, a revival of colonial lifestyles and values seemed to be the ideal panacea for the country's ills. As immigrants arrived speaking a multitude of foreign tongues and practicing an array of unusual customs, a common response was to promote values that members of established families held to be traditionally American. Most of the societies that embodied these notions emerged in the 1890s, including the Daughters of the American Revolution, the Colonial Dames of America, and the Society of Mayflower Descendants.[17]

The trend toward colonial revival furnishings in the early years of the twentieth century also demonstrated an attempt by Americans to recapture a fleeting past. If they were able to create an eighteenth-century atmosphere at home, perhaps they would be able to instill traditional values in their friends and families. In a nation increasingly influenced by immigrants, older American families looked to traditional furnishings and household designs to express their heritage and their fealty to national values. By separating themselves from the crowds of recent immigrants walking America's streets, they acted as keepers of the past and its ideals.[18]

In building styles as well, many Americans began to turn to colonial-style structures as they developed a greater understanding and interest in the architecture of the eighteenth century. In this way, people could create dwellings that replicated the styles of ancestors or admired colonial figures. These buildings also served as bulwarks against the perceived intrusion of foreign peoples and unacceptable ideas. Although initially viewed as a fad, this trend took root and grew in popularity throughout the first three decades of the twentieth century. Communities took it upon themselves to promote their colonial heritage, in some cases to an overwhelming degree, perhaps creating a stronger colonial legacy than actually existed in the eighteenth century.[19]

In addition, many Americans looked to the nation's Founding Fathers for inspiration in troubled times. During much of the twentieth century, George Washington stood for the American ideals of honesty, courage, and the strength of the individual. Washington was portrayed as embodying these qualities throughout his life, whether or not he truly did; indeed, the reality of Washington's behavior was less important than people's perception of him. His ability to inspire Americans and to give them a sense of national pride and purpose was the most important thing. Goodwin and Rockefeller sought to promote these perceptions about Washington and the other Founding Fathers in American society through the restoration of Colonial Williamsburg. By invigorating the present with ideals from the past, Williamsburg's founders hoped to regenerate a lost Americanism that prided itself on the accomplishments and sacrifices of those who had lived in the eighteenth century. Since the former Virginia capital had been at least a part-time home to so many of these individuals, including Washington, Thomas Jefferson, Patrick Henry, and town resident George Wythe, it was natural to promote the memory of their actions by restoring and rebuilding those structures that were associated with them, thereby creating a shrine to their deeds.[20]

National shrines have played an important role in the way that Americans have perceived their country's past. The Washington Monument, the Lincoln Memorial, Monticello, and Mount Vernon exemplify the ways in which Americans have used buildings to promote a sense of national identity and purpose. These buildings have substituted for a national religious orthodoxy by providing Americans with places to honor the accomplishments of their nation's forefathers. A newer creation like Colonial Williamsburg, which combined historic architecture with famous and inspirational individuals, served the need of a generation that some Americans, like John D. Rockefeller 3d (JDR 3d), believed had lost the essentials of the American character.[21]

The eldest of JDR Jr.'s five sons, JDR 3d was born in 1906. As the principal heir to the family name, JDR 3d felt an obligation to continue the family's role in philanthropy, a tradition that was started by his grandfather. Yet he took a more aggressive approach to the promotion of the family's ideology, believing that sites like Williamsburg should not simply be used passively to inform but actively to indoctrinate visitors in the importance of American ideals. He felt that his countrymen needed a place to reorient themselves toward an appreciation of past struggles and ideals, and Colonial Williamsburg filled that need. In Williamsburg, the glory and hardships of the past had been resurrected for a population that had no living memory of these events. The restoration created a chance to physically interact with a sanitized version of the past and to gain a better appreciation of the restoration founders' view of what it meant to be an American. Indeed, a variety of philanthropic efforts at re-creating the past, such as Henry Ford's Greenfield Village, were aimed at eliciting a sense of patriotism in Americans. Although many of these movements were on a much smaller scale than Colonial Williamsburg, the principal argument remained the same— namely, that if historic sites were not preserved, Americans would lose their sense of history as well as an understanding of their past.[22]

At the core of this concept of Americanism was the belief in the superiority of the past and its ideals. Through the representation of the "great white men" of the eighteenth century, some Americanists of the early 1900s hoped to shape a modern society that embodied not only industrial might but also the values of yesteryear. They effected a combination of both Jeffersonian and Hamiltonian ideals, and in doing so they wished to create an America that was not only industrially powerful but also virtuous. For the restoration's founders, it was time that Americans, native and foreign born, recognized their unique heritage and used it in their everyday lives, emphasizing those beliefs that the founders felt were uniquely American in origin. The past had been used to promote American values for more than one hundred years before the restoration began, and Rockefeller and Goodwin drew on this use, adding to it their own notions of what American history should represent. These ideals, including democracy and republican government, needed to be preserved while at the same time educating Americans in the meaning of their country. From Colonial Williamsburg's inception to the present day, a variety of manifestations of Americanism have bolstered its role as a shrine to American beliefs.[23]

The decade of the 1920s was a period of upheaval and uncertainty in American life, and even before the restoration was complete, the ideals that Colonial Williamsburg was to promote were considered highly important. The growth of technology, rapid urbanization, and the emphasis on science meant that the traditional world of the nineteenth century was about to disappear. For those who valued the ideals of this earlier period, modern America must have been quite alarming. Americanism, therefore, was important in maintaining a hold on earlier ways; the fear of the spread of Bolshevism following World War I and the concerns of American nativists enhanced the importance of this ideology. Williamsburg stood as a symbol of the cornerstones of American values that promoted a respect for the past in an ever-changing world.[24]

JDR Jr. and W. A. R. Goodwin also meant Colonial Williamsburg to be an educational landmark. Its teaching was meant to be subtle, though clear in its purpose. When people were able to transport themselves back in time to the eighteenth century, they would gain a better appreciation of the importance of the movement for independence. This change in people's perception of the past was clear from early visitors. No longer was history the dry, boring stuff of textbooks. In Williamsburg history was novel and exciting, as the restoration inspired people to learn more about how their country began.

Colonial Williamsburg persisted in following this path of public education throughout much of the Cold War. During World War II, soldiers and sailors from nearby military bases were the guests of the Rockefellers in one-day education programs to inform them of the values that the armed forces were fighting for in Europe and Asia. These educational sessions for male and female members of the armed forces strove to elicit patriotic feelings, as well as to keep the restoration active during a period of low civilian participation due to wartime travel restrictions. Apparently the restoration's efforts were successful, since many servicemen subsequently wrote of their great appreciation for the struggles of the past after seeing Williamsburg. In letters full of grandiloquent phrases, a true respect for history emerged. Many soldiers and sailors who visited the restoration during the war returned afterward, bringing their wives and families, and introducing a new generation to the town and its message. As middle-class families journeyed to the town in large numbers following the end of World War II, the restoration helped to institutionalize a respect for the past in American life. The restored town also emerged as a major tourist destination for couples and families, many of whom made trips to surrounding historic sites or stopped on their way to Florida and other southern destinations. This role highlighted a continuing issue for the restoration, for although Colonial Williamsburg wished to represent the eighteenth century to its visitors, it also wanted them to enjoy their stays and to come back. But combining a historical restoration with a vacation destination necessarily impaired Colonial Williamsburg's presentation of eighteenth-century life.[25]

The town of Williamsburg and its inhabitants were important actors in this historical drama, too. For many of them, the restoration meant a complete change of life. People sold their homes and lost schools and businesses all in the name of the project's success. Many saw the changes in the town as positive, but there was also a touch of sadness in their recollections in addition to the hostility projected by a few community members. For while Williamsburg itself was immortalized, many families, both black and white, lost part of their heritage. Residents spoke of leaving Williamsburg and returning later to find a ghost town devoid of its last 150 years of history. It was as though time had stopped, yet the families of Williamsburg grew older, losing a large section of their past, which had to be sacrificed to return the town to its eighteenth-century form.

As a venture whose primary goal was not to make money, Colonial Williamsburg clearly needed to have another purpose—one in keeping with its position as a living museum. First as a bulwark against foreign ideas in the 1920s and as a promoter of individual initiative in the 1930s, then as an active participant in World War II and the Cold War, the restoration sought to keep its role alive, tailoring its presentation to the political climate of the times. It did so by bringing to the American public an inspiration to fight for traditional American values and to encourage the growth of democracy and representative government throughout the world. By the 1970s, however, this traditional interpretation of the colonial town and its people had grown stale. The changing social climate of the country forced Colonial Williamsburg to incorporate the history of African Americans, women, and the working class into its presentation. That would not be an easy task, however, because the restoration ran the risk of offending some of its strongest supporters. It also faced the wrath of critics who argued that this new line of interpretation was insufficient in detailing the lives of these previously neglected groups. Colonial Williamsburg was forced to become a social history museum, but it did not leave behind all of its previous message. To an extent, the old message was grafted uncomfortably onto the new, which failed to please all of the restoration's patrons. The restoration also faced monetary problems, which forced it to reexamine its presentations and later to form alliances with nearby theme parks that provided more amusement than education.

Overall, an examination of the transformation of Colonial Williamsburg is an excellent means of understanding the changing modern American character. In its role as a shrine that was conceived by a cleric and the heir to the nation's greatest industrial fortune and that has become one of the nation's leading centers for the study of colonial life, the restoration serves as a useful conduit for understanding the changing nature of twentieth-century American society. In the history of the past seventy-five years of the restoration, we can see not only a changing understanding of the past but also a reflection of the nature of American life. As a result, by studying the transformation of Colonial Williamsburg we can better understand the United States during the last three-quarters of the twentieth century.[26]

I

The Birth of a Dream

Reverend W. A. R. Goodwin intended to catapult Williamsburg onto the national scene through a restoration and reconstruction of its historic buildings, using the town's architectural landmarks to recall its prestigious roots in the eighteenth century. Although the massive infusion of outside funding needed to accomplish this endeavor would inevitably set up a confrontation between the local population and the restoration forces, the importance of the restoration was so strong that there was good justification for going ahead with the plan. The result would be the rebirth of Virginia's eighteenth-century capital as a landmark of what Goodwin and JDR Jr. believed to be the core values of American society.

In the early years of the twentieth century, Williamsburg was a vestige of its former self. Although the town was not wholly divided by race, the interaction between whites and African Americans was circumscribed as much by custom as by law. In a locale where poverty was the rule rather than the exception, African Americans generally bore a greater burden than did whites. On the whole, however, relationships between the races were amicable, and Williamsburg was never a place of great racial tension, even during the charged years of the civil rights movement that disrupted so much of the American south.[1]

During the first two decades of the twentieth century, the "keepers of the past" in Williamsburg were the members of the Association for the Preservation of Virginia Antiquities (APVA). Modeled on the Mount Vernon Ladies' Association, which was created in 1856 to preserve the home and memory of George Washington, the APVA admitted members who were in good standing in the community but successfully protected the association from those who were not "in society." The APVA served primarily as a means to preserve genteel culture against a variety of changes in the post–Civil War era. By keeping the memory of the past alive, upper-class Virginians were able to hold onto a vestige of their history. This desire to venerate the past helped smooth the transition of Williamsburg from a small, isolated backwater early in the century to a town that by the 1930s embraced a full-scale restoration and rebuilding process. The APVA initially controlled some of the town's historic properties, such as the foundations of the Capitol and the unrestored Public Magazine, which Colonial Williamsburg would eventually want to present under its own auspices. In general, the relations between the APVA and Colonial Williamsburg were amicable. The APVA felt that even though JDR Jr. and his associates were Northerners, they were helping to re-create a period of history of which many locals were especially proud. In addition, many APVA members were pleased to see the restoration and rebuilding of many of the town's historic buildings. Nevertheless, they tended to resent the power and influence that this new Rockefeller corporation wielded. In the process, this new organization would take much of the original passion away from previous attempts at local historic preservation and make Williamsburg into a corporate entity.[2]

Although the APVA was primarily interested in maintaining Williamsburg's historic sites as a reminder of the town's glorious past, W. A. R. Goodwin was more interested in the ways that Williamsburg could be used as an educational landmark. Goodwin believed that America needed to go back to its roots for a regeneration of the true national spirit. In his book on Bruton Parish Church, he wrote of the role that Williamsburg and the nearby historic sites of Jamestown and Yorktown could play in such a movement: "Here the value of our free institutions may be measured. . . . [F]or on this soil are the tokens which recall the toil, the tears, the blood, and the birth pangs of our civilization and our liberty."[3]

Goodwin had conceived of the importance of Williamsburg and the local area early in the century during the restoration of Bruton Parish Church, but it was not until he returned to Williamsburg in 1923 from a pastorate in Rochester, New York, that he began to implement his plans for Williamsburg's rebirth. He wanted a more sophisticated and organized plan of restoration and preservation than was possible under the APVA. While he was formulating this plan, Goodwin attended a Phi Beta Kappa dinner in New

African American youths playing at the Williamsburg railroad yard, ca. 1900 (Courtesy of the Colonial Williamsburg Foundation)

York City in February 1924 where he first met JDR Jr. He initially asked the philanthropist only for the funds to build Phi Beta Kappa Memorial Hall at the College of William and Mary, where the honorary society was founded in 1776. But his plans for a broader participation by JDR Jr. were already under way. In late 1924 Goodwin founded the Colonial Holding Corporation, along with two other prominent town residents, attorney Channing Hall, and William and Mary law professor William Shewmake. This organization was set up to buy buildings that Goodwin wanted to acquire for the restoration. JDR Jr. and his family first informally visited the Tidewater area in the spring of 1926 and gained a better appreciation for the area and its historic significance. When JDR Jr. attended the dedication of the Phi Beta Kappa Memorial Hall at the College of William and Mary in the fall of that year, Goodwin attempted to lure him into his vision of a restored Williamsburg. Goodwin slowly impressed JDR Jr. with the beauty of the town but refrained from asking for a specific financial commitment. Later during that visit, JDR Jr. agreed to the hiring of an architect to pre-

Mrs. George P. Coleman, wife of Williamsburg mayor George
P. Coleman, and her daughters, Janet and Cynthia, ca. 1910
(Courtesy of the Colonial Williamsburg Foundation)

pare drawings that would depict a restored Williamsburg, but that would be
the extent of his involvement for the time being.[4]

As was common for him, JDR Jr. did not make the decision to mount the
restoration in haste. He carefully considered the amount of money that
would have to be spent and the value of the project after it was completed.
His early correspondence with Goodwin demonstrated great interest in the
restoration but a reluctance to firmly commit to it. In writing to Goodwin
on 29 November 1926, JDR Jr. thanked the rector for the assistance shown
to him in getting the project started with the understanding that "I am committed to nothing, either now or later on." He went on to say that this
arrangement "is greatly appreciated by me and will make any such consideration of the problem as we may jointly give it a pleasure entirely free from
any possible embarrassment."[5]

Duke of Gloucester Street before the restoration, 1920s (Courtesy of the Colonial Williamsburg Foundation)

Impressed with what Williamsburg could become, JDR Jr. was slowly drawn into Goodwin's vision and in December 1926 authorized the purchase of the Ludwell-Paradise House, a noted Williamsburg property from the early eighteenth century. The architectural firm of Perry, Shaw, and Hepburn of Boston was employed to draw up preliminary plans, while Goodwin continued purchasing properties in the historic area. Buoyed by successful land purchases and an enthusiastic Goodwin, JDR Jr. had decided to support the project completely. This commitment would entail purchasing virtually all of the private residences and businesses along the Duke of Gloucester Street, the main thoroughfare in colonial times. Eventually, the restoration would control almost all the properties in a one-square-mile area of the town. JDR Jr. wrote to Col. Arthur Woods, a close associate and the first president of the restoration, that the purpose of the project was "to restore Williamsburg, so far as that may be possible, to what it was in the old colonial days and to make it a great centre for historical study and inspiration." JDR Jr. realized that the restoration would cost at least $3 million and possibly even $4 or $5 million. Little could he have predicted that twenty-five years later the figure would approach $30 million, with a need of $15 million more.[6]

JDR Jr.'s initial involvement in Williamsburg had to remain a secret; otherwise he would have been forced to pay highly inflated prices for the houses he wished to acquire for the restoration. This fact forced Goodwin to be the front man for the purchasing effort, which led to suspicion as a less-than-prosperous clergyman was attempting to buy large tracts of the town. Goodwin's story was that a small amount of money had been provided to him to preserve major historic sites in the name of the College of William and Mary. But as the number of houses he purchased increased, this activity did not go unnoticed in the community, and rumors started to circulate as to who was actually behind this large effort. Local residents thought it might be Henry Ford or Harvey Firestone, both prominent industrialists of the era. They realized that to purchase such a large section of the town would require financial means far beyond those of an ordinary individual.[7]

Goodwin wrote to express his concerns to JDR Jr. in December 1927, after an article in the *Richmond Times-Dispatch* suggested that JDR Jr. was part of the plan to buy large tracts of Williamsburg. The publicity at this time was of particular concern as Goodwin was about to close several large real estate deals and any rumor of Rockefeller money would probably send prices sky high. The rector personally approached many businessmen, encouraging them not to sell their property to real estate shysters but to deal only with him, thereby keeping prices reasonable.[8]

To calm fears and to gain support from local businessmen, Goodwin wrote an open letter that December to clarify misconceptions and to put many rumors to rest. He assured these entrepreneurs that his recent purchases would not do great damage to their financial interests. "It will be clearly to the interest of all business and professional men to cooperate in the plan which is being worked out," he wrote. Goodwin sought to acquire support from town leaders early on, hoping that their backing would help him sell the idea of the restoration to the rest of the town.[9]

Despite attempts to keep JDR Jr.'s identity a secret, his name became more and more closely associated with the process as Goodwin continued to buy more houses. Townspeople speculated that only a man with the wealth of a Rockefeller could possess the capital needed to buy up almost a whole town in Virginia. Goodwin's ability to keep JDR Jr.'s identity a secret was quite remarkable, as was his ability to make such a large number of purchases and deal with groups as diverse as the APVA and the College of William and Mary. At a segregated town meeting on 12 June 1928, Goodwin finally disclosed that JDR Jr. was purchasing the properties with an eye toward restoring the town to its colonial state. In so doing, Goodwin told the assembled townspeople, JDR Jr. would present to the people of the

United States a monument to the ideals and self-sacrifice of those who strove for American independence over a century before.[10]

The reaction of most of the attendees was supportive, with little open opposition to the sale, once the purchaser and his motives had been revealed, as the vote of 150 for the project and 5 against it indicated. Maj. Samuel D. Freeman, chairman of the school board, felt that both sides of the question should be aired, however, and rose to express "the minority side." He asked the people of Williamsburg to question what would happen after the transfer had taken place and the land that they once had owned was in the hands of a private corporation: "[H]ave you all been hypnotized by five million dollars dangled before your eyes? Can any of you talk back to five million dollars?"[11]

Furthermore, he wondered, what would happen once the project passed out of the control of Goodwin and JDR Jr. He cautioned the townspeople to consider some issues that he felt had been ignored. He asked, "[W]ill you not be in the position of a butterfly pinned to a card in a glass cabinet, or like a mummy unearthed in the tomb of Tutenkhamon [*sic*]?" Yet the vast majority of those present supported the measure. Although Williamsburg would become a tourist showplace, it would also be markedly improved by the millions of dollars provided to it by the restoration. Goodwin proceeded to explain the division of the two charters of the organization, one to control the profit-making entity and one to be strictly nonprofit and research oriented. Goodwin commented that "the Corporations are formed in the interest of preserving historic Williamsburg. If there had been any danger the State Corporation Commission would surely have pointed it out."[12]

Thus, with relatively little vocal dissent, Colonial Williamsburg began that evening on a course to make it a landmark in historic preservation and a potent institution for the promotion of American ideals. For JDR Jr. it was the beginning of an enormous undertaking that would last until the end of his life, and for W. A. R. Goodwin it was the culmination of a quest to preserve the beliefs that he felt Williamsburg embodied.

Nevertheless, the required rebuilding and restoration process was not going to be an easy task. Although the revelation of the benefactor eased some minds, it also led to greater tensions and further questions about how this powerful northern family would alter this traditionally southern town. One local citizen, John Arthur Hundley, was inclined to verse upon hearing of the massive buyout that allowed JDR Jr. to control 95 percent of the colonial area:

My God! They've sold the town,
The streets will all come up,
The poles will all come down.
They've sold the Church, the vestry too,
The Sexton and the steeple;
They've sold the Court House and the Greens,
They've even sold the people.
And you will hear from miles around
From people poor and of renown
My God! They've sold the town.[13]

For many in the Rockefeller organization, JDR Jr.'s decision to restore Williamsburg seemed far too hasty, especially when it became apparent in the fall of 1928 that a complete and fully accurate representation of Williamsburg in colonial times would be an impossible task. Charles O. Heydt, a Rockefeller aid, wrote to Goodwin in November that "the City has naturally adopted modern things that cannot be discarded even for this great ideal, and we must face and deal with the practical nature of the problem as well as the sentimental." Fear of a lack of local cooperation also beset Heydt. If the community was unwilling to work with the architects, contractors, and landscapers, the townspeople would make the work far more difficult: "[T]his whole enterprise cannot be made the success it should be unless the local people show a willingness to meet [JDR Jr.] half way. It is for them to extend the friendly hand of cooperation."[14]

Much of the population was willing to meet the philanthropist halfway, especially because his property purchases had in many cases improved their lives. Poorer families who had been previously unable to afford medical care were now able to do so. The money paid for the properties also gave financial security to many of those who sold their homes. Some residents indulged their desires for new clothes and automobiles, paid for out of the proceeds from the sale of their property. Many residents who sold to the restoration built homes in the outlying sections of the city. Others were offered life tenancies by the restoration if they owned homes that would not be torn down because of their historic significance. These life tenancies, numbering thirty-four in all, allowed people to sell their homes and turn the maintenance of the structure over to Colonial Williamsburg. Upon their death, the restoration would assume control of the building, which might be used for exhibition purposes or rented out to employees to give the town a "lived in feel." This solution was generally agreeable for all concerned, although there were minor disputes along the way. Although there was some inconvenience to those who sold their houses, there was generally strong support for the project in the community, as well as a sense that something important was being accomplished for Williamsburg and the nation.[15]

In addition to the money they received, many residents were happy to see some of the older, less attractive buildings removed. The town elite had often viewed the poorer houses as a blight on the community. In general, the homes of the local African American population were poorly constructed shacks that were unpopular with the white residents. Thirty-eight of these "negro dwellings" were purchased by the restoration and their residents re-located. But as one black resident, Eliza Baker, a former slave born in 1845, recalled, many of the African Americans' new homes were often "so small people [could not] get their furniture in." In addition, whereas white residents were free to decide where they would move after selling their dwellings, blacks were restricted as to where they could relocate. A. Edwin Kendrew, principal architect of the restoration, and later a vice president of Colonial Williamsburg, recalled that "we tried to keep the costs reasonable in order to make the houses somewhat similar to what the Negroes were accustomed to . . . not making larger rooms but making them compact." Many blacks, however, viewed the restoration with ambivalence, because it was clear that its purpose was simply to re-create the lives of prominent white Virginians. While many whites profited from the restoration, the wealth and position of African Americans in the town remained essentially unchanged, as they were forced to continue in subservient roles. Some black residents felt that the situation had gotten worse as a result of the restoration, for as Kendrew noted, "I heard criticism from Negroes even way back in the forties, saying the Restoration was responsible for promoting segregation. That we had broken up this wonderful situation of the Negroes living on the same street with whites."[16]

Many long-term white residents, including Elizabeth Lee Henderson, noticed that something was missing in this newly reconstructed town. In an interview in 1975, she said: "I don't think that charm has gone. But as a hometown, in a certain sense, it doesn't exist anymore." But Henderson did feel that the restoration had done more good than harm. As Colonial Williamsburg was thrust into the national and later international spotlight, it created great pride among the town's residents. She recalled, "Williamsburg . . . is not just the Mecca of America: it is a shrine for . . . peoples all over the world; and they *come* [emphasis in original] from all over the world."[17]

For Henderson, the presence of the Rockefeller family during much of the restoration and early years of the presentation to the public gave the project an important personal touch. "Mr. Rockefeller himself, I think, is greatly responsible for [the acceptance of the restoration]. He made it known that he wanted nothing to do with it unless the people of Williamsburg wanted it." Of the two founders, JDR Jr., in Henderson's view, was more interested in the development of the project and its effect on people. "Dr. Goodwin seemed to have less interest in [the] project after it was started and progressing. He had the whole vision and the detailed process of making that vision materialize seemed less important to him," she commented. Indeed, by the time the project was under way in the mid-1930s, Goodwin, who was in his sixties, was increasingly concerned about provisions for his wife and children after his death and therefore began to plan for that eventuality. This concern was probably a major factor in his turning over most of the work of the restoration to Colonial Williamsburg, in addition to the fact that once the initial plans for the restoration had been completed, the rebuilding process was largely in the hands of the architects and contractors.[18]

Most townspeople were excited about the future that the restoration promised and probably held sentiments similar to those expressed in the *Virginia Gazette,* which had begun publishing again in 1930. The newspaper held that "here in the cradle of the republic will be preserved for all time the shrines made sacred by hallow associations, pregnant with the lives of men who made America the land of the free." Later that year, an editorial proclaimed the future that Williamsburg would have once the restoration was completed. No longer would the townspeople feel inadequate, and the world would see a different type of Williamsburg, one that would be "the mecca for thousands of tourists and visitors in the years to come." The paper argued that "Williamsburg will be the most attractive place in America for those who love old traditions and are proud of their Anglo-Saxon lineage and of the men and women who made America what it is today." Undoubtedly this promotionalism played an important part in developing the image of Williamsburg, as did the emphasis on people of Anglo-Saxon lineage. In light of the large wave of immigrants who landed on America's shores from eastern and southern Europe in the late nineteenth and early twentieth centuries, Williamsburg offered people of British ancestry a place they could call their own, as well as one they could use to educate others in the heritage of America's first settlers.[19]

But everything did not go smoothly during the restoration process. Although the majority of the townspeople were generally supportive of the plan, a minority, especially among the older established families, resented the disruption to their way of life and the power of a wealthy northern benefactor. These older families had been the purveyors of the spirit of the past of Williamsburg before the restoration. They also resented the fact that their control of the past would be wrestled from them. Although this minority did not organize enough opposition to disband the restoration, Elizabeth Henderson noted that they were "perhaps rather violent in a small way." Much of the opposition that the restoration faced was intransigence from some residents who opposed the restoration completely or who wanted to get as much as they could from JDR Jr. and Colonial Williamsburg. Some were genuinely concerned about what the restoration might do to their town, whereas others were more than likely simply obstructionist and opposed in principle to the process that was transforming the town. For those who disliked the restoration, "Colonial Williamsburg had to push . . . to guide them and keep them from becoming obstinate because of their resistance to change. . . . [W]e had to make them feel they were in control and that Colonial Williamsburg was a good citizen," noted A. Edwin Kendrew.[20]

Within the architectural offices of the Williamsburg Holding Corporation, the early name for the restoration organization, thousands of questions needed to be answered about how far accuracy should extend in the project. The restoration wanted to promote the notion that patrons would be visiting an accurate representation of the eighteenth-century town. Much of how particular buildings looked in the colonial period could be garnered from old sketches, exterior drawings, and residents' descriptions, but the interiors were often a mystery. An important aid in understanding the layout of the eighteenth-century town was the "Frenchman's Map," which was drawn in 1782 for the purpose of billeting French soldiers in the town. This map helped the architects accurately reconstruct the dimensions of buildings and their relative placement in the colonial period.[21]

In addition, accommodation was required in accord with the twentieth-century needs of the project. For example, the restoration was forced to include fire hydrants in the restored area, although they would not have been there in the colonial period. Kendrew noted, "[W]e . . . compromised on a low type of hydrant, . . . we then painted them all green to be less conspic-

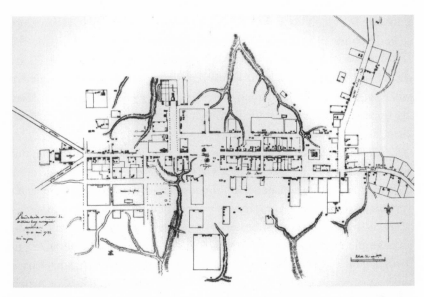

The Frenchman's Map of Williamsburg from 1782, discovered at the library of the College of William and Mary in 1927 (Courtesy of the Swem Library, College of William and Mary)

uous and even hid some in bushes which confounded the firemen." As the restoration progressed, strict guidelines were set up to ensure that all work be done with *"fidelity to an ideal, rather than fidelity to a time schedule"* [emphasis in original]. Although money seemed plentiful, there was not a limitless supply, and JDR Jr. insisted on economy wherever possible. In such cases where money was an issue, both sides were to be weighed, as there would arise situations where "compromises would doubtless have to be made, but they should not be made until the elements of beauty and art are fully weighed against the economic consideration." Indeed, such compromises were at the heart of the restoration process. To re-create the eighteenth century in the twentieth would clearly be impossible. Therefore there needed to be accommodations that took into consideration public health laws, safety factors, and common conveniences that were part of modern life. Once visitors started to arrive, further considerations had to be given to safety and comfort to ensure that they would enjoy their stay, appreciate the ideals that the restoration promoted, and afterward recommend it to their friends.[22]

The restoration's workers realized that they were making something for posterity. They understood that most of the other major colonial cities—

primarily Boston, New York, and Philadelphia—were too large and modern to undergo any type of large-scale restoration, and so Williamsburg was the last chance to recapture America's colonial past. As an article in the *Virginia Gazette* in June 1930 noted, "[P]eople realize the importance Williamsburg will have throughout the United States when the work is finished. . . . Here are practically the only historic ruins that have been undefiled by the ever-changing American civilization."[23]

Even though Williamsburg was, perhaps, colonial history's last stand, this situation did not mean that all aspects of the past were to be fully re-created. A. Edwin Kendrew indicated that "the restoration was not considered a reversion to the original necessarily. It was considered fixing it up and saving what you had and making it better." The question of "negro servants" was an example of this attitude. Although the restoration did symbolize primarily an ideal of the past, thought was given to the reconstruction of slave quarters early in the restoration. In April 1930 Goodwin wrote to Col. Arthur Woods, detailing plans for the building of slave quarters. Goodwin recognized that slaves were an integral part of colonial life. Yet the question of how to portray slavery would be one of the most enduring of the restoration's challenges.[24]

Goodwin understood that although the question of portraying slave housing was a difficult one, "a great mistake would be made if we did not reproduce a sufficient number of these houses to recall the ancient atmosphere and this aspect of the ancient civilization." He suggested that this idea could be considered in connection with exhibition houses "near which log cabins or primitive type of houses might be erected, in which some old negroes might be placed." In addition, he indicated that these African Americans could be given some menial work to do to keep the grounds in order or to scrub the floors of the houses. He concluded, "[T]o exile them completely from the Colonial area would, I am convinced, be a mistake which we could not justify."[25]

Although Goodwin's proposal did not meet with much success, it indicated that at least one individual in the restoration recognized the importance of including African Americans in the project. JDR Jr., however, was mostly interested in the architectural portion of the plan and was not particularly concerned with sociohistorical problems. Therefore, although the role of African Americans in colonial times was always understood, not until the late 1950s was a serious attempt made to understand the importance of bondsmen in eighteenth-century Williamsburg. In fact, the move to treat

W. A. R. Goodwin and John D. Rockefeller Jr., ca. 1930
(Courtesy of the Colonial Williamsburg Foundation)

African American history at Colonial Williamsburg in a serious fashion did not begin until the mid-1960s, and even then the presentation was in its most rudimentary form. Only after 1976 did the restoration truly treat African American history as an integral part of its interpretation program.

In addition to internal questions of authenticity and practicality, Colonial Williamsburg found itself in the middle of a heated debate about the role of the federal government and the preservation of two other important local historical sites: Jamestown and Yorktown. In January 1930 Congressman Louis Cramton of Michigan introduced a bill in the House of Representatives to create a colonial national monument. He sought to include Williamsburg in a plan to create a national monument to patriotic ideals involving not only Williamsburg but also Yorktown and Jamestown. The creation of a highway running from Jamestown, through (or eventually below) Williamsburg, to Yorktown would enable easy passage between these historic landmarks and would enhance the experience for visitors.

Cramton and a group of approximately fifty congressmen toured the Williamsburg area in early April 1930 to see the possibilities inherent in the creation of such a plan. He made every effort to reassure the Williamsburg inhabitants that the purpose of the bill and the fact-finding expedition were solely in the best interest of the town and should not be viewed as government meddling in local affairs. The monument, he argued, would bring nothing but benefits to a region of the state struggling under the burden of the Great Depression. Many of the locals, however, considered further outside incursion dangerous. They had just become accustomed to the sight of the Rockefeller men and were anxious not to allow too many outsiders into the locality. It was hard enough to accept the presence of one outside man, but for many residents the sight of fifty politicians traipsing around their community caused alarm. To be certain that the congressman kept his promise, some of the town's residents planned to attend the congressional hearings on the bill to ensure that any parts unfavorable to Williamsburg would be thrown out. Furthermore, Cramton assured the town that he would be willing to amend the bill in any way so as to win the support of the community. The legislation clearly made concessions for the restoration and made it readily apparent that there would be little federal incursion into Williamsburg. In fact, only the land needed for a thoroughfare between Jamestown and Yorktown had to be provided by Williamsburg. In addition, section seven of the bill provided that there would be a reimbursement under which the "United States shall pay . . . Williamsburg 25 per cent of any rentals included in said revenues . . . such payment into the treasury of the city of Williamsburg not to exceed $20,000 in any year." With such assurances, Williamsburg residents more easily accepted the federal plan, described by one congressman as creating a "shrine for American patriots."[26]

On 3 March 1931, President Herbert Hoover signed into law the bill to create the Colonial National Monument. The federal government dedicated the monument on 16 October 1931 in Yorktown, Virginia, in connection with the celebration of the sesquicentennial of the Battle of Yorktown. Speaking at the dedication was Congressman Robert Luce of Massachusetts, whose address characterized the shrinelike aura many gave to the monument. Luce described the three-city area as a special place for all Americans that "will arouse remembrance and awaken gratitude in matters of pioneering, government, the higher education, military prowess, the winning of independence—in sum, the essentials from which and by which grew a nation." An article in the April 1931 edition of the *National Republic* referred to the monument as a "triple shrine of history," further reinforcing the religious feeling that would become an intricate part of the restoration and the surrounding historic area.[27]

The restoration of Colonial Williamsburg certainly played an important part in the promotion and eventual passage of Cramton's legislation, for Goodwin had proclaimed that "Williamsburg is the continuation of Jamestown and Yorktown is the vindication of Williamsburg." Although locals were extremely wary of any federal intervention, the promise of payment by the federal government for commerce lost from Williamsburg eased the minds of many businessmen. As Horace Albright, a former director of the National Park Service and subsequently a member of the Board of Directors of Colonial Williamsburg, recalled, "[T]he people of Williamsburg didn't know for sure that they liked [the park]; we had to have a good many conferences with the Williamsburg officials." Yet strong support from Cramton and the Rockefeller organization convinced the town to support the plan.[28]

Also included in Cramton's bill was the provision that at any time in the future the restoration could become part of the National Park Service if such an arrangement was desired by JDR Jr. or his heirs. This provision was to ensure that should he or his family be unwilling to manage the project in the future, its control would then fall to the federal government. Albright, with his twenty-one-year tenure with the National Park Service, acted as liaison between the government and the restoration in this matter. Since JDR Jr. brought Albright onto the board, he clearly wanted to establish good ties with the Park Service and to ensure a lasting relationship between the federal government and Colonial Williamsburg.[29]

The Commonwealth of Virginia also had an eye on the restoration work at Williamsburg. In the late twenties and early thirties, there was strong support in the state government for the development of Virginia's natural resources—its forests and waterways—as well as its historic sites. The State Commission on Conservation and Development worked for seven and a half years from 1926 to 1934 to develop a far-ranging program that would draw tourists and their dollars to the state; the commission hoped that businesses would fall in love with the surroundings and consider the region for future industrial development. The state government, and especially Gov. Harry F. Byrd, saw the need to bring Virginia into the twentieth century and hoped to do so primarily with private funds. Therefore, Byrd and his administration were greatly appreciative of the Rockefeller-funded restoration of Colonial Williamsburg.[30]

In the Williamsburg community, local leaders realized the important economic role that tourism was to play in their future. The boost would, of course, be particularly noticeable in the traditional tourist trades—restaurants and hostelries—but businesses in virtually all sectors of society could benefit from the greater number of people visiting the town. Comparisons with other sites indicated that tourist rates had steadily increased during the 1920s. Of course, the Great Depression would probably dampen these figures, but clearly citizens had the desire, if not the financial means, to view historic monuments. Thus, although national economic forecasts were still bleak, local entrepreneurs hoped that by the time the restoration opened enough visitors would come to boost Williamsburg's businesses.[31]

By August 1931 the restoration had published a booklet that posed a variety of questions and answers geared to those who desired more information about the technical and ideological purposes of the project. The publication proclaimed that the restoration would provide "a composite representation of the original forms of a number of buildings and areas known or, on good authority, believed to have existed in Williamsburg between the years 1699 and 1840." In addition to supplying the public with an as-close-as-possible reconstruction of a colonial town, the project would also speak to the patriotic elements of American history. "It will supply a shrine where great events in early American history and the lives of many of the men who made it may be visualized in their proper setting."[32]

The economic and social effects of the restoration no doubt greatly altered Williamsburg and the surrounding community. As much of the restoration work took place during the early years of the depression, the funds from the Rockefellers did much to raise the living standards of Williamsburg residents. As Mrs. George P. Coleman recalled, "[T]he depression of 1930–1935 did much to make us satisfied with the [restoration], for our community scarcely felt it. There was no unemployment to speak of, in comparison with what we knew existed elsewhere." That much of the restoration work took place during the depression is an important fact to

Excavation of the remains of the Governor's Palace (Courtesy of the Colonial Williamsburg Foundation)

consider. The poor economy meant that the money expended by the Rockefeller family helped to alleviate hard times and perhaps persuaded people to support the restoration. Had the economy been good, and the jobs less economically necessary, there might have been less support for the work. The local Williamsburg newspaper, the *Virginia Gazette*, also felt that the restoration had done much to ease the depression in the town. As it noted in an editorial in July 1930, Williamsburg was among the most fortunate of American towns, since there was a rapid increase in unemployment in the United States, yet the small Tidewater village was spared some of these problems due to the restoration.[33]

Not only were there more jobs, but also the town took on a fresh, new appearance due to the restoration work. As the *Virginia Gazette* commented in May 1931, "[T]he Restoration is rapidly changing Williamsburg from a lazy tumbled down village to an enterprising new-old historical center." Although those who were interested in authenticity might have looked down

Excavation work for the tunnel connecting Colonial Williamsburg with Jamestown and Yorktown. The Public Magazine is on the left, and the Courthouse of 1770 is on the right. (Courtesy of the Colonial Williamsburg Foundation)

on certain measures, such as filling in holes, paving streets, and installing sewers and running water, the beautification and modernization of local facilities were important to the local population. Residents felt they could take pride in their community and finally join the twentieth century.[34]

Although it is difficult to assess fully the effect that the restoration had on all residents during the early years, there is no doubt that the availability of local employment increased substantially. Andrew H. Hepburn, one of the main architects involved with the project, recalled that "most of the construction personnel came from the surrounding area." Some of the steel men came from New York, but the actual craftsmen—the carpenters, the plasterers, and the brick masons—were local men. "They knew nothing to start with but they were willing to learn." The availability of large sums of money, in addition to plentiful local labor, also made the work go more smoothly. "We never had to ask for anything after we had made sure that was the thing to do. We were not restricted even when it cost $10,000 to refurbish the steel on the Wren Building roof."[35]

The immediate psychological effects of the alteration of the town were more difficult to judge. Reactions varied from an inability to grasp the larger concept of the restoration to a gradual feeling that a dead town was being created. The houses, shops, and taverns of two hundred years ago were to be faithfully re-created, but the actual inhabitants who called Williamsburg home during this period were long dead. The Great Depression also probably contributed to this eerie feeling. Although the residents of the town suffered less from the economic hard times than others in neighboring communities and many across the country, outsiders were going to be the ones who would be providing the income for the project from their visitation fees. Yet a lingering question was that although considerable time and energy were being spent on the town's re-creation, would anyone ever come to see it?[36]

Although Goodwin and JDR Jr. remained ideologically committed to the restoration, the depression had forced JDR Jr. to make some sobering decisions about his finances. By 1934 his net worth had been cut nearly in half, and by 1939 it was down to $291.1 million. The work on Colonial Williamsburg was to continue at full force, however, since this project occupied more of JDR Jr.'s time and interest than virtually anything else in his control during this period. It was no exaggeration to refer to restored Williamsburg as Mr. Rockefeller's village, for it was, in fact, his—he bought it, built it, and cherished it almost as much as his children. No matter the insecurities that many townspeople felt at the start of the project, most were soon convinced that he was not interested in merely promoting his own self-interest but rather that he had primarily altruistic feelings about Williamsburg.[37]

Articles in popular magazines spoke of the changes taking place in this small Tidewater town. Writing in *St. Nicholas Magazine*, Anne Hard detailed the restoration for thousands of young readers. Hard likened JDR Jr. to a prince who had awakened a "sleeping beauty" out of a lifeless 150-year trance. With clarity and simplicity, she detailed the changes taking place, shaping her article to entrance a youthful audience. She also emphasized the importance of Americanism in viewing Williamsburg. "It is not only beauty they are restoring, recreating, there in Williamsburg. They are not only preserving sacred historic sites. . . . [They] are giving us one more chance, when we visit it, to be proud we are Americans."[38]

The first building accessible to the public was the Raleigh Tavern, opened on 16 September 1932. Standing in front of a lectern draped with the American flag, Gov. John Pollard addressed a crowd at the opening of

Governor John G. Pollard giving an address at the opening of the reconstructed
Raleigh Tavern, September 1932 (Courtesy of the Colonial Williamsburg Foundation)

the tavern. The Raleigh Tavern provided the public with their first opportunity to look at a completed building in the restoration area. The site
needed to make a good impression to ensure that visitors would be interested enough to come back to see the Capitol and the Governor's Palace,
which were due to open a few months later.[39]

But even before the buildings were opened for viewing, visitors came to
Colonial Williamsburg to glimpse the changes that were taking place in the
town. In April 1932, Howard M. Canoune, one of the town's first visitors,
wrote to the restoration to express his fascination with the transformation
of the town. "I was greatly privileged and inspired to observe the magnificent work which is to the American people the cradle of their civilization,"
he wrote. Canoune noted that although the colonial heritage of the town
had been neglected for decades, a concentrated effort at rectifying the situation could lead to spectacular results when propelled by "intelligence, taste,
patriotism and high grade citizenship." He felt that Colonial Williamsburg
was "a source of new hope to everyone with a heart for the things of our cultural tradition . . . and our peculiar American culture in general." Canoune's

thinking was echoed by many who saw the town before the great prewar wave of visitors began to arrive starting in early 1934. Charles J. Breck expressed similar sentiments writing in June 1932: "I would say that Mrs. Breck and I . . . enjoyed our short visit in Williamsburg. We are all heartily in accord with the plan of the restoration. . . . [W]e are all old time Americans and look with pride at the manner in which our ancestors lived in the far distant past." By recalling their family histories, these visitors attempted to create a lasting bond between the past and themselves and to use that relationship to promote Americanist ideals.[40]

Other writers addressed the future of the restoration and predicted a national mecca for those who wished to demonstrate a love of country. Henry Breckenridge wrote to Goodwin that "it is highly probable that the restoration will have a profound and permanent effect. It brings to the American mind a vivid and true conception of the nation's genesis. Not the fortitude alone but the grace of life and good taste of our founders are . . . perfectly manifested." Such a letter exemplified the belief that some visitors had about Colonial Williamsburg's future position. Breckenridge had accurately predicted the restoration's role through the Great Depression, World War II, and the Cold War.[41]

Others praised Colonial Williamsburg's uniqueness among restoration efforts for the care and scholarly manner that guided the project. The director of the history and archaeology division of the Virginia State Commission on Conservation and Development held such a view. "I consider the restoration the most unique project ever attempted in this country, and one of the most beneficent. . . . It teaches history in the most practical manner and so adds to the stability of American institutions."[42]

Therefore, even before a massive wave of publicity had enveloped Colonial Williamsburg, many people hailed it as a "shrine," an "ancient relic" brought back to life to inspire the twentieth century with the values and dreams of the eighteenth century. Colonial Williamsburg was not the only place in America to achieve this status, but its rebirth was made all the more exciting because it was completely privately run and financed by the leading philanthropist of the day.

For the people of the local community, the restoration meant a great change in their way of life. Although many received a good price for their homes, residents lost some of the sense of community that helped bind them together. The loss of a hometown for Elizabeth Henderson was particularly painful. The growth of Colonial Williamsburg placed the town in

The reconstructed Capitol, which was rebuilt from 1932 to 1933 on its original foundations, based upon the Bodleian Plate, which was discovered in the Bodleian Library at Oxford University. The plate also answered questions about the exterior of the Governor's Palace and the three original buildings of the College of William and Mary. (Courtesy of the Colonial Williamsburg Foundation)

a national spotlight, one that was to grow more prominent during World War II and the Cold War. Although many residents were proud to see their town used as an example of "proper" American values, some residents resented the intrusion. One older woman referred to the restoration of the town as a "reconstruction," resignedly saying that she had lived through one Yankee reconstruction and could probably survive another.[43]

Yet this reconstruction held more of a future for Williamsburg than the one that followed the Civil War. The restoration represented the glorious antebellum period that many Southerners longed to revive. Although it might have been a "Yankee reconstruction," Colonial Williamsburg sought to take its visitors back to yesteryear and to provide them with a taste of the town's history before the Civil War. This was no doubt a positive goal in the minds of many of Williamsburg's residents. The restoration would be preserving the values of the colonial era and with it the lure of the antebellum South.

In addition, millions of Americans whose families had immigrated to the United States in the decades following the Civil War were now able to participate in America's colonial past, as Colonial Williamsburg re-created it for them. By bringing the eighteenth century to life in the twentieth century, JDR Jr. linked those who created the nation and those who shared in the fruits of its later successes. Like other forms of Americanism, Colonial Williamsburg was created to inspire in Americans a greater love of country and an appreciation of traditional values. In a period of great change, the restoration helped to represent tradition and to repudiate the fast-paced world of the jazz age. For a conservative Baptist like JDR Jr., Colonial Williamsburg embodied ideals that modern society was carelessly casting away.

When the restored Capitol was opened on 24 February 1934, JDR Jr. addressed the members of the House of Delegates and the Senate of the Commonwealth of Virginia, who met in the building in a joint session. In referring to the men who had helped propel American independence, JDR Jr. noted that their legacy was still essential in the twentieth century. After the ceremony, JDR Jr. gave a luncheon and reception for the dignitaries who had attended the opening. Back in New York City, JDR Jr. wrote to his father to inform him of the day's events. "Everything went off most satisfactorily at Williamsburg. . . . [T]he session which [was] held in the reconstructed Capitol was dignified, impressive and in every way appropriate."[44]

2

Creating the Faith

A lthough the main buildings of the restoration—including the Capitol, the Governor's Palace, and the Raleigh Tavern—had opened by the spring of 1934, Colonial Williamsburg's mission as a shrine to the American faith still needed to be expanded and the visitors enthralled. As the restoration gained in popularity and notoriety, greater numbers of people began to flock to the town, if for no other reason than to see what all the excitement was about. Clearly distinct from those who viewed the restoration during and after World War II, Colonial Williamsburg's first visitors were of a higher socioeconomic class, were better educated, and often had personal ties to those who were founders of the colony or were prominent figures in Virginia politics. This group was especially interested in the patriotic message that Colonial Williamsburg supplied, and they were anxious to imbue the local area—and the country as a whole—with the importance of Tidewater Virginia's role in America's quest for independence.

These first visitors often came with precise and detailed questions that the restoration's hostesses and guides labored to answer to the best of their ability. Early visitors were often interested in the history of particular artifacts and desired to know if any old legends had any basis in fact. Often they were disappointed to learn that the furnishings were reproductions or merely period pieces and not originals from the collections of the royal governors. For these visitors, sociohistorical concerns were less important than the history of architecture, furnishings, or horticultural designs. They viewed the past as primarily centering around the lives and living quarters of the great white men. Thus the lives and living conditions of less prominent people were generally of far less interest for them.

During the early years of the restoration, both press reports and visitors' commentaries used terms such as "shrine" or "religious spirit," popularizing this identification and using it commonly in writing about the restoration. No doubt, this constant religious identification cemented a certain perception of the restoration in people's minds, drawing on a common bond that most Americans would be able to relate to in one form or another. An article in *American Home*, entitled "Williamsburg—A Shrine for American Patriots," emphasized this view of the colonial past. The introduction promised the story of a "restored city that rises again to link our present and the future with a *living* [emphasis in original] 18th century whose decades are glorious with historic significance and inspiration." Barbara Trigg Brown, the article's author, proceeded to discuss the process of the restoration and concluded that the project had effectively linked 1934 with 1734, providing twentieth-century Americans with a better understanding of the world of two hundred years ago.[1]

A furthering of the popular notice of the restoration came on 20 October 1934 when President Franklin Roosevelt traveled to Colonial Williamsburg to dedicate the Duke of Gloucester Street, which he referred to as the "most historic avenue in all America." Over fifteen thousand people watched as Roosevelt's motorcade made its way from the Capitol to the College of William and Mary, where he spoke at the inaugural ceremonies for the college's new president, John Stewart Bryan. Roosevelt's implied support for the restoration served to anchor it in the public's mind as an important undertaking worthy of a presidential visit.[2]

The visitors during these years were primarily prosperous, yet this did not necessarily reflect JDR Jr.'s interest in restoring the town. The "snob appeal" that many associated with the early years of the restoration was not intentional, argued Thomas G. McCaskey, a restoration employee. For McCaskey, Colonial Williamsburg had to appeal to all parts of the American populace and to touch all of them equally with its message of traditional values. "I think Mr. Rockefeller built this in order to have as many Americans as possible come and touch it and be touched by it, and the snob appeal is not for *this* [emphasis in original] project as I see it." McCaskey readily admitted, however, that the popular perception of Colonial Williamsburg was of a place for only the well-to-do. In Virginia, at least, the restoration was considered a place where people with ample means could gather and enjoy the beauty of the colonial past. Yet it was obvious to those traveling to Colonial Williamsburg that it was primarily a haunt of the very well-to-do. "Cadillacs and chauffeurs were common sights all over the place, at the Williamsburg Inn particularly. It seemed to be a wealthier, slightly older audience; you saw very few children," McCaskey recounted.[3]

Although those connected with the restoration were reluctant to talk about money, preferring to emphasize ideas of Americanism and national heritage, the press was quick to seize on the cost of the work. An article in *Fortune* in July 1935, entitled "Mr. Rockefeller's $14,000,000 Idyl," cast JDR Jr. as a free spender, ready to finance even the most detailed and painstaking work to assure an accurate restoration. The fact that Colonial Williamsburg drew about sixty thousand visitors at that time, each paying about $1.25 to visit the restoration buildings, which totaled about $75,000 a year in proceeds from admissions, clearly demonstrated that the restoration could not keep progressing at a good pace by admission fees alone.[4]

Although admission fees did not generate a great deal of money, officials were reluctant to overly commercialize the restoration. There needed to be a balance between making money and promoting the ideals of Colonial Williamsburg, though most officials generally assumed that once the restoration was complete it should be self-supporting. As Thomas McCaskey noted, "I have always been of the school that we should break even and delighted when we were able to do it. . . . I think that the watch word here is that we have no *obligation* [emphasis in original] to make money. But likewise we have had no privilege to lose it."[5]

The question of how much advertising should be put out by the restoration was a much-debated problem. Although articles in magazines and newspapers carried free publicity, some officials were concerned that those articles would exaggerate the scope of the restoration and lead to disappointment for visitors who had expected a much more advanced project. Two problems that officials feared would occur were difficulties in housing and controlling large crowds, reasonable concerns for a village that ten years earlier was a small college town with few outside visitors. When the tourists did come, however, the restoration was concerned with providing them with a good experience; administrators were careful to listen to criticisms and often tried to rectify the visitors' complaints.[6]

The local community also tried to accommodate visitors. The town's reputation of southern hospitality needed to be upheld, as well as the desire to operate tourist businesses at a profit. The *Virginia Gazette* realized this as well, noting that "tourists are our best assets." The newspaper realized that if the town wished to leave a positive impression on its visitors, it "must be prepared to take care of them as befitting a colonial city whose hospitality should . . . be in keeping with the good fame of Virginia." In addition, the building of a new local airport provided another means by which visitors could journey to the restoration, further increasing its tourist potential. Obviously, most of those who would come to see the restoration were fairly wealthy to be able to afford to travel during the years of the Great Depression.[7]

Virtually all of those who journeyed to Colonial Williamsburg before World War II had nothing but praise for the efforts of the architects, contractors, and landscape artists who had turned a small Tidewater village into a landmark of national importance. From lay people to professional historians, most had a positive view of the work and its importance in inspiring Americans' spirit. Since most Americans' perception of colonial history in the 1930s closely mirrored that presented by the restoration and did not encompass a broader understanding of the lives of laborers, African Americans, and women, there was little criticism directed at the restoration's presentation of the past. As one Colonial Williamsburg supporter, George deBenneville Kiem, noted in a speech at the dinner of the General Council of the General Society of Colonial Wars in 1935, "[W]ho can see what we have seen . . . without being born again in the spirit of true American patriotism and feel in himself a new devotion to those ideals and principles that have made the English-speaking race significant in the development of the spiritual life of the human race." Kiem's views confirmed the goals of the restoration—a recognition by those who visited it that the town embodied the ability to stir people's emotions and promote patriotic ideas.[8]

The sight of the newly restored village must have been quite a spectacle in the mid-1930s. For a town that was a combination of ramshackle older buildings and unattractive modern edifices, the new Colonial Williamsburg was a welcome relief for many in the local population and undoubtedly a welcome surprise for the restoration's early visitors. The town, which only a few years before had been rundown, could now be viewed as a beautiful spot both by its residents and its new visitors. One could stand halfway down the mile-long Duke of Gloucester Street, Colonial Williamsburg's main thoroughfare, and see the cupola of the Capitol at one end and the Wren Building at the College of William and Mary at the other, with no unsightly poles or wires to mar the view since they had been placed underground. From the same spot, one could look to the north over Palace Green "where the mansion of the Royal Governors flanked by noble buildings and high brick walls can easily be seen looking as it did in Colonial days." In addition, taverns, houses, and stores were being rebuilt or restored. These smaller buildings fleshed out the town and brought its appearance more closely in line with the colonial village.[9]

Through the efforts of the restoration, visitors could grasp what life would have been like in the eighteenth century when Williamsburg's more famous residents trod its streets. The modern version, however, was far more sanitized, without animals, mud, or manure. The *Virginia Gazette* claimed that all that would be needed when the restoration was complete would be "people dressed as in colonial times, the Raleigh Tavern again open as a public house, . . . and good fellowship which our forefathers were noted for." Such boosterism was typical of many local newspapers, which sought to encourage local residents and visitors to speak well of the restoration. These comments demonstrated that many people outside the restoration's organization also understood the great potential of the project and the benefit that it could provide to the local economy.[10]

But the *Virginia Gazette* was not always complimentary. It criticized the town's apparent indifference to the new waves of tourists who were coming to see the restoration. Although some concessions to the new arrivals were being made, the Williamsburg area still lacked important tourist aids. The newspaper called for a chamber of commerce office in Williamsburg that would help coordinate guest activities and provide vital information on the town, its attractions, and the local businesses. As the *Virginia Gazette* commented, "[A] mere information bureau is not enough. We must do bigger things and show our visitors who come from the north, the south, and the west that not only are we glad to have them, but we desire to see that their stay among us is enjoyable." Tourists, the newspaper felt, would spread news about the restoration, making Colonial Williamsburg "the mecca for millions in the years to come."[11]

Most of the hundreds of letters written by visitors to restoration officials indicated public satisfaction with the town's transformation and mentioned no difficulties due to any lack of amenities. Writing on Thanksgiving Day, 1935, Elizabeth Pontefrace commented to Mr. and Mrs. John D. Rockefeller Jr. that "not beauty alone is being served in this Williamsburg that bears your imprint more than any other living souls." She apparently took something away with her from the visit as she commented that "whatever the luxury of those days, ours, though sometimes troubled, are better ones in which to be alive." Pontefrace demonstrated a sentiment common to many early Colonial Williamsburg visitors, namely, that Colonial Williamsburg served to remind people of the struggles of the past, comparing them with the economic troubles of the 1930s. Clearly she believed that these difficult days of the depression were better ones in which to be alive than those of the Revolutionary period.[12]

This promotion of a better understanding of the struggles of the eighteenth century was the primary goal of the restoration and was clearly discussed in internal correspondence. W. A. R. Goodwin realized that a strong Americanist sentiment was the primary message that the project should convey. He wrote to JDR 3d in March 1934 that although it was impossible to re-create the past fully and accurately, "we can, however, reproduce the symbols and sacraments of the past." Such religious imagery indicated the connection that Goodwin made between the restoration and the spiritual importance of the colonial age. The restoration performed not merely a secular role but also a sacred one because it recalled the struggles of the American Revolution and the desire for Americans to live free lives, which, according to Thomas Jefferson, were granted to them by God. Goodwin further wrote that "this reproduction is more stimulating and more appealing when these symbols have co[m]e down to us through the centuries, bringing with them the associations which somehow seem to continue to live in brick and mortar and furniture and portraits."[13]

But visitors would not be able to appreciate fully the restoration without some type of guide service to ensure that they were adequately informed about the significance of the buildings, furnishings, and gardens that had been so carefully re-created. Before the creation of the Colonial Williamsburg guide service, a city ordinance in Williamsburg provided a standard for guides—the main component of which was an examination. If this hurdle was successfully passed, a guide could then purchase a license from the city for an annual fee of five dollars. These city guides were not permitted, however, to lead groups inside any private buildings in Williamsburg, including those of the restoration. Because of problems with the guides, reports of overcharging, and subsequent bad publicity for the restoration, Kenneth Chorley recommended that Colonial Williamsburg establish its own guide service. This move would ensure that visitors would receive properly trained guides who could show off the town to the high standards required by the restoration.[14]

Guides would be trained in the same program used for hostesses and would take the city exam; if they passed and were acceptable to Colonial Williamsburg, they would be commissioned as an Official Colonial Williamsburg Guide. Education for the guides consisted of "a course of reading not only the historic but the social background of Colonial Virginia, and more especially Colonial Williamsburg." The guides were to be used solely to escort visitors outside and between the exhibition buildings, because an intricate network of trained hostesses was already established to assist the guests inside the buildings. Whereas the hostesses were long-time white female residents of the town, both men and women could be trained as guides, opening up the employment ranks to large segments of Williamsburg's population, including students from the College of William and Mary.[15]

Not realizing the great appeal that the town would have once it became widely known, officials first assumed that Williamsburg would draw only modest numbers of people. But the public responded with greater enthusiasm than anyone had expected. As the restoration progressed and more buildings began to open to visitors, a more concrete vision of what Colonial Williamsburg was to become emerged. JDR Jr. became more and more interested in the process as time passed and attempted to create one more thing that would associate the family name with positive enterprises. The desire to wash away the stain of irresponsibility from the family image, as well as his interest in a personal legacy, compelled him to spend far more money on the town, making the restoration as grand as possible.[16]

As attendance grew, the restoration needed to promote more contact between visitors and the Colonial Williamsburg organization. Imparting Colonial Williamsburg's message needed to be in the hands of skilled and educated guides and hostesses who were not only trained in customer relations but also capable of answering difficult, complicated questions from knowledgeable people. A letter from Fielding Robinson to JDR Jr. indicated the taste and restraint that were embodied in the restoration. Robinson wrote that "you have captured the spiritual charm which must have been a part of the early civilization." He went on to comment on the high quality of the hostesses and the fact that the "beauty of the flower arrangements in the buildings [and] the quiet atmosphere which lingers throughout the entire area are all the result of excellent and careful thinking."[17]

The courtesy of the hostesses was a common theme, and for many visitors the relationship with them was the most important part of the visit. Officials realized that visitors would be in close contact with these employees and would shape their impressions of the restoration directly around these women. In light of this, a thorough hostess training program was instituted under the direction of Rutherfoord Goodwin, W. A. R. Goodwin's son. To project a suitable air of gentility, only older white women were chosen for these positions. These women were from the more prominent families of Tidewater Virginia and with their heritage and training could often command respect from a wide variety of visitors, most of whom wanted to find old-time civility in Colonial Williamsburg and would be disconcerted if they were shortchanged.

In an address to the new hostesses in December 1934, Kenneth Chorley clearly spelled out their responsibilities. He detailed the history of the restoration up to the present, indicating how a dead city was revitalized to imbue the American people with a greater appreciation of the ordeals of the past. Most important, he indicated that the vast majority of visitors who came to Colonial Williamsburg during this early period came without previous preparation. As he commented, "[T]hey come either out of curiosity or a desire to learn—but what they are to learn and how they are to learn it is to them a more or less puzzling and indefinite thing."[18]

Therefore the hostesses were responsible for aiding these people in their passage back in time to ensure that they understood and fully appreciated their visit. Chorley argued that in dealing with a guest "we must give him a general idea or understanding of the whole, . . . we must give him something of the spirit—we must at least introduce him to the great ghosts of those who built this place, and from it reached out to aid so greatly in the building of a nation."[19]

Because Colonial Williamsburg was a Rockefeller-funded project, people expected that no expense would be spared in the restoration and that it would be a truly splendid affair. When disappointment did occur, it was usually because the town did not live up to some of the visitors' more stringent standards. But more often than not the hostesses and other employees elicited a positive response from the patrons, such as the comment by Mary S. Hazel in 1939 that "every where we found courtesy, patience, a deep interest in the development itself, and a sincere desire to be helpful wherever possible."[20]

Elizabeth Lee Henderson, a hostess for the restoration for many years, recalled that the hostesses did as much as they could to offer the guests the best information on each building. Hostesses also tried to connect eigh-

teenth-century events with those in the twentieth century to indicate how
the past affected the present day. She recalled that the first tourists were
often well-educated people who had heard about the restoration by word
of mouth and had come to see how things were progressing. She indicated
that although some of the visitors did not have a strong academic background, "we don't have many of the usual types of tourist as a rule. We have
some of them I know, but the average Williamsburg tourist is certainly far
superior to the average [visitor] at Coney Island, for instance."[21]

Coney Island attracted the working and middle classes from New York
City, but Colonial Williamsburg clearly catered to a far wealthier audience
who could afford more than a day's excursion to Coney Island. Colonial
Williamsburg not only catered to the well-to-do but also provided a more
intellectual type of recreation than did the "Sodom by the sea," as Coney
Island was referred to earlier in the century. While Coney Island showed off
the extravagant, geared to impressing its less wealthy audience, Colonial
Williamsburg projected a refined opulence that, through the purchase of
restoration replicas, could be re-created in homes across the country. This
re-creation would help to promote the message of the restoration, since
Americans who brought Williamsburg furniture into their homes were furthering the cause of Americanism by creating mini-Williamsburgs across the
country.[22]

The development of the craft shops in 1937 took the restoration in a new
direction. Not only buildings but also old techniques of craft production
would be preserved to retain "something really worthwhile . . . which coming generations will appreciate." Such an emphasis placed an importance
on the role of the individual craftsman, whose influence was lost during industrialization. As a result, not only did these crafts retain a lost art, but they
also promoted Colonial Williamsburg's political message, which sought to
foster a strong sense of individual accomplishment—a necessary ingredient
in thwarting any trend toward a socialist system, which some political con-
servatives feared could emerge in the 1930s.[23]

The influence of the restoration extended far beyond the borders of the
town, as people all over the country began to adopt Colonial Williamsburg
styles in gardens, furnishings, and home decoration. Colonial Williamsburg
reproductions became increasingly popular with wealthier Americans who
were anxious to demonstrate their Americanism through the purchase of a
variety of objects. As the *Virginia Gazette* noted in July 1936 about these reproductions, "[T]he research department of the Restoration has brought to

light many important phases of Colonial days whereby not only the style and type of the buildings have been duplicated but the furnishings of the buildings as well." So popular had the style and material of eighteenth-century furnishings become, they spread to cities where factories were making reproductions and advising that "it is fashionable to buy and use furniture and furnishings such as used in the colonial days." This practice continued well past the early stages of the restoration. *Look* magazine indicated in 1958 that since the official Williamsburg Reproduction Program began in 1937, public enthusiasm for the plan had been so great that more than five hundred items were available for purchase.[24]

By promoting the popularization of the colonial revival style of architecture and furnishings, Colonial Williamsburg created not only a shrine to Americanism but also a precedent for home builders and interior designers across the country. In evoking the spirit of the restoration through the styles of Colonial Williamsburg, those builders and designers spread the ideals of the restoration and ignited further popular interest in the work. The dissemination of the restoration's ideology was part of the founders' original intent, but the popularity of these designs indicated how fully Colonial Williamsburg became incorporated into American life. Through the purchase of these replicas, families felt that they were keeping in touch with their colonial past and at the same time rejuvenating old values and ideals. In addition, families who lacked their own colonial heritage could purchase these items and in so doing promote their Americanist sentiment, even if their ancestors had come to the United States more recently.[25]

In November 1937, *House and Garden* devoted thirty pages of that month's issue to the Colonial Williamsburg restoration. In examining the influence that the project had on architecture, gardening, and decoration, the magazine noted that "both the spirit of ancient Williamsburg and the actuality of its splendid public buildings and homes now restored have a definite, necessary and vital message for our times." For those who were wealthy enough to build their own homes, the Colonial Williamsburg styles presented a compelling option in the late 1930s. *House and Garden* felt that the influence of Colonial Williamsburg upon American architecture would be deep and long lasting. If for no other reason, the revived colonial style gave America's builders a chance to study another form of architecture and possibly to incorporate it into their designs.[26]

Alterations in garden styles, of course, would be easier to accomplish than architectural ones, and they would also give homeowners a chance to re-create some part of Colonial Williamsburg in their backyards. The restoration's gardens departed from the usual American style, however. Those of the Governor's Palace, for example, had been designed by British gardeners, whose style was noticeably different from that of American gardeners. Some of Colonial Williamsburg's architects questioned whether all the town's gardens had been as elaborate as the modern gardeners made them, but since the critics could not prove that the original gardens were not ornate, those styles remained. This adornment drew many visitors who found the horticultural beauty of the restoration to be one of its biggest attractions.[27]

Perhaps the easiest way to make one's home resemble those in Colonial Williamsburg would be to use official restoration paints and furniture replicas. Although an accurate re-creation of the Palace ballroom would be beyond the means of most Americans, the use of a few antique replicas and some cans of Colonial Williamsburg paint could effectively re-create the air of the eighteenth century in a previously twentieth-century-style living or dining room. The imitation of these styles and their popularity, as attested by the amount of attention paid to them, indicated the interest that many Americans had in the country's colonial past.[28]

With the purchase of Bassett Hall, the most elegant manor house in the city, JDR Jr. became a part-time resident of Williamsburg, coming there for two months each year for the rest of his life. He liked to walk among the workers as they completed the restoration, allowing himself to get a good feel for what he was creating. He was pleased that he could walk the streets and enjoy the changes taking place in the town, much like all the other residents and tourists. He also played an important role in the presentation of the restoration. He had frequent discussions with the president of the restoration, Kenneth Chorley, and the lead architect, A. Edwin Kendrew, about the construction and restoration of the buildings, as well as the arrangement of much of the town's plants, trees, and shrubs. He was also interested in providing scenic views and seating arrangements for the visitors, even if those arrangements were not historically accurate.[29]

In addition to the attention Colonial Williamsburg received nationally, the growing number of tourists meant an increase in revenue for the town. Mrs. Henry M. Stryker recalled that the extra fifty dollars a month she earned as a hostess meant a better standard of living for her family. But the benefit to the town was not solely financial; the restoration changed people's attitudes in a number of ways. Residents gained ideas from the restoration about everything from furnishings to flower arrangements, which helped to

The garden of the Governor's Palace in full bloom (Courtesy of the Colonial Williamsburg Foundation)

brighten the homes of those who lived in the vicinity. Overall, the local standard of living increased as the town became a mecca for the idealization of the American past.[30]

But not all of the town's residents were overjoyed with the interest that the restoration received. Before the start of the project, the College of

William and Mary was the most popular tourist attraction in the town. The restoration, however, took attention away from the college and made it merely a part of the overall project. Thomas McCaskey felt that this caused a certain amount of resentment toward the restoration among college officials. But the college was an integral part of the attraction for many visitors, and the restoration of the Wren Building, Brafferton Hall, and the President's House were important parts of the presentation. Without the cooperation of the college, the restoration would have lacked a proper perspective of Williamsburg in the eighteenth century.[31]

As greater numbers of people came to see how Colonial Williamsburg had been transformed in the preceding ten years, a housing and food service shortage, which would need to be rectified as soon as possible, became apparent. Originally, the small number of visitors who were forecast to come could have been easily handled by the inns and motels in the town. To serve wealthier visitors, the Williamsburg Inn, a luxury hotel, was opened by the restoration in 1937. But the question of providing both food and rooms for the large groups coming into the town remained a major planning issue for the restoration. Private houses could be used to some extent, but many of those available lacked bathrooms, a drawback for many visitors.

The food situation was handled a bit more easily: the plan was to construct a one-story addition to the north end of the Williamsburg Inn dining room, at a cost of approximately $4,600. To help alleviate the lack of rooms, the *Virginia Gazette* called for the building of more tourist houses or apartment blocks with modern amenities that could house these visitors. If the restoration was to keep the crowds coming, it would need a great increase in all types of accommodations because not all patrons could afford to stay at the Williamsburg Inn. JDR Jr. was wary about building more hotels at Colonial Williamsburg and preferred that private ventures provide the accommodations needed by the growing number of tourists venturing to see the town. He did agree, however, to the building of the Williamsburg Lodge, which would be less expensive than the Inn. The Lodge was thrown up in a hurry, leading to criticism that its more modern architectural style did not blend into the restoration, especially since it was located so close to the Georgian-style Inn. But the Lodge turned out to be a great help in easing the strain of the large numbers of visitors who came to the town, especially during World War II, and it later became a thriving conference center that broadened the facilities the restoration had to offer.[32]

In the spring of 1937, the *National Geographic* magazine published an ar-

The Williamsburg Inn (Courtesy of the Colonial Williamsburg Foundation)

ticle in which JDR Jr. made his first widespread public announcement of
the reasons why he had begun the restoration a decade ago. JDR Jr. could
have used his family's wealth in many other ways, but his interest in the
American past, as well as its art and architecture, made Williamsburg a logical choice for such a large personal investment. Unlike Rockefeller Center
in New York City, which stood for the family's business interests, Colonial
Williamsburg embodied JDR Jr.'s ideas and inclinations. He wrote that the
restoration received his interest and support because "to see beautiful and
historic places and buildings disintegrating had long caused me very real
distress." The restoration of Colonial Williamsburg, however, offered JDR
Jr. the opportunity to restore a complete area and "free it entirely from alien
or inharmonious surroundings" in addition to preserving "the beauty and
charm of the old buildings of the city and its historic significance." He went
on to note that as the work progressed he came to feel that "perhaps an even
greater value is the lesson that it teaches of the patriotism, high purpose,
and unselfish devotion of our forefathers for the common good. If this
proves to be true, any expenditure made there will be amply justified."[33]

With the last words of his article, JDR Jr.'s position became clear. If any
expense would be justified in promoting the "spirit" at Colonial Williams-

burg, clearly this lesson in Americanism was to be an integral part of the operation. He saw Colonial Williamsburg as an important ingredient in the promotion of his brand of Americanism early in the restoration process. Promoting this ideology was so important, in fact, that he was willing to spend as much money as was necessary to convey this ideology to those who came to visit the restoration.

The *Virginia Gazette* also weighed in that spring, evoking a religious tone in calling Colonial Williamsburg the "Mecca for the thousands who wish to see this sacred and historic spot." The *Gazette* claimed that since almost everyday "one may see cars with foreign licenses from every state in the Union as well as Canada," Colonial Williamsburg was becoming a true national and international shrine. But this did not surprise the newspaper, because in its view "here in Williamsburg one can live again as in the past, with the voices now stilled, echoing in our souls." The *Gazette* further asked, "[I]s it any wonder that tourists and visitors from the ends of the earth come here to dwell for a short space of time, to breathe once gain in this twentieth century the very air of centuries gone by?"[34]

Earlier that year, speakers at a Colonial Williamsburg restoration conference urged Americans to look to "'the glorious pioneer spirit, the intrepid courage and steadfast fidelity to high ideals' of their forefathers for guidance and inspiration in meeting the complex problems of the present day." This desire to create a symbiotic relationship between the peoples of the eighteenth and twentieth centuries was preserved as a common theme during the next seventeen years of the restoration, as domestic and international struggles forced Americans to search for an inner strength to allow them to perpetuate American ideals.[35]

By July 1937 the restoration had reached such a stage that W. A. R. Goodwin wrote to JDR Jr. that "it would appear that the structural, material side of the undertaking has been well nigh brought to completion." But some problems still remained. The most prominent of those related to the "conservation of essential values of the restoration, to the educational and interpretive side of the endeavor and to the preservation and further development of public confidence." Goodwin argued that the interpretive side of the restoration needed to be bolstered to ensure the proper presentation of Colonial Williamsburg. He suggested that specialists be put in charge of the interpretation program to ensure the continued success of this portion of the endeavor. He was particularly concerned by a comment made by a visitor that indicated the danger of commercializing the restoration to the point where it would lose its value as a beacon of Americanist ideas. He was fearful of "obscuring spiritual values by injudicious commercial methods" and the loss of public confidence if people perceived that Colonial Williamsburg was intent on becoming more of a money-making enterprise than one devoted to perpetuating the aura of the past. "Nothing could be more vital than to scrupulously safeguard the integrity of the Restoration," he wrote, arguing that the future of the project depended upon a strong interpretive program.[36]

To assure public satisfaction and to mute criticism, Goodwin proposed that a board be created, the members of which were experts in the fields "of Architecture, creative Literature, History, Education and Interpretation." He warned JDR Jr. that, above all, Colonial Williamsburg had to project a voice of "truth and beauty and of inherent integrity. . . . You have here created a sacred Shrine. It must be maintained in its integrity. It must be defended lest it lose its sanctity."[37]

Goodwin feared that all he had worked for would be lost if visitors found the town too commercial. A few visitors were quick to seize on any indication that the restoration was becoming even the least bit commercialized, mostly because of the association of the Rockefeller family. The more cynical tourists failed to believe that Colonial Williamsburg was truly a philanthropic enterprise; they saw it as another way to add to the already enormous Rockefeller fortune. Thus, it appeared that JDR Jr.'s grand scheme to give something back to the people was in danger of backfiring. This fear provided another reason for the restoration to make a strong effort to sell the spiritual side of the project, while de-emphasizing the amount of money spent on its completion.

Late in 1939, in an attempt to reconcile the financial needs of the restoration with the desire to cater to an audience of modest as well as substantial means, the staff committee on admissions proposed a three-tiered ticket system for entrance into the colonial area. The adult day ticket cost $1.50 and allowed entrance to "six Exhibition Buildings, four Craft shops and accompanying daytime activities—good for a date on which stamped." For fifty cents more, one could extend the visit for one week and have unlimited access to six buildings and four shops during that time. The annual ticket cost $5.00 and allowed entrance to all buildings and craft shops for one calendar year.[38]

This plan had three main aims: to continue to attract visitors, to provide a fair income for the restoration, and to encourage visitors to stay longer.

Staying longer, of course, meant that tourists were more likely to spend more money in the inns and taverns in the town. This would be particularly beneficial because businesses owned by the restoration plowed their profits back into the further development of the project. The committee's goal was that "admissions should continue at such a level as to enable the greatest number to obtain the greatest benefit (whether this is designated enjoyment, inspiration or education) from visits to these buildings." The committee also took into account Colonial Williamsburg's unique position as a public educational resource. "In its relations to the public as an educational organization, we of the Restoration are mindful of the distinction between a purely commercial enterprise and one whose support and continuing usefulness depend upon undiminished public support." As the country began to come out of the Great Depression, Colonial Williamsburg's officials anticipated a greater increase in travel and visitation. Even more important, as fascism took its toll in Europe, Colonial Williamsburg's role as a defender of democracy became paramount and the restoration began to gear itself to that presentation.[39]

Although five years had passed since the first visitors walked through the town, the restoration still projected a special aura, one that transcended the merely historical. Francis Bemiss Mason wrote to Kenneth Chorley that although the restoration had historical value, "it has a much greater moral and educational importance. . . . Though it has taken time for the spirit of the Restoration to permeate the thought of the nation [that] is one more proof of its sincerity and stability." He continued, arguing the long-lasting effect that Colonial Williamsburg would have: "It is really an institution, and one in which we can deposit historical treasures with the assurance they will again be woven into the interests of active generations." In May of that year, Alice O. Kay wrote to JDR Jr. to express similar sentiments. "I think you have achieved something far beyond a perfect reconstruction of a Colonial capital of the eighteenth century." She went on to say that she felt "in Williamsburg as one feels in a great cathedral or on the height of a mountain, grateful for the identification with a force, fundamental and spiritually beautiful."[40]

Key to a greater diffusion of the belief in Americanism was a greater promotion of what Colonial Williamsburg had to offer. Both economic and educational concerns centered on bringing the restoration and the public closer together for mutual benefit. From the start, the problem of the variation in seasonal attendance had beset the restoration. Differences between winter and spring proceeds were so large as to require some type of remedy. One way to alleviate this problem was the start of the Christmas celebration in Colonial Williamsburg, which began in December 1939. Kenneth Chorley felt that there must have been some interesting Christmas customs in colonial times and hoped through a revival of these traditions to attract visitors to spend the holiday season in the eighteenth century. Thomas McCaskey recalled that the first year of the Williamsburg Christmas program was small but was well received by the visitors, many of whom did not get in until the "wee hours of the morning."[41]

Early in 1940 Chorley turned to Raymond Rich Associates of New York City to plot a promotional program for Colonial Williamsburg. Rich proposed a six-step plan to bring the restoration to the public's attention, including an on-site assessment by several associates and a review of such things as national, state, and local publicity, hotel and admission rates, recreation and entertainment facilities, cooperation with travel agents, and several other categories closely related to the public's image of and knowledge about Colonial Williamsburg. The estimated price for the first four stages, essentially the ones needed before finalizing the recommendations, would cost between $6,000 and $7,500. Finalization of the project was predicted to cost between $1,000 and $3,000, depending on the amount of time needed to fuse all the different calculations from different areas.[42]

Internally, restoration officials also looked to "realize the full possibilities of the Williamsburg enterprise." Louis Wirth, a prominent sociologist of the period who was a consultant to Colonial Williamsburg, felt that it was necessary to see more than the contemporary status of the restoration as a museum piece or a monument but that instead there should be an attempt to understand "what the community of Williamsburg stood for in the day of its glory and what it might conceivably stand for as a symbol today." Wirth cogently argued that Colonial Williamsburg could not be used to demonstrate colonial America as a whole. In addition, as he correctly pointed out, "Williamsburg represents the aristocratic strain in American colonial civilization. It was the seat of government of Virginia up to about the 1780's and the home of the favored classes of society." Having thoroughly disputed the notion that the eighteenth-century Williamsburg could be viewed as a paradigm, Wirth supported a presentation that showed Colonial Williamsburg as an example of the leisurely life of the eighteenth century from which "we might be able to dramatize, if we are ingenious enough, the possibilities of such a leisurely life for all or most of the people of today." He felt that another way to present Williamsburg was from an intellectual standpoint, capitalizing on the town's heritage of having housed such people as Thomas Jefferson, George Wythe, and Patrick Henry, demonstrating that in Williamsburg many of the Founding Fathers had conceived their notions of liberty.[43]

Wirth argued that to make Colonial Williamsburg a more potent force in American life it was necessary to look forward and to use the restoration to project a better life in the present rather than merely to reminisce about the past. "Above all," he argued, "its educational value for American youth and for the American citizenry generally should not be confined to the function of serving as a place of pilgrimage." Colonial Williamsburg needed to go beyond this situation because if it was "to become merely a mecca to which relatively few can travel, and even fewer can be admitted, (by virtue of the dollar and a quarter admission charge), its major possibilities will not be realized."[44]

The proximity to the College of William and Mary and the large supply of colonial documents at Williamsburg made it clear that the town should also have an important role to play in the promotion of the study of early American history and culture. Beyond this role, it would be possible to promote the "effectiveness of the restoration buildings to stimulate study and reflection . . . of the meaning of democracy." This promotion was extremely important because it "would provide a very strong motivation for the kind of intelligent effort required of the citizen of the democratic state." This reflection would probably lead the visitor to "rededicate himself to constructive service as a citizen in behalf of freedom, liberty, and democracy." Even beyond that, further contributions to the understanding of American values could be obtained by bringing community leaders from around the country to the restoration for a week or so, under the assumption that such visits would "produce an effect upon the attitudes and thinking of these council members that would go far toward developing a better democracy throughout the country." Thus, Colonial Williamsburg was truly taking shape as the beacon for the promotion of democracy. The restoration still embodied the struggles of the past but combined with that was a mission to promote the importance of democracy in a world that was fast coming under the control of fascism.[45]

During the 1930s, Colonial Williamsburg sought to define its identity as its officials created a shrine that would promote Americanism. From W. A. R. Goodwin to Louis Wirth, restoration planners worked to project a suitable image for Colonial Williamsburg—one that combined public appeal with historical authenticity. At first, the restoration was able to count on free publicity from the popular press, which was fascinated with the transformation being effected in Virginia. But Colonial Williamsburg needed to ensure that visitors would still come once the novelty had worn off. As the restoration created a faith that supported American ideals against the deprivations of the depression, the war in Europe forced Americans to look outward and to think about protecting their country from external attack as well as from internal economic difficulties.

This reality would enforce an important change on the restoration. It would have to reach out and join the cause of the war. In so doing, Colonial Williamsburg would serve as a means to portray the past in a way that would be useful to the war effort. As the perilous situation abroad became more and more obvious to Americans, Colonial Williamsburg could help satisfy the national need for security. The struggles of the colonial era could provide solace for a country battling to remove the specter of fascism from Europe and Asia. Just as the cause of the earlier era was the attainment of liberty, the greatest confrontation of the twentieth century was also a battle to preserve that most basic American ideal.

3

To Preserve a Nation

The promotion of Americanism had always been high on the list of Colonial Williamsburg's responsibilities, but in 1941 its role became more urgent than ever, as the tension of an impending national emergency spread across the country. In this time of crisis, feelings of national pride and the role of the country's past struggles rose higher than before. Americans both inside and outside of government began to feel that the United States would eventually have to enter the war, and to help ensure victory, the preparation for battle would have to include some type of indoctrination program. Such a program would teach the soldiers and sailors what their country and its allies were fighting for and why this battle was so important for the preservation of liberty at home and abroad. This program would highlight the Americanist ideals of the restoration's founders and serve as a means to instill a sense of the responsibility modern Americans had to the past. Soldiers and sailors would then take away stronger feelings of national duty and obligation.

Comparisons between the Revolutionary struggle and the ravages of the Great Depression were common in Colonial Williamsburg in the 1930s, but as World War II grew closer, a more accurate analogy was drawn between the American War of Independence and the need to defeat fascism. The promotion of Americanism at Colonial Williamsburg was primarily an educational mission, and the organization's internal memoranda discussed the best way to create a greater appreciation for the past as well as a stronger love of country. The more bombastic approach centering simply on famous leaders was discarded in exchange for one with a greater emphasis on the people as a whole. This approach would make visitors feel more a part of the restoration and show them that the fight for freedom needed the participation of more than just a special few. To ensure that people would remember the issues well past the time of their visit, Colonial Williamsburg wished to elicit a visceral reaction from its visitors, not merely an intellectual one.[1]

Restoration officials also favored presentations that would permit "self-identification with the dramatic characters." The key was to strive for reality and not present these characters of the past in too favorable a light. They should be shown to possess weaknesses and failings, qualities that would more readily allow the audience to identify with individuals who lived almost two hundred years ago. Another means of communicating the past was to have buildings "speak" of their role in the past and explain the great events that had occurred within their walls. Organized by the roles of the buildings, these presentations were to cover important events in the life of Williamsburg and the colony of Virginia. The Capitol would represent economic and political developments, the Wren Building education, Raleigh Tavern social gatherings, the Court House the law, and Bruton Parish Church religion and faith.[2]

Questions also centered on the presentation of historical material in the restoration, primarily which aspects of the past were to be emphasized and which were to be given less importance. A memorandum about the guiding principles of Colonial Williamsburg noted that all education relating to history involved a selective process influenced by the motive of the educator. "That motive may range from the extreme of propaganda . . . to the scholar's 'completely balanced presentation,' which is designed to produce comprehensive intellectual knowledge." The path for Colonial Williamsburg was to be neither of these, because propaganda would probably weaken the attempted message, whereas a scholarly approach would preclude an "inspirational emphasis" that was held to be an important part of the message. Officials also felt that "the volume of facts essential to a 'completely balanced presentation' is, in practice, excessive." Therefore, the notion of presenting an accurate slice of eighteenth-century life in colonial Virginia never got a full hearing during this time. In the minds of the restoration's officials, the public could not, or would not, fully appreciate the complexity of the past.[3]

Colonial Williamsburg's role also needed to change with the times and to present the past in a way that related to the most important problems of the American people. That meant that during a given period it might be advisable to emphasize the basic freedoms of speech, press, and religion promulgated in eighteenth-century Williamsburg. At another time it would be preferable to stress the fact that the colonials faced serious economic maladjustments, which they either solved or successfully survived. This point explained the changes that took place in Colonial Williamsburg from the 1930s to the 1940s. Because the restoration's goal was to blend the meaning of the past with present-day events, its presentation changed over time. Yet at all times its goal was to be inspirational and supportive of American ideals.[4]

In addition to the social and economic status of the country, the restoration needed to take into account its varied audience. Officials identified three main audience types and the different types of presentations that needed to be prepared for all three. Because these groups had a variety of tastes, interests, and backgrounds, the restoration needed to account for the differences between these people. One obviously could not treat someone with a Ph.D. in the same manner in which one might treat a young school child. Therefore, the restoration required different approaches so that each audience could get the most out of the Colonial Williamsburg experience.

The first audience was composed of "post-graduate historians and those with a substantial interest and prior knowledge in history, architecture, furnishings, crafts, gardens, flower arrangements, etc." These people required a sophisticated program that included guides who were extremely knowledgeable and well prepared to answer probing questions. These individuals could be expected to dedicate a long period of time to the intricate study of minute details of the restoration. They often took a professional interest in the subject and could be expected to linger for quite a while, as they attempted to absorb all that the restoration had to offer.[5]

The second audience was composed of students from grade schools, high schools, preparatory schools, and colleges. These individuals would evince some interest in the specifics yet would also search for a broader understanding of the restoration. Younger children would be captivated by stories of exciting deeds and anecdotes about George Washington, Thomas Jefferson, or Patrick Henry. Older students would be able to grasp much more sophisticated information: perhaps they would be able to see the restoration both as a representation of the town and also as a paradigm for the ideals of the nation as a whole.[6]

Finally, the third and largest audience was composed of adults who had little knowledge of colonial history and little time to devote to its study. Therefore, "to start an educational program for this group at a level beyond its reach would seriously weaken the effectiveness of the program." Clearly the restoration's officials believed that any attempt to relay too sophisticated information to such people would compromise their ability to understand and to enjoy the restoration. The restoration's purpose for this audience would be to interest and to entertain but not to overeducate them.[7]

Of course, a necessary component of the plan for increasing the educational potential of the restoration revolved around building an audience at Colonial Williamsburg. Because visitors provided much of the essential income for current maintenance of the restoration's educational activities, and because Colonial Williamsburg's message was most effectively communicated through a personal visit, the restoration's officials recognized that audience building was an essential part of a successful educational program. Three elements were crucial to this audience building: attracting visitors, conveying the information to them, and reaching as many people outside of Williamsburg as possible.[8]

The most important means of ensuring a growing audience was to maintain the public's interest in the project and to demonstrate Colonial Williamsburg's relevance to modern events. At all times, the restoration had to be presented in an attractive way so as to generate goodwill among the visitors that would result, officials hoped, in positive word-of-mouth advertising. Fees should be kept as low as possible to encourage visitations, although some charge was necessary to help defray the costs of the restoration and to encourage people to respect their experience. Important, too, was facilitating visits to ensure that viewers derived as much as possible from the undertaking. To accomplish this, the restoration needed to provide maps, accessible information on transportation facilities, and a suitable range of accommodations in Williamsburg to encourage people to come and to stay as long as possible. Once visitors arrived in town, informational signs, guide maps, hostesses, and escorts helped to educate the public about the restoration's message. In addition, evening entertainments were proposed to occupy people once the buildings and stores had closed for the night. All these plans were important for increasing the potential audience for Colonial Williamsburg.[9]

The Rockefellers also wanted to get the most out of the money that they had donated to Colonial Williamsburg. JDR Jr. was anxious that the restoration be able to support itself, a sentiment that was also shared by JDR 3d. The 1940 operating budget was balanced, with a strong hope that this would continue into the future. Hoping to continue the work that his father had done drawing the American public closer to the restoration to benefit from its ideology, JDR 3d tentatively offered to assist in the managerial and promotional sides of Colonial Williamsburg. He argued that due to the New Deal the American people had become dependent on the federal government. If the people felt that the country owed them more than they owed *it*, traditional American values—"those individual qualities such as self-reliance, initiative, courage and sacrifice and . . . the principles of democracy and freedom"—would erode. With that assertion, JDR 3d encapsulated much of the ideological framework surrounding the restoration.[10]

But an understanding of the need for these values could only take place by means of an educational program that stressed the importance of traditional beliefs. Qualities such as leadership, self-reliance, versatility, practical skill, dignity, justice, personal cultivation, and self-control were supposedly promoted by the Virginia aristocracy of the eighteenth century but were, in the mind of JDR 3d, lacking in the world of the early 1940s. A study of these ideals and their popularization through Colonial Williamsburg would do much to re-create a "sense of civic obligation." If merely the aesthetic qualities of the past were recalled, then only part of the picture would be complete. No doubt the restoration's officials idealized the figures of the past, but in believing that the Founding Fathers possessed these qualities, the founders of Colonial Williamsburg strove to create an ideal world where people embodied the values held to be important by the Rockefellers and their associates.[11]

Harold D. Lasswell of the federal government's experimental Division for the Study of War Time Communications wrote to JDR 3d in March 1942 to suggest a possible role for Colonial Williamsburg. Lasswell claimed that Colonial Williamsburg "offers many opportunities to dramatize the Four Freedoms stated by the President—Freedom to Live, Work, Speak, Worship. These were what the Virginians lived for." In a time of national emergency, disputes or bickering had no place. The most important part of the presentation, however, was to steer between the extremes of "dull exposition on the one hand and cheap wisecrack dramatization on the other." The challenge was to reach a broad audience and leave something worthwhile behind.[12]

Morale building was also important within the organization of Colonial Williamsburg. Discontinuance of the publication of "Restoration News," the employees' newspaper, was received poorly by the organization's workers. In this case, economy did not yield positive results. The newspaper's most important job was to keep former employees currently serving in the armed forces in touch with the changes taking place in Colonial Williamsburg. For this reason, Kenneth Chorley requested that JDR Jr. grant $400 to defray the cost of publication. Such a sum would show that Colonial Williamsburg was tied closely to the war effort and was serious about pursuing its goals. Employees on leave to serve their country could share the news of the restoration with their peers, encourage them to promote the restoration's objectives, and create a desire to visit the restoration after the war. The fact that from all the Rockefeller millions Chorley had to beg for $400 to keep the newspaper going demonstrates the up-and-down nature of funding at Colonial Williamsburg. For some parts funds were more than adequate, yet for others shortfalls were a serious problem. Efforts at cost control during the war sometimes hit the organization in the wrong place, the best example of which was the debate over the employee newspaper.[13]

To inspire the country and to remind it what the war was all about, Colonial Williamsburg became the focal point of planning for a nationwide radio program that would inform Americans that the infringements on their liberties were only short lived. When the war was over, freedom of the press and freedom of speech would return to their normal, prewar levels. A committee consisting of officials from the army, the National Education Association, the Library of Congress, and Colonial Williamsburg agreed that the best way to bolster public morale would be to use Colonial Williamsburg to remind people of the country's origins. The committee proposed that initially there be a radio program aimed at adults; this format would be edited to fifteen minutes and played in schools on records or broadcast through radio stations. This plan would reach the greatest number of people in the shortest period of time at relatively little cost, thereby fulfilling the restoration's goal of promoting a sense of Americanism in this national emergency.[14]

Many visitors, however, felt that seeing the restoration was important and lamented that Colonial Williamsburg was not better advertised in the national media. Word of mouth, which was the initial means of promoting the restoration, seemed inadequate. As Ethel B. Bellsmith suggested to JDR Jr. in the spring of 1941, "the historical value is of course important but the demonstration of a culture strongly motivated and moving with religious force to objectives of freedom and democracy is I think its greatest value." Bellsmith also argued for a strong promotional campaign that would attract people to the restoration and make its effect more widely felt.[15]

Once the war began, many Americans found comfort in Colonial Williamsburg because it forced people to envision the struggles of the past as they had often done during the depression. Now fascism, not economic hardship, needed to be fought. People such as C. Kenneth Snyder found that "today as we fight to maintain . . . liberty and freedom, the beauty of the 'harvest' reaped so many years ago in the struggle and work becomes even more strongly important." He further argued that in the battle to defeat fascism Americans would better understand their rights and gain an appreciation of the fight for freedom in the colonial era.[16]

The *Virginia Gazette* felt that due to the patriotic nature of Colonial Williamsburg's presentation, people should come to see the restoration during the war: "as long as cars can be run, it will be to the advantage of all who live within a restricted area and desire a vacation, to come to Williamsburg which can be easily reached in a few hours." The newspaper also noted that the local chamber of commerce had reported that thirty-six thousand tourists had passed through its doors in 1941 and five thousand had written for information on Colonial Williamsburg and the Tidewater peninsula. Although the national tourist traffic would be greatly diminished due to the war restrictions on leisure travel, those who lived close by—and perhaps had never seen the restoration—had the chance to experience Colonial Williamsburg without being overwhelmed by large crowds. Thus even in wartime, Colonial Williamsburg could still be the "mecca for tourists" that the *Virginia Gazette* claimed it should be.[17]

The plans for radio programs to enlighten Americans about their history also took on a new importance in the wake of the United States's entry into World War II. In July 1942 JDR 3d contacted William S. Paley, president of the Columbia Broadcasting System (cbs), to propose a plan for thirteen such radio programs that would be scheduled to be released in October. With the army and the National Education Association already on board, JDR 3d hoped to win over cbs to the cause. He was unsuccessful, however, because cbs was unwilling to add another morale-boosting program to its fall program since, in Paley's words, "we have already selected about as many shows of a 'morale' building and patriotic character as we feel our schedule should contain."[18]

Soldiers from Fort Eustis in Merchant's Square during their visit to Colonial Williamsburg, ca. 1943 (Courtesy of the Colonial Williamsburg Foundation)

At the same time that the radio programs were being planned, arrangements for soldiers and sailors from nearby military bases to visit the restoration were being finalized. These men and women were to be indoctrinated in much the same way that the civilian population was. If they could be made to understand that the "principles which were established . . . at Jamestown, Williamsburg and Yorktown in the eighteenth century are exactly the same as those we are fighting to maintain, they will be benefitted by the knowledge and Williamsburg will be accomplishing a worthwhile purpose in the national emergency." Three hundred servicemen and women would visit Colonial Williamsburg daily, Monday through Saturday, from nine o'clock A.M. to four o'clock P.M. Such a schedule would ensure that all the troops had a chance to visit the restoration during their stay at Fort Eustis, allowing them to better understand their role in the war against fascism.[19]

These young men and women who were indoctrinated by the restoration were given an intense one-day tour of the area. The entire day's group would assemble in the Williamsburg Theatre and be welcomed by an offi-

Vernon Geddy Sr., a Williamsburg lawyer who served as an
important link between the restoration and the local population (Courtesy of the Colonial Williamsburg Foundation)

cer of the restoration as the personal guests of Mr. and Mrs. John D. Rockefeller Jr. This greeting was followed by an hour-long lecture on the history
of the region and a movie showing the various steps in the restoration of the
town. After this session the larger group divided into smaller classes of
twenty-five or thirty who spent the rest of the day visiting the most important historical buildings in Colonial Williamsburg. They would first visit the
Capitol "in which they are shown the Speaker's Chair in the House of
Burgesses and the benches from which such utterances as Patrick Henry's
famous 'Caesar had his Brutus' speech were delivered." The next stop was
the Raleigh Tavern, where the soldiers viewed the rooms where the
burgesses met after they were dissolved by the royal governor and where
they passed resolutions, corresponded with the other colonies, and elected
delegates to the several continental congresses. Visits to Bruton Parish
Church and the Wren Building at the College of William and Mary em-

phasized the freedom to worship God and to pursue knowledge and truth, "which are such important elements in the American way of life."[20]

Vernon Geddy, a local lawyer and Rockefeller aid, further explained the purpose of the soldiers' visits. They came to Colonial Williamsburg to find inspiration for their overseas battles for patriotism and justice, rights that Americans, in Geddy's eyes, had taken far too much for granted. "In Williamsburg they see an accurate and intelligent reminder of the principles its founders sought to establish." Imbued with the desire to perpetuate these ideas, the soldiers and sailors would fight even harder for their country—or at least that is what the restoration's officials hoped.[21]

JDR Jr. authorized a payment of up to $300 per week for the soldiers' educational program, which he had increased from $200 to provide guides for the troops, serve them coffee, and pay for attendants during the film presentations. He was highly supportive of the plan of troop education, especially since fewer civilians could travel to the restoration because of wartime restrictions due to gasoline rationing and space limitations on trains and buses. Military education, therefore, served an important purpose for keeping the restoration active and the local workers employed, especially since the rebuilding and restoration program was halted because all building supplies were needed for the war effort. Starting in October 1944, JDR Jr. agreed to have soldiers and sailors in the military hospitals in the vicinity of Colonial Williamsburg take tours of the restoration as his guests. This additional group included those from Camps Peary and Lee as well as those from the Portsmouth Hospital, Fort Story Hospital, and the Fort Eustis Hospital. This further extension of the program demonstrated that Colonial Williamsburg could be instrumental not only as a place of military education but also as a recreational facility for those who had been wounded in the service of their country.[22]

JDR Jr.'s plans did not go unappreciated by these military visitors, and for many the effect of the restoration was what he had hoped it would be. Cpl. Art Froehly wrote to JDR Jr. in November 1942 to describe how instructive the tour was for him. "I find it most difficult to find words that describe this beautifully restored settlement. It is so rich in history that one could listen for hours and yet not have covered everything. . . . Everything is so real as it was in those colonial days that it really and truly makes us proud to be an American."[23]

Far more grandiloquent was the letter by Pfc. Richard Korn who wrote from the hospital at Camp Lee in August 1944. Korn's effusive phrasing demonstrated the effect that the restoration had on at least some of its visitors. "[Y]ou worked with an age so great that it could compel even the dead mortar and the unfeeling utensils of daily life to proclaim its story—written on its stones and on those silent tongues tolling forever, 'that the future may learn from the past.'"[24]

As Korn saw it, future generations would only be able to comprehend events like World War II through the use of historical shrines like Colonial Williamsburg. The restoration would be able to relate to its audiences the struggle for freedom during both the colonial era and the mid-twentieth century, as well as the ideals and values of both eras. Such a tradition of historical shrines dated well back into the nineteenth century, as visitors ascribed religious meaning to sites across the country. In visiting these attractions, ranging from historic buildings to natural wonders such as Niagara Falls and Yosemite, many tourists felt a sense of renewal and a feeling of liberation. Korn's description of Colonial Williamsburg paralleled this ideology and demonstrated the restoration's position as a modern-day national shrine.[25]

Perhaps the most famous letter received by the restoration during the war came from Robert Friedberg. He wrote, "Of all the sights I've seen, and the books I have read, and the speeches I have heard, none of them made me see the greatness of this country with more force and clearness than when I saw Williamsburg slumbering peacefully on its old foundations." The restoration widely publicized this letter as an illustration of Colonial Williamsburg's good work and its ability to influence Americans to regard the importance of the colonial past. In addition, the letter demonstrated how restored and reconstructed buildings could promote an appreciation for the eighteenth century. These structures stood as symbols of an era whose ideology was being reinforced in a new international battle.[26]

An anonymous navy serviceman stationed at Camp Peary wrote an article for the *Virginia Gazette* in March 1945 that detailed his visit to the restoration. This sailor generally supported the restoration and felt that it enlivened the past and provided a good perspective on the role of Williamsburg in the colonial era. He noted that the architecture of the restoration was not necessarily so influential in promoting these ideas but rather that its spirit had the greatest effect on its visitors. He wrote, "[T]he serviceman . . . views this all with the climactic thought 'so this is what we're fighting for,' calm and quaint peaceful living, the church, [and] shops of plenty."[27]

All these letters evoked similar themes. They demonstrated the sense

A Women's Army Corps contingent viewing a portrait of
George Washington in the Capitol, ca. 1943 (Courtesy of
the Colonial Williamsburg Foundation)

that although Colonial Williamsburg was restored and rebuilt, it still embodied a quality of stillness and quiet reminiscent of the colonial era. This quietude contrasted with the modern world, which, especially because of the war, seemed more hurried than usual. But the difference between the centuries was nevertheless quite apparent. The restoration's founders wished to present such a contrast to allow modern-day Americans to appreciate life in the pretechnological age.

Soldiers and sailors also discovered a new interest in history in Colonial Williamsburg. Mary F. McWilliams wrote to JDR Jr. in the fall of 1945 to tell of a young sailor who when told about Colonial Williamsburg replied that he had no interest in anything historical: "'The only three places that interest a soldier are Frisco, Diego and Scolley's square.'" Later that afternoon, though, he went to Colonial Williamsburg with two other sailors to be "exposed to the beauties of the palace." Servicemen and women who were cynical about the restoration either did not write about their skepticism or perhaps had it muted by superiors. One may assume that not all sailors and soldiers were as ecstatic about Colonial Williamsburg as Korn or Froehly. Nevertheless, the most important point for the restoration was that the exposure these men and women received during the war made them potential candidates to revisit the restoration later on. As A. Edwin Kendrew commented, "I think the exposure of all these thousands of men . . . to Williamsburg has brought many . . . back to us as visitors."[28]

As a result of the war, Colonial Williamsburg had a problem attracting and keeping qualified workers for the restoration. Many of the maintenance people who remained on the job were African American, and there was a need for a dormitory to house these men, as the situation in the town itself was quite poor: "[T]hey are sleeping three and four in a room and sleeping on porches. With the labor situation as it is, these men are not going to put up with that sort of thing." The solution to the problem, as Chorley saw it, was to build a dormitory to ensure that the workers would remain with the restoration. Due to manpower shortages African Americans found ever-increasing employment opportunities during the war. To keep the restoration running, Colonial Williamsburg recruited workers from the farming areas of North and South Carolina and brought them to Williamsburg for seasonal work. They had little opportunity to do much except work in the buildings and return to the dormitory, which was "almost like a chicken house for people to live in." When the heavy season was over, these workers returned to their home areas and waited to be hired again for the next year.[29]

Although the restoration was interested in having African American workers, the same could not be said for visitors of the same race, highlighting an essential contradiction of a project that was geared to the promotion of American democracy. JDR Jr. drafted a form letter in May 1943 that was to be sent to all nonwhites who inquired about accommodations at one of the restoration-run hostelries: "The management has not thus far found it practicable to provide for both colored and white guests. I (or we are) am [*sic*] sorry we cannot accommodate you (or cannot take care of you; or cannot offer you hospitality)." In making this pronouncement, Colonial Williamsburg retained the local provision of housing blacks and whites separately, feeling that there was no need for the restoration to provide black accommodation.[30]

With the end of the war in August 1945, JDR Jr. and Kenneth Chorley could finally start to put into action their plans for further improving the restoration. JDR Jr. realized that the several millions of dollars he had contributed up to that time were insufficient to complete the work to the standard that he and the top officials desired. As A. Edwin Kendrew observed, "During the war years he . . . had a chance on his spring and fall visits to . . . [establish] some pretty firm ideas about how the presentation of Williamsburg . . . should be handled in the future." JDR Jr. turned seventy-one that year and wanted to see Colonial Williamsburg completed during his lifetime for several reasons, but especially because "the chances of it being completed by succeeding generations were small because of lack of funds and also because no one else would be apt to have the same interest in doing so that I have." Since the extension of the educational scope of the restoration depended on the completion of the physical aspects, JDR Jr. decided to invest in this part of the venture first. "I have felt right along . . . that until the physical restoration has been completed, neither surplus capital nor even surplus income or earnings should be used for that purpose lest the larger project might fail of completion."[31]

JDR Jr. understood the importance of the restoration's educational work, however, and fully supported its goals. His main purpose, though, was to ensure that the physical side of the restoration—the buildings, furnishings, and gardens—were authentically reproduced. As he pointed out, this aspect required the largest capital outlay and therefore needed to be financed before other expenditures. JDR Jr. felt that Colonial Williamsburg should teach and inform quietly, not boldly or ostentatiously. In this belief, he was remaining true to Goodwin's original plan. Colonial Williamsburg's message was still "that the future may learn from the past," but the education was to be more in the form of a gentle reminder rather than a stern lecture. But the restoration needed more facilities to help people better understand the town. Edward P. Alexander, who was head of educational programs for the restoration, began to push for "a visitor information and interpretive center where an indoctrination could be made right at the outset of a person's visit."[32]

A further development that occurred during the war helped raise the prominence of the restoration. In collaboration with the College of William and Mary, the restoration sponsored the development of the Institute of Early American History and Culture in January 1944, the purpose of which was to "establish Williamsburg as a major center for the study of early American history." Directed by an advisory panel of historians, which initially included such well-known scholars as Samuel Eliot Morison, Arthur Schlesinger, and Thomas Wertenbaker, the institute would seek to develop a greater appreciation for the study of colonial history and would sponsor fellowships for young historians who wished to perform research in American colonial and early national history. The *William and Mary Quarterly*, an important journal in early American history already in operation, would be sponsored by both the college and the restoration and would further raise the prominence of the collaborative work of both parties. The institute would make Colonial Williamsburg a laboratory for the study of early America and "a center of great interest for its art, architecture, crafts and broad culture touching every aspect of the lives of early Virginians and their relationships to the life and leaders of other American colonies."[33]

By the spring of 1946, Colonial Williamsburg was finally beginning to create the integrated demonstration of the past that many had sought for so long. Arthur Shurcliff, one of the original landscape architects, told Kenneth Chorley that "the Williamsburg scene you were trying out and perfected last week with the many horses and carriages . . . traveling past the ancient dwellings and town setting, was doubtless the most perfect 18th century scene since those old days themselves." Since automobiles still traveled the streets of the restoration in the mid-1940s, special arrangements had to be made to ensure such a scene unfolded. Yet Shurcliff's idea—to have carriages traversing the restoration's streets on a regular basis—was a step toward presenting a more authentic portrayal of life in the past.[34]

Yet the "Negro problem," as it was commonly called, could not disappear because a few black families participated in Colonial Williamsburg pageants. The paradox of promoting Colonial Williamsburg as a shrine to democracy yet forbidding the service of African Americans in restoration-owned hotels and restaurants became even more painful after the war. The summer of 1946 saw the first of many internal debates on how to handle this delicate question. Aware of the tone that Colonial Williamsburg would set in excluding blacks and the danger of losing white visitors if blacks were admitted, Kenneth Chorley decided to "duck the problem" and say in reply to questions from the American Association of Adult Education and the Federal Council of the Churches of Christ in America, both of which had black members, that Colonial Williamsburg would not be able to handle their groups at the time requested.[35]

Not all members of Colonial Williamsburg's Board of Directors agreed with Chorley, however. Vernon Geddy wrote to Chorley in September 1946 to argue that evading the problem would not solve anything. After consulting with other officials, Geddy recommended that the policy of segregation be maintained, that blacks be admitted to neither the Williamsburg Inn nor the Williamsburg Lodge, and that racially mixed groups be informed that as the town did not have any hotels to accommodate blacks, African American members would have to be housed and fed at the homes of local black residents. Although restoration officials did not necessarily believe in the separation of the races, they feared negative repercussions for the restoration should they back away from accepted state practices.[36]

Their fears were well grounded as some visitors complained to the restoration about the presence of African Americans in the town. Although many tourists probably kept their feelings to themselves, Joanna L. S. Priest was moved enough to write and comment that although her stay was "lovely," she noticed that "at noon-time . . . literally hundreds of negroes would appear along the main thoroughfare, standing in large groups, talking and laughing or just lounging against the buildings. . . . [It] made us wonder if you have a colored unemployment problem." Priest was probably not alone in her preferences, but Colonial Williamsburg did not make an attempt to explain that African Americans had always been a part of the Williamsburg community and that their presence should not be viewed as inharmonious with the surroundings.[37]

As Colonial Williamsburg successfully weathered the storm of World War II, it entered another era, one where the questions of race would play an ever-important role. Over the next five years, Colonial Williamsburg would live uncomfortably between the two forces of integration and segregation until it could no longer resist a growing reality. At the same time, the postwar peace of mind that many Americans had hoped they would find dissolved with the start of the Cold War and the fears of internal communism. On these two vital issues of the postwar era Colonial Williamsburg would take center stage.

Because the restoration had become a shrine of growing prominence, the nation looked toward it for leadership in the proper promotion of American ideals in the postwar United States. At a time of increasing internal and international tension, Colonial Williamsburg represented traditional America. It could be held up as a beacon of the country's values to help orient Americans toward the glory of its past. As an article in the *New York Sun* proclaimed, Colonial Williamsburg "is a possession of the whole nation, it is a part of the fabric of American culture being woven on the loom of the centuries, whose cosmopolitan vari-colored woofs are bound by the warp of English tradition."[38]

During the war years, Colonial Williamsburg was able to be a truly potent force in promoting the nation's welfare. Many of the soldiers and sailors who visited the restoration took away with them a better understanding of Williamsburg's role in the nation's past and the ideals that the nation was fighting for in World War II. Doubtless, this conception mostly emphasized the deeds of prominent individuals and generally played down those of ordinary people. Even though there was a stated aim by restoration officials to broaden the focus of Colonial Williamsburg, by its very nature it remained a shrine. It had moved a bit toward a broader interpretation of the past, but it still had a long way to go. Even after the end of their military service, many soldiers and sailors remembered what they had seen in the restored village, and in the years to come, a large number of them returned with their wives and families to broaden the experience of Colonial Williamsburg and to make it an institution that had a wide appeal for much of American society. They reinforced the notion of return visits, establishing a tradition that the restoration hoped to encourage with all its visitors. Many who were intrigued by the restoration in their youth would return to see the rebuilding and restoration process make progress. In so doing, these individuals would help support a project that through the Cold War and the tensions of the 1960s and 1970s would fight to promote its ideals yet slowly would change to accommodate a more accurate interpretation of the colonial past.

4

A Growing Prominence

The growth of the Cold War with the Soviet Union in the late 1940s propelled Colonial Williamsburg into yet another realm of Americanist activity. Once again the restoration was called upon to do what it did best: stir the hearts and minds of Americans toward a love of country and its ideals. In so doing, Colonial Williamsburg advanced a dynamic Americanism that actively promoted the virtues of the United States rather than merely warning of the evils of communism. The restoration became a focal point in the growing war against Soviet aggression. This change in the town's purpose caused a rift between father and son. The perception of JDR Jr. and much of his generation was that Colonial Williamsburg should teach, but without any type of bold ostentation. JDR 3d, however, felt that the time was ripe to exploit Colonial Williamsburg's opportunities and to give it a chance to be a global force in the movement to prevent the spread of communism.

Greater publicity in newspapers and magazines meant that the public was more aware of the restoration than at any time in the past. With the end of wartime travel restrictions, and because of higher wages and wartime savings, many Americans were able to travel over long distances for the first time in over a decade. This freedom meant that Colonial Williamsburg would have an even greater audience than before, giving it the chance to educate a growing number of visitors in the virtues of the country's colonial past. In addition, the restoration had to consider its position as a tourist destination in promoting its presentation. To the restoration's benefit, popular magazines began to run even more articles on Colonial Williamsburg. Most articles appeared in traditional women's magazines such as *House and Garden,* but other periodicals such as *Popular Mechanics* also carried features about the restoration. Education journals also published pieces in the hope of eliciting the interest of teachers and their students. One such article in the January 1947 edition of *School Arts* lauded the accomplishments of the restoration and emphasized the great pains taken in re-creating the colonial town from its early twentieth-century form. The craft shops were particularly highlighted as examples of what the restoration had to offer. But most important of all, the author Gerald Horton Bath concluded, was the "evolution of present-day Williamsburg into a living laboratory of early American history which is providing inspiration for countless Americans today and which is likely to be of increasing significance in the years to come."[1]

Visitors tended to agree with Bath's perception, as D. E. Watkins indicated in 1947. After visiting the restoration, Watkins came away "fully convinced that one's education on the history of our country is incomplete without a visit to Williamsburg, and a visit to the homes and buildings where our forefathers lived and planned." He compared his trip to Colonial Williamsburg with one he had taken ten years earlier to Europe and concluded that "I don't recall any tour in my entire life that impressed me like this one to Williamsburg, and that is saying something when it comes from a Californian." Such a letter indicated the sentiment of Americans who felt that their country possessed a historic singularity worthy of international note; for them, Colonial Williamsburg was such an important place that all Europe paled in comparison. Even the physical splendor of California was not nearly as impressive as this "birth place of the nation." Watkins clearly placed Colonial Williamsburg in a class all its own, and in so doing, he echoed the viewpoint of those who argued that the restoration should be elevated to the status of an international secular shrine. As such, Colonial Williamsburg could appeal to all people, regardless of their religious beliefs. The restoration promoted a unity of belief in a democratic governmental system, an ideal that encompassed all historical periods and crossed all international boundaries.[2]

Olive A. Knight was similarly inspired to write after spending "four idyllic weeks" in Colonial Williamsburg. Knight concurred with Watkins's assessment of the town, calling the restoration "the most perfect and inspiring gift ever presented to any great nation." But she was not content merely to laud the restoration's accomplishments. For her, Colonial Williamsburg had a deeper meaning that she revealed in closing her letter to JDR Jr.: "Forgive me for taking the liberty of writing—but I do so strongly feel that every right-thinking American should at least attempt to thank you." Knight expressed a sentiment that became even more prevalent in the years following World War II: the duty of "good" Americans to visit Colonial Williamsburg and to engage in other activities that proved one's patriotism.[3]

Such a desire to distinguish between "good" and "bad" Americans probably originated in the congressional investigations into domestic communism from the mid-1930s through the early 1950s. By establishing proper norms of behavior, congressional investigative committees, such as the House of Representatives' Un-American Activities Committee and Joseph McCarthy's U.S. Senate investigations, compelled citizens to distinguish thoughts and actions that proved that one was a good American. Colonial Williamsburg, serving as a beacon of liberty and a remembrance of past glories, easily fit the bill of an important patriotic landmark. Thus, "good" Americans visited Colonial Williamsburg and appreciated its glory and importance. Just as these congressional investigations encouraged people to inform on others who had past or present communist ties, some visitors wanted to inform on those who said negative things about the restoration or the Rockefellers. The culture of suspicion that surrounded suspected communists throughout the country also encroached on Americans' perceptions about a national landmark like Colonial Williamsburg. As Americans were often compelled to make declarations about their national loyalty, they found Colonial Williamsburg to be a ready icon to incorporate into their perception of proper citizenship.[4]

In addition, Colonial Williamsburg's proximity to Washington, D.C., played an important part in its postwar role, one that had begun by the late 1940s. Colonial Williamsburg was often incorporated in the tours given to foreign dignitaries and was also a popular spot for government officials on vacation from Washington. One of those who heard quite a bit of reaction to the restoration was Sen. Harry F. Byrd of Virginia. Many of Byrd's colleagues and associates who made the trip to Colonial Williamsburg from Washington commented to him on what they found there. As Byrd noted to restoration vice president Bela W. Norton in 1949, "I do not believe that anything has been done that has accomplished more than the restoration of Williamsburg in giving inspiration to the people of America." Byrd went on to extoll the restoration and to thank JDR Jr. for his efforts in restoring this piece of Americana.[5]

During this period of growing interest in the restoration, changes were under discussion within the business offices of the organization. The offices were divided between the nonprofit Colonial Williamsburg, Inc., which was responsible for the noncommercial properties in the historic area, and Williamsburg Restoration, Inc., which managed the profit-making parts of the restoration, including the hotels, restaurants, and gift shops. One of the most important of these postwar issues was the creation of a new ticket policy. Colonial Williamsburg was again confronted with the dilemma of setting ticket prices to ensure maximum visitation and the least dissatisfaction among visitors while at the same time helping to provide for the financial needs of the restoration. The block ticket, which would allow entrance to all the structures, cost $1.75, which was not much of an increase over prewar rates. Such a fee, officials hoped, would draw visitors from all over the country and encourage return visits. This accessibility would serve to embed Colonial Williamsburg even more firmly in the mind of each visitor and would provide an effective base for Americanist efforts.[6]

In fact, there was an appreciable increase in the number of families who came to see the restoration in the postwar period, especially former soldiers who had since married and brought their wives and children with them. An influx of middle-class families changed the makeup of visitors from the wealthier set that had come before the war to a broader assortment of Americans. No longer did just the local people or those with a great expertise and interest in the colonial period come to Colonial Williamsburg; a more democratic cross section of the country appeared on the streets of the restored village. This group was composed not simply of experts interested in garden design and draperies but of those who wished to see something of the restoration that had won so much national acclaim. These individuals wished to get a sense of their national heritage and to bask in the glory of the colonial era. For them, a trip to Colonial Williamsburg was a good family outing, combining fun and relaxation with an educational experience.[7]

This move signaled the change in Colonial Williamsburg's role from that of an exclusive club for the wealthy to an important educational landmark that was open and accessible to middle-class Americans. If Colonial Williamsburg was to be an important player in the promotion of Cold War Americanism, it needed to reach a wide audience, one that would be receptive to its message and not one that saw the restoration as an exclusive enterprise built on a whim with Rockefeller money. The larger number of visitors meant a greater income for the restoration, the chance to expand its

A couple at Chowning's Tavern, ca. 1948 (Courtesy of the Colonial Williamsburg Foundation)

interpretative programs, and therefore an opportunity to be even more influential in the everyday lives of Americans.

More important, Colonial Williamsburg had to have a good plan of what its future would hold. A good deal of logistical planning was necessary to ensure that visitors got the most out of the restoration. To this end, Colonial Williamsburg pushed to develop an idea of what the final project would look like, how many buildings there would be, and how visitors would interact with the project. As head of the architectural department, A. Edwin Kendrew played a key role in bringing this final idea into focus. This plan involved "filling in the gaps" by reconstructing buildings between those that were already in place, as well as further promoting the role of the craft shops and broadening the interpretation of the restoration with the "so-called 'Life on the Scene' activity." The overall purpose was to give the restoration more of a lived-in feel, moving it away from a traditional museum and closer to a living history presentation. Of course, as the restoration became more popular, some officials feared that in an attempt to lure more visitors Colonial Williamsburg might overly compromise its ideals of an accurate physical restoration of the town. This compromise would have gone against JDR Jr.'s original goals for the restoration. Ever faithful to the founders' original vision, Kendrew worked assiduously to keep this from happening. As he remarked, "[I]t's been a constant battle all during my association with Colonial Williamsburg to hold down the pressures of popularity."[8]

With the rising number of tourists, however, came the feeling that Colonial Williamsburg was becoming overcommercialized. The aura of a small town recaptured from the past was losing ground in the late 1940s. It appeared to many both inside and outside the town that Colonial Williamsburg was more interested in the public's pocketbook than in its understanding of the past. Robert Morris informed Raymond Fosdick, JDR Jr.'s biographer and a Rockefeller aid, of the impressions he and his family had acquired from a trip to Colonial Williamsburg. "[As] we continued our visit about the town, [we gained] further impressions that the [postwar] Williamsburg is regarded by the residents of the town not as a national shrine . . . but rather that the visitor is but a poor lamb primed for the fleecing."[9]

Yet this overcommercialization was certainly not the experience of all tourists, many of whom still carried with them extremely positive views of the restoration. One example was Beatrice S. Kahn, who felt very strongly that the town had an important message to bring to the American people. "A spiritual quality is developing in Williamsburg, either because of the educational service or because of the type of men who are in charge of the restoration and the foundation." Kahn went on to conclude that she, and other Colonial Williamsburg visitors, she hoped, carried away a sense of the restoration's importance.[10]

Some visitors, however, did not find commercialization to be the problem; instead they felt that the restoration as a whole was overrated and simply not worth all the fuss accorded to it. For those who hoped Colonial Williamsburg would be free and easily accessible, the charges for admission were antithetical to the main purpose of the project. Others found the prices reasonable and the experience to be invaluable. The consensus of the majority was guardedly positive, with most people feeling that a trip to see the restoration was an expensive but generally worthwhile experience that brought them a greater understanding of American history and the struggles of the colonial era.[11]

Whether or not Colonial Williamsburg was overcommercialized, it did provide a lesson in history for many Americans. Granted, the portrayal failed to acknowledge the role of a large part of the working population, but it did provide a useful education in basic colonial political history. Children and adults who had never thought much about the beginnings of their country at least received a cursory introduction to American life on the eve of the Revolution. F. Lloyd Adams certainly felt that he, his wife, and his son had gained a lot from the restoration; "I think my son learned more about early American history after spending a week end in Williamsburg than he learned from books over a full semester." Adams's experience was typical of that of many visitors who came to see Colonial Williamsburg in the late 1940s and early 1950s. They came more to have fun than to investigate colonial fabric patterns or garden designs and were perhaps more susceptible to the influences of the restoration than some of the earlier tourists.[12]

Colonial Williamsburg continued to educate people outside the borders of the town with films it sent across the country to be viewed by wide-ranging audiences in many locales. These films allowed people who lacked the means or the inclination to travel to the restored village to get a glimpse of the restoration and to understand its work. The films conveyed the message of the restoration, highlighting life in the colonial era and educating modern-day Americans on their responsibilities as good citizens. For example, one film, *Eighteenth Century Life in Colonial Williamsburg,* netted 2,806 viewers in forty-one showings in Gary, Indiana, not including a number of other high school showings. These presentations demonstrated the important role and the continuing appeal of the restoration, as its message was widely disseminated in the postwar years. For a nation fearful of possible communist incursion, such screenings helped to reinforce an ideology that comforted those who feared the worst from the Soviet Union. The media agreed with the prominence of the restoration, and as the *New York Times* remarked in January 1948, "the Restoration has been a wise investment in the re-education of Americans."[13]

Colonial Williamsburg also received attention in other newspapers across the country. The *Virginia Gazette* published an editorial in October 1947 that was a reprint of a column by Louis Spilman who wrote for the *Waynesboro (Va.) News-Virginian.* Spilman argued that Colonial Williamsburg should inspire every man, woman, and child in the United States. "Here, at this spot on one little peninsula in the eastern part of the country, has been reconstructed a breath of colonial atmosphere of incomparable authenticity," he wrote. In Spilman's view, nobody with the slightest imagination could walk the streets of Colonial Williamsburg without feeling "the emotion and strain that accompanied the early days of the city." In addition, he indicated, "no one, with even a modicum of pride in this country, can help having that pride expanded and strengthened after a visit to Williamsburg." In his eyes, Colonial Williamsburg was a vital ingredient in the promotion of American culture and in the demonstration of one's loyalty to the United States.[14]

This editorial is an excellent example of the veneration that was accorded the restoration. In a time of growing fears of international and internal communist incursions, Colonial Williamsburg—in the eyes of many—offered the best opportunity to give Americans "unity and singleness of purpose." To unite the country against the threats of loss of national identity, Colonial Williamsburg provided a focal point of Americanist teachings. In so doing, it was an important instrument in the perpetuation of the nation's Cold War doctrine of extolling the greatness of the American system and decrying the evils of communism.[15]

Although World War II had precluded the continuance of the building program, in peacetime development could resume with a budget of $10 million. The new construction was concentrated along the Duke of Gloucester Street during 1948 and focused primarily on the extensive reconstruction of two of the main structures in the area: the guard house at the Public Magazine and the extensive rehabilitation of the Debtor's Prison. As an editorial from the *Sheboygan (Wisc.) Press* reprinted in the *Virginia Gazette* commented, "[A]lready an influx of our citizens have [*sic*] visited reconstructed Williamsburg, but in the future there will be a pilgrimage there every year. Like New Salem and Philadelphia, Williamsburg will take on the atmosphere of days when our early history was being made." This increase in tourists diversified the type of visitor that the restoration received. More and more frequently those who journeyed to the town were young couples, many of whom had married shortly after the end of the war. In many cases the husbands were servicemen who had visited Colonial Williamsburg during the war years and were returning to show the restoration to their friends and family.[16]

The increased publicity and word-of-mouth advertising further cemented the role of the restoration in the public's perception of the American past. Many Americans, whose principal contact with the colonial era was what they read, saw, and heard about Colonial Williamsburg, necessarily received a bit of the Rockefeller ideal of that era and its importance in the modern world. As the national press was quick to seize upon this presentation, the Americanist message of Colonial Williamsburg became even further embedded in the public's mind.

But Colonial Williamsburg was more than an Americanist tourist attraction; it held a national political significance as well. This meaning was well demonstrated in Harry S. Truman's proclamation of a worldwide "Good Neighbor Policy" at Colonial Williamsburg in April 1948. Truman was under attack from southern Democrats for his promotion of federal civil rights legislation, and so his visit to the restoration was an attempt to demonstrate the South's history of democratic action. This use of Colonial Williamsburg as a locale for the declaration of presidential policy demonstrated the extent to which the restoration was held up as a symbol of the national past. As such, the restoration was not merely a stop on the tourist's trip to mid-Atlantic historic spots, which often included Washington, D.C., and Charlottesville, Virginia, but it was also a potent political symbol that would be used again and again in years to come.[17]

The *Virginia Gazette* also noted Colonial Williamsburg's importance as an international political symbol of the Cold War. In reminding its readers of Hitler's aggressions in the late 1930s, the *Gazette* cautioned that the United States was facing its own confrontation with the Soviet Union. The newspaper noted that "in 1939 it was apparent that the aggressors would continue their course until definitely checkmated by the other powers of the world." The newspaper asked its readers to "learn from the past," utilizing the motto of the restoration. In conclusion, the *Gazette* urged that "here we can learn much from the lives and works of those great men who contributed so much to Williamsburg and to the Nation in America's early days of the 18th century." The newspaper went on to point out that "we can apply the motto to our own present times in striving to work out the best solution to the tense and troubled international situation prevailing today."[18]

As Colonial Williamsburg's role as a political symbol grew, the restoration also attempted to present an appealing picture of the American past to the public. Walter Dorwin Teague, a New York public relations firm, was commissioned in 1948 to assess Colonial Williamsburg's presentation and to suggest ways to better project the restoration's attributes. By the middle of that year, Colonial Williamsburg had passed the five million visitors mark and wanted to ensure its presentation would remain fresh for the coming generations. The firm's assessment was essentially that Colonial Williamsburg had an effective presentation, except that "we felt that we were in the midst of a magnificent stage setting but that the drama had not yet begun."[19]

The Teague report of 1948 went on to argue that it was time for Colonial Williamsburg to shift away from the physical restoration and toward the *"values which made Williamsburg so greatly worth restoring"* [emphasis in original]. Colonial Williamsburg should become a shrine of the American past, much like Independence Hall in Philadelphia, Faneuil Hall in Boston, and George Washington's home at Mount Vernon, the report argued. But Colonial Williamsburg had several characteristics that allowed it to surpass these other landmarks as it provided a more complete vision of the past than one building or home did. As a planned re-creation of a whole colonial town, Colonial Williamsburg could recapture an aura of the past and bring history to life in a way that these other sites could never hope to do.[20]

The desire to move Colonial Williamsburg into a new era, one that focused on visitors' imaginations and their conceptions of the past, meant that Colonial Williamsburg needed to alter the structure of the restoration. If visitors were to walk the streets of the restored town and to believe themselves to be in the eighteenth century, automobiles had to be excluded from the historic area. A bus line would have to be added to provide transportation to and around the restored area as well as to the parking lots, inns, and lodges. To accompany these changes, a main reception area was needed to accommodate visitors and to provide them with a chance to get well acquainted with the restoration before entering the historic area. Essential to this presentation in the visitor's center would be a film that covered the highlights of Williamsburg's colonial past and its role in the promotion of independence.[21]

The Teague report marked an important turning point in the presentation of Colonial Williamsburg. More than fifty years after this report was issued, Colonial Williamsburg still follows its basic principles. The closing of the restoration's streets to traffic, along with the use of a bus system and a main visitor's center, all exist much as Teague and his associates suggested. These factors were instrumental in shaping the restoration's presentation of the past as well as its role in promoting Americanism. Visitors could more readily feel that they were going back in time to the eighteenth century, and as such they would be better able to recognize the town's historical importance. In writing to restoration vice president Bela W. Norton in January 1949, JDR Jr. noted that "the task to which we have all committed ourselves is a task of national and world significance. It is an unending challenge."[22]

Many officials saw the need to keep Colonial Williamsburg high in the public's mind not only as a recreational and educational site but also as a shrine and a symbol of democratic ideals. This view was held by numerous visitors as well. As Dorothy Hanson Gillikin remarked to JDR Jr. in May 1949, "[M]y little boy sat in the pew that bore George Washington's name and I think he has been walking in the clouds ever since. . . . When my son used to say his prayers at bedtime always at the end he said God bless George Washington, Abe Lincoln . . . and now he adds . . . Mr. Rockefeller and Mr. Goodwin." Apparently, both W. A. R. Goodwin and JDR Jr. became ranked, at least in the mind of one child, as important figures in the American past, equal in stature to Washington and Lincoln. These men who were responsible for bringing the past back to life encouraged Americans of all ages to examine their nation and themselves more closely.[23]

The relationship between the town of Williamsburg and the restoration generally remained strong throughout this period of expansion. Nevertheless, the two parties needed to exchange ideas to avoid rifts and confrontations in policy. In writing to Henry M. Stryker, the mayor of Williamsburg, in April 1949, JDR Jr. commented on the good relationship that both parties had maintained: "With each passing year I am increasingly conscious of the fact that [Colonial] Williamsburg could never have been accomplished without the interest, understanding and cooperation of the citizens of Williamsburg." On the whole, the town's citizens supported the restoration's wider appeal, although they, like some of the visitors, noted an increase in the commercialization of the restoration.[24]

In July 1949 the *Virginia Gazette* published a special section that took an in-depth look at the restoration. In covering broad aspects of Colonial Williamsburg and the town that it called home, the paper sought to put the work of the restoration in historical perspective. As the *Gazette* noted, Colonial Williamsburg's purpose was not only to detail life in the eighteenth century but also to ensure that "Americans of today will understand their present problems better by seeing them in the perspective of their tradition, [and] will be more clearheaded and purposeful in making choices today. This is what is meant by the motto of Colonial Williamsburg 'That the future may learn from the past.'"[25]

The end of 1949 saw the transition of JDR Jr. out of the majority of Colonial Williamsburg's affairs. Although he had officially retired ten years earlier, the soldiers' education program during the war and the postwar building and expansion program occupied a good deal of his time. Under the leadership of JDR 3d, Colonial Williamsburg expanded to send its message

of American ideals and values overseas to an audience hungry for the bless-
ings of liberty. As the century's midpoint dawned, JDR 3d strove to make
Colonial Williamsburg and its ideals as well known abroad as they were
at home.[26]

The restoration was able to appeal to people's feelings of national pride
even during a time of peace and economic success. Its ability to do so was
testimony to its endurance and strength in holding an audience. As the
1950s arrived, many visitors still remarked on the charm and beauty of the
restoration, although it was reaching the quarter-century mark. Some still
felt that it was overly commercial and that it catered to the well-to-do trav-
eler more than to the one of average income—but far more visitors com-
plimented the ideals portrayed in the restoration. Those who commented
on the restored village repeatedly noted its beauty and historic importance.
As Elihu S. Wing wrote to Colonial Williamsburg in November 1950, "You
have given America or should I say restored for us a priceless heritage."[27]

The restoration also served an important function in the days when
people would drive, rather than fly, to Florida and other southern locations
for their vacations. As a suitable stopping-off point between New York and
more southerly destinations, Colonial Williamsburg drew quite a few au-
tumn travelers to its exhibits. During the fall months, the restoration was
quieter than in the summer, which served to better represent its idealized
view of the quaintness of the past. In addition, as most children were back
in school at this time, the restored village was populated mostly by adults.
This audience created a more sophisticated atmosphere that many of these
travelers probably found attractive. To aid in this promotion, the restoration
received the help of the *New York Times*, which on 12 November 1950 profiled Colonial Williamsburg as a perfect rest stop for "winter travelers to and
from the South or Southwest."[28]

For those who toured the traditional sites of Washington, D.C., and Charlottesville, Virginia, Colonial Williamsburg became a natural addition to this
tour of the upper South. Ideally situated, Colonial Williamsburg's year-
round program benefited from a variety of tourists who ventured to the town
for a number of reasons. These travelers found many positive things to admire as they visited the reborn town. From those who admired the architecture to those who were partial to the spirit of the past, Colonial Williamsburg drew enthusiastic responses.[29]

Yet the question of racial equality still dogged the restoration and its officials. The problem of presenting a town that embodied the notion of lib-

erty while at the same time it denied basic rights to people of color was a paradox that several visitors noted. A satisfactory answer to such a dilemma was slow in coming and required an appreciation of the variety of views involved. The problem of reaching an accommodation between the town's democratic ideals and the laws and customs of Virginia continually presented difficulties for the restoration officials making policy in the early 1950s.

Typical of such difficulties was the letter from George E. Cohron that detailed the experiences of a black couple who visited the restoration early in 1950. Cohron related that while he and his wife were provided with room and board by one of the African American families in town, they were not satisfied with the accommodations and implied that they would have preferred the comforts of the Williamsburg Inn or some other hotel. Cohron also noted the difficulty in obtaining food from the local establishments while they were visiting the town. As he commented, noting the barriers that existed for blacks, "the Negro suffers these embarrassments, discomforts and disadvantages only because a national project privately financed adheres to local public policies. Is it not irony that Williamsburg, restored and publicized as the place democracy was founded, should permit discrimination or democracy in reverse?" While Colonial Williamsburg adhered to its policy to restrict the Inn and other hotel and dining properties to whites only, the restoration's building tours were not segregated. Thus although it was possible for blacks to view the exhibits and to purchase items in the shops on equal terms with white visitors, they were forced to stay with and to eat their meals with other black families.[30]

The case of the senior class of Mercersburg High School from Mercersburg, Pennsylvania, illustrates how the local community viewed Colonial Williamsburg's discriminatory practices. Hampton Institute, a black university located in nearby Hampton, Virginia, was approached by the high school's class secretary concerning housing for three African American girls who were to accompany their classmates to Colonial Williamsburg for a week's visit in May 1950. Hampton's president, Alonzo G. Moron, agreed to accommodate a section of the class that would include up to thirty students, both black and white, but refused to house solely the black students, arguing that "to separate these girls from their classmates would be destructive of the educational purposes of the trip." In closing his letter, he evoked a sentiment that had become prevalent among antisegregationists during the 1950s, namely, that "in these days when we are trying to hold on to world leadership and to demonstrate the superiority of democracy over other forms of government, we cannot afford to give aid and comfort to any attempt to spread racial discrimination and segregation."[31]

In April 1950 Colonial Williamsburg official John D. Green reported to Kenneth Chorley that in the months since 1 January 1949 six biracial groups had visited the restoration, that all were dealt with carefully, and that the groups were kept away from the other restoration visitors while they used the dining facilities at Colonial Williamsburg. The restoration was obviously mindful not to offend the white visitors who composed the majority of its clientele. Although officials did their best to offend neither blacks nor whites, it was evident that this custom would be difficult to maintain, and the creation of a broader policy that addressed Colonial Williamsburg's position on this highly provocative issue was extremely important.[32]

The wheels were put into motion to effect such a change in the spring of 1950. In a conversation with restoration official John Dickey that May, JDR 3d realized that the two or three changes that were needed to open all facilities to visitors made a neat package and could be introduced at the beginning of the next year. JDR 3d, who hoped to extend Colonial Williamsburg's influence past the borders of the United States, was particularly sensitive to international criticism of an institution that professed to be a beacon of democracy but failed to accord basic rights to all people. Dickey felt that the change would have to be made within the next five years to keep the organization's program on track. This inevitability probably weighed heavily in JDR 3d's decision to proceed with desegregation sooner rather than later, hoping that the negative effects that would probably occur in the South would be offset by international gains.[33]

In a draft of a policy statement concerning integration written in 1950, JDR 3d spelled out the ideological reasons why Colonial Williamsburg needed to promote a nonsegregationist policy, stating that "in answer to the questions we have been asked by many people, we now therefore say that all people, as they come here to draw inspiration from this Restoration, will be welcomed and housed and fed in our facilities without regard to race, creed or color." In making this statement, JDR 3d recognized that this idea might conflict with others' view of race relations, but he felt that to be honest to the "founders of eighteenth century Williamsburg" these changes in policy needed to be made. Of course, many of Williamsburg's original founders were slaveholders who supported the separation of the races, something that JDR 3d failed to acknowledge.[34]

This change did not necessarily mean that either the public at large or members of the restoration staff would immediately accept the proposition. One particular incident over a luncheon in May 1951 proved to be a stress point for this policy. Lloyd H. Williams of Williamsburg wrote to JDR 3d on 24 May to say that he had boycotted the luncheon given nine days before by Colonial Williamsburg because he had learned only a "few minutes prior to the luncheon that it was to be an interracial affair. Had I known earlier I would not have accepted the invitation extended to me jointly by you and Mr. Chorley." A later interview with Williams revealed that he harbored no ill will toward the restoration as a whole, nor toward JDR 3d and Chorley in particular, but rather that he was opposed to a demonstration of social equality between the races. Although he had eaten at restaurants where blacks were served next to whites, the social context of the luncheon at Colonial Williamsburg was different. Williams indicated that a number of people who were at the luncheon complained to him because African Americans were present, although those whites had not left the meal. Evidently, Colonial Williamsburg's policy of interracial gatherings was still not well received by some of the community, although Chorley saw no reason to alter the restoration's practice of admitting blacks and whites together.[35]

Although the question of entertaining interracial groups together was still a difficult one, Colonial Williamsburg did make some strides in promoting integration. In most cases, whites did not object to a small number of African Americans at the hotels or in the restaurants, but some restoration officials did fear repercussions from the white community if Colonial Williamsburg was "overrun." This prospect, however unlikely it might be, forced the restoration to keep an eye on the proportion of blacks at the hotels and restaurants, although there was little evidence that there was any type of crisis concerning the integration policy.

While the racial question was brewing, Colonial Williamsburg was making important strides as an educational landmark for many Americans. Key to this educational role was JDR 3d's belief in a dynamic Americanism, one that not only preached the evils of communism but also elevated the virtues of American society to their highest level. In the fall of 1950, JDR 3d proposed to the secretary of the army that Colonial Williamsburg organize an orientation program for American troops, much along the lines of the scheme that JDR Jr. had funded during World War II. This program would promote to soldiers the idea that the United States was not involved in

Crown Prince Akihito of Japan with JDR 3d and a coachman,
1953 (Courtesy of the Colonial Williamsburg Foundation)

world affairs merely because it was "against this or that" but because it stood for certain values and ideals, ones that the soldiers could also proclaim to the enemy if captured.[36]

Even for civilians, dynamic Americanism was significant because it gave everyday Americans a better appreciation of the values Colonial Williamsburg was trying to project. This active component of the restoration, promoted by JDR 3d, ran in direct contrast to the views of his father. JDR Jr. had supported the idea of an educational experience that informed but did not lecture to the restoration's visitors. The differences in opinion about how Colonial Williamsburg was to be portrayed and the conflict over the integration of the hotels and restaurants were the main dividing points between father and son. Although JDR Jr. was approaching his eightieth year, he still had strong views about Colonial Williamsburg's direction. He refused to allocate funds for elaborate educational or orientation programs when more work still had to be done to ensure the project's physical completeness.[37]

Aside from these internal difficulties, visitors were still enchanted by Colonial Williamsburg and took to heart a variety of meanings from their visits to the restoration. A common reaction was the feeling that the exhibits, the films, and virtually everything about Colonial Williamsburg should be "seen by every American," as New York governor Thomas E. Dewey put it. Many thanked JDR Jr. for his vision and humanitarian service in the aid of democracy. Especially common was the desire that those who lacked an appreciation for the rigors of the past and the sacrifices of the last war should gain a better understanding of what it meant to be an American. Elders wanted to ensure that those of the younger generations would come to realize the importance of the colonial era in their own lives.[38]

In the years directly following World War II, Colonial Williamsburg became a prominent institution in American life as larger numbers of people from many parts of the American social strata visited the restoration. In addition, the restoration was at the forefront of two of the most important movements of postwar America, the crusades against racism and communism. As the restoration drew both praise and criticism for its policies, it was shaped by the complex forces of a new postwar America, a country torn between its racist traditions and the values it had fought to preserve in World War II. In truth, American life would never be as simple and straightforward as the restoration preferred to portray it.[39]

The organization's fits and starts during this era were only natural for an organization that was in the forefront of the historical preservation movement. Instead of remaining aloof from national and international issues, Colonial Williamsburg became embroiled in two of the mid-century's most divisive battles. Much of this involvement was due to the restoration's location and the prominence of the family that funded it. Had Colonial Williamsburg been in the North, the racial issue would probably have been far less important. Also, had the restoration's backers been less prominent, less attention might have been paid to the restoration's political position. But Colonial Williamsburg—advertised as one of the birthplaces of the nation, promoted as a shrine by its government, situated in the leading state of the Confederacy, and founded and funded by one of the nation's preeminent families—could not shrink from public scrutiny. Faced with such realities, the restoration would struggle to promote its message without offending its audience. In a country obsessed with the fears of communist incursion, Colonial Williamsburg complemented other attempts to promote a love of country. Yet the restoration still had to work to teach its visitors and supporters that America's story was not complete without an understanding of the historic role of *all* its citizens.

5

For the Greater Good

As the century reached its midpoint, the restoration grew steadily as more tourists than ever before came to see the restored village. JDR 3d believed that through its growing influence Colonial Williamsburg could become an international landmark, a city that would contain the world's hope for freedom for all mankind. Others, frequent visitors especially, were concerned with the future of the restoration because they felt it might be losing its popular appeal. The increasing size of the restored area, as well as the growing number of tourists, left many of those who recalled Colonial Williamsburg before the war recounting the loss of its previously quaint atmosphere. Charles D. Faulkner expressed such sentiments in a letter to JDR Jr.: "[T]he danger that I am convinced faces the Restoration is that the continued addition of structures . . . is fast threatening Williamsburg with congestion and a . . . loss of dignity." As Colonial Williamsburg grew, the town took on a different appearance as the rebuilding process began in earnest after the end of wartime rationing. These constructions were primarily aimed at making the restoration appear more complete as an eighteenth-century town in order to give a more realistic impression to its visitors. The greater number of tourists also changed the ambiance of the village. For Faulkner, "[t]he great appeal of Williamsburg, as it was restored up to 1950, was found in its freedom from congestion and its direct tie with the past."[1]

Not all visitors shared this view, however. Significant numbers—many of whom were visiting the town for the first time and were therefore unaware of previous conditions—still wrote of enjoyable experiences in postwar Colonial Williamsburg. A small percentage still felt that the broader commercialization of the restoration affected its message, but they remained in the minority. In contrast to Charles Faulkner's letter, J. L. Underhill noted that he had just returned from a trip "to historic Williamsburg where I was greatly impressed by the changes and additions made since an earlier trip in 1940. Williamsburg has truly become America's greatest shrine." There was clearly no set popular perception of Colonial Williamsburg. The individual experiences of visitors could vary, as at any tourist spot. More than likely, prior trips or preconceived notions about what the restoration had to offer were part of the individual visitor's overall perception as well.[2]

Allene Veitch echoed these sentiments in her comments from August 1952: "We enjoyed our stay in Williamsburg very much and we feel that no matter how much effort and work were put into the restoration of Williamsburg it will remain a shrine[,] a dream of the good things in life that the early colonists [en]visioned for the future generations of America." Chester F. Collier was not so easily swayed by Colonial Williamsburg's importance, however. He argued that there were many other locales that had as much or more claim to fame than Colonial Williamsburg. "During extensive travel I have found many more interesting historical sites with *true* [emphasis in original] significance—not just a private dwelling or beer tavern (ale-house). I have been terribly disappointed in my trip to Williamsburg and feel that Mr. Rockefeller certainly misplaced his funds."[3]

For someone like Collier, Colonial Williamsburg was little more than an expensive museum, with little or no value being imparted from its buildings, furnishings, and gardens. For those who could not or would not imagine the village of the eighteenth century, the restoration could do little more than chronicle the styles of the period. Most visitors, however, probably took with them a deeper meaning, as evidenced by Laurence M. Gould's letter. He wrote to JDR Jr. in December 1951: "I had never been in the city before, and so what has been taking place over the last few years was a revelation to me. It seems to me, as I absorbed the atmosphere of the place during the two days that I was there, that it has become one of the most meaningful of all American shrines."[4]

Not all visitors felt the special aura that the restoration hoped to provide, but those who were moved to write often did so with great passion. Those who commented negatively usually did so out of a feeling of exploitation. They believed that Colonial Williamsburg was nothing more than an elaborately conceived commercial enterprise aimed at fleecing unsuspecting travelers. Increasing numbers of visitors in the 1950s also tended to make the restoration more congested, taking away the more relaxed appeal that it had possessed in the prewar era. For many Americans who took to the road to see the country in the 1950s, Colonial Williamsburg served as both a natural shrine and an attractive vacation spot. But as costs rose after the war, prices of admission, food, and lodging also naturally increased. As a result, for those visitors who failed to realize the enormous cost of the restoration, admission prices may have seemed exorbitant.[5]

In the early 1950s, JDR 3d turned his attention to the international importance of the restoration. Colonial Williamsburg's ability to transcend the boundaries of the United States meant that it could become a worldwide force in the promotion of democracy and republican ideals. The Special Survey Committee was founded by JDR 3d in February 1950 to promote this international aspect of the restoration. Initially the committee was to assess the importance and effect of Colonial Williamsburg nationally and internationally, to create a program for Colonial Williamsburg based on that survey, and finally to execute that plan of action. JDR 3d's move to integrate the restoration into the framework of Cold War diplomacy indicated the extent to which he sought to foster American ideals around the globe and to promote the restoration's growing agenda.[6]

JDR 3d's vision of an expanding role for Colonial Williamsburg was a part of his overall perspective on world affairs. A committed internationalist, he sought to bolster the role of the United States as an agent for suppressing communism. In promoting his ideal of a dynamic Americanism, JDR 3d sought to bring a new import to the Rockefeller name. Just as JDR Jr. wanted to break away from his father's legacy, JDR 3d hoped to establish his own reputation and to create a Colonial Williamsburg that would meet the needs of the postwar era. He proposed that his father take care of the expenses surrounding the structural completion of the restoration, while he would be in charge of the educational aspect. "I don't need to tell you of my interest in Colonial Williamsburg. To me it has tremendous potentials for public service," JDR 3d wrote to his father, indicating that he, too, saw a future for the dream of promoting the ideals of the Founding Fathers, albeit in a more overt way. He wanted to make Colonial Williamsburg an international beacon for the family's beliefs.[7]

Although the father-son relationship was strained over the restoration, the underlying ideal of what the project represented did not change. It was still to promote the same basic goals—an appreciation of the struggles of the past and the importance of democracy—but now Colonial Williamsburg was going to take its message to the public forcefully and to proselytize its views. Such a move, however, ran counter to the Rockefeller tradition of effecting change discretely and quietly, and this disparity caused friction between father and son and their individual beliefs about what Colonial Williamsburg should ultimately represent.

The Special Survey Committee was the most important step that JDR 3d took to promote his ideal of an international dynamic Americanism. This form of nationalism was geared not only to inform but also to convert. JDR 3d wanted his international contribution to be not only financially beneficial, as in his work with the Rockefeller Foundation, but also spiritually uplifting. The international promotion of American ideals needed to go hand-in-hand with other areas that the Rockefellers were interested in overseas, such as education and disease control. By basing his view of an ideal world on the complete acceptance of the American political process, JDR 3d helped to institutionalize the international promotion of American doctrine. Indeed, in much of the Third World the exportation of American money and technology was linked directly to the promotion of the American political agenda. In this way, Colonial Williamsburg complemented U.S. foreign policy during the Cold War.[8]

The Special Survey Committee became the way for JDR 3d and Colonial Williamsburg to enter more fully into the volatile postwar world. By showing that Colonial Williamsburg could be more than merely a symbol of the past, JDR 3d took it to a new height. The restoration could help fashion a political climate instead of merely representing one. International attention focused on the small town, and it had to do its best to be worthy of the role of the birthplace of American democracy. The committee presented its interim report in November 1950, spelling out its reasons for existence and its goals. Both the near-completeness of the restoration and the world situation were compelling factors for the committee's creation. Discussions between committee members and prominent Americans revealed a need for a vigorous democratic faith, along with the impetus to "express the historical concepts of Williamsburg's past in a contemporary context." Such a desire for patriotic programs, however, needed to be balanced with the recognition of a possible negative public reaction if the restoration went too far.[9]

Since freedom was the key ingredient of Colonial Williamsburg's message and its strongest promotion point, the committee traveled overseas to see "those areas where freedom was undergoing its most severe test." The group went behind the Iron Curtain to talk to communists and former communists. In trying to understand the "curious appeal" of communism, they sought to understand the role that Colonial Williamsburg could play in an international attempt to promote democracy. By studying the primary aspects of the authoritarian political system, the committee sought a better understanding of its importance and effectiveness. The principal points of conflict between communism and republicanism were summarized as follows: "The will of the state vs. the will of the individual; materialism vs. idealism; no God vs. God; a communist controlled world state vs. self-determination; imperialism (Russian variety) vs. nationalism; security vs. freedom."[10]

By establishing a dichotomy between the two political forces, the committee effectively created a good versus evil confrontation, attempting to demonstrate how a good system of government (republicanism) could defeat a bad one (authoritarian communism). Through a study of eighteenth-century political beliefs and their effects on the modern world, the committee demonstrated how the message of Colonial Williamsburg could be used to advance republican ideals. By focusing on such points as dignity and integrity of the individual, individual freedom and responsibility, opportunity, self-government, and faith, the Special Survey Committee stressed the primary difference between the democratic republicanism and authoritative communism: the control of the individual over the state as opposed to the control of the state over the individual.[11]

To make Colonial Williamsburg's message more meaningful, the committee recommended that the nature of the world political system, and the threat of communism in particular, be emphasized in all aspects of the restoration's presentation. The point of this message was to be grounded in the "development of a positive, affirmative faith which the free nations of today can or should share." Therefore, this program was geared to stress what Colonial Williamsburg was *for*, not what it was *against*. This idea was to be implemented first through those who visited Colonial Williamsburg, then those in the United States who could be reached but could not come to the restoration, and finally the international community. Obviously, the third sector would be much harder to reach, and so emphasis was to be placed on the first two groups.[12]

One facet of public service that Colonial Williamsburg was able to provide in support of this international role was to give tours to distinguished foreign visitors while they were in the United States. JDR 3d wrote to Undersecretary of State James E. Webb in April 1950 suggesting that such tours would be useful; "because of the emphasis we Americans so often attach to technology and progress, we are sometimes misjudged by visitors who would assume that our native traditions go no deeper than our automobiles and television sets." He further indicated the fact that Colonial Williamsburg stood at the core of the American political system because it emphasized the role of the individual and self-government. In this way, the restoration not only could demonstrate the American interest in the past, but also it could serve as an educational medium for these foreign guests.[13]

As a result, Colonial Williamsburg would focus on its traditional domestic audience, but it would also, through a liaison with the State Department, seek to bring more foreign dignitaries to the restoration. By gearing itself to further the political education of Americans during the Cold War, Colonial Williamsburg established the promotion of a dynamic Americanism that it planned to disseminate throughout the country. As such, it became an integral player in the formation of American Cold War ideology and a strong proponent of anticommunism. To cement a stronger relationship with the federal government and to gain greater publicity for the work of the restoration, JDR 3d invited President Harry S. Truman to visit Colonial Williamsburg in the spring of 1951. Truman replied that he would attempt to make the visit if he was not bogged down with other responsibilities, commenting, "I am very much interested in Williamsburg and its historical significance for our great Republic."[14]

To further its message, Colonial Williamsburg brought the Voice of Democracy winners to visit the restoration in 1949. Sponsored by the U.S. Junior Chamber of Commerce and radio and television groups, the Voice of Democracy awarded prizes to four high school students from across the nation for essays on the theme of democratic government. The program attempted to lure teenagers into a greater appreciation of the country's past and its democratic heritage, involving more than two million students throughout the United States and its territories. Those students wrote and recorded essays entitled "I speak for Democracy," and the winners traveled to Colonial Williamsburg and Washington, D.C., where they had the opportunity to learn more about American government. The *Virginia Gazette* had high esteem for such a program, arguing that "if every boy and girl would take time out to consider the ideals and principles of democracy there would be fewer 'juvenile delinquents' in the nation and . . . America will have a better chance to stand up against communism." Such conventions in the restored city were part of a concerted effort to bring young people into the discussion about democracy and republicanism, using eighteenth-century Virginia as a model for the forum. The restoration felt that the youthful portion of the population was particularly impressionable and perhaps the most likely to be swayed by communism, so a special emphasis needed to be placed on encouraging children's understanding of democratic principles.[15]

The first big step that was taken to introduce Colonial Williamsburg into the global political fray was the planning of the Williamsburg Conferences on International Affairs. The goals of these conferences were "to examine objectively some major problem on the international level facing the American people today, . . . to stimulate constructive . . . thinking about the problem; [and] to foster a mutual better understanding among Americans and people of other nations of the issues involved in the problem and of the diverse opinions held about them." Bringing together approximately fifty of the world's leaders, half from the United States, the other half from foreign countries, these conferences would tackle major questions of the state of democracy as well as other related issues in foreign policy. These meetings would then bring international prestige and recognition to Colonial Williamsburg, making it an important player in world affairs. Men such as John Foster Dulles and Dag Hammarskjöld were participants in these meetings during the 1950s. Their presence helped to bolster Colonial Williamsburg's reputation, thereby increasing the interest in the restoration of both Americans and others across the globe. In this way, the Rockefeller name was further associated with internationalism and with it came an inherent promotion of the family's political beliefs.[16]

In addition to the restoration's growing international function, JDR 3d was interested in revitalizing Colonial Williamsburg's role during World War II: that of an educator of soldiers and sailors from nearby military bases. Although it was fought on a much smaller scale, the Korean War had the same urgent need for servicemen who were educated in the political goals of the United States. As JDR 3d indicated, "[W]e feel that a real contribution can be made through a program of this character toward giving the men in the Armed Forces a better understanding of what they are being asked to fight for and maybe die for. So many of us in this country know very clearly what we are against but do not fully appreciate what we are for." Although the program would be centered in the Colonial Williamsburg area, it would also include soldiers and sailors from other parts of the country through a variety of media presentations.[17]

Although the work of the Special Survey Committee appeared to be going well, during a staff meeting on 18 May 1951, JDR 3d announced that the committee would cease to exist as of that date. He felt that the group had made a significant contribution to the future of the project—creating a restoration that did not simply represent the past but propelled people to action to improve the future. Nevertheless, the committee's work was too far outside the normal operations of the restoration. Though the committee officially ceased as of that date, JDR 3d still harbored the desire to pursue a program of dynamic Americanism at Colonial Williamsburg. His continual assertion of this idea brought him into conflict with his father and probably led, in part, to his resignation as chairman of the board a year later.[18]

Two months later, in July 1951, JDR Jr. received a letter from Elizabeth Rapelye, who, upon seeing Colonial Williamsburg, was moved to put her future savings into United States Defense Bonds. She indicated that she had wondered what she could give to her grandchildren: "I want to leave them something to remember—that will mold their characters and make them proud to be born here. . . . I shall endeavor to save enough so that [they] . . . have such a trip as I have just had through . . . Williamsburg. This, I am sure, will make them aware of their true heritage."[19]

Rapelye might have made JDR 3d happier by addressing her remarks to him, instead of to his father, for she was acting in the way that JDR 3d would have wanted—using the inspiration one received from Colonial Williamsburg to create something for the future, something that would promote American values, especially in young children. Such reactions to Colonial Williamsburg were probably common; even without the input of the Special Survey Committee, many Americans sought to keep alive the ideals of Colonial Williamsburg in their children and grandchildren. Those who wrote during this period did so to give their thanks for what the restoration was doing for America or to report on events in the restoration that might be interesting to the founders or to restoration officials. Gladys O. Jaquith wrote to JDR Jr. in September 1951 to relate a story of a foreign family who had derived a good deal from their visit to the restoration. "I was very much interested in a conversation I heard one morning. . . . [I]t was between a mother, father and a boy about ten years old. . . . [T]he mother said 'that

Williamsburg was the most beautiful place she had seen since she was in America,' and the father voiced the wish that [if] people . . . behind the Iron Curtain could see Williamsburg, he thought they would understand us better and feel differently about the American people."[20]

Not only did JDR 3d attempt to make Colonial Williamsburg into an international icon, but some of its visitors also echoed this sentiment. Even if the younger Rockefeller had not pushed to promote Colonial Williamsburg internationally, it may have become well known overseas. One visitor, R. C. Boyce of Greensboro, North Carolina, had such a positive reaction to the restoration that he wanted JDR Jr. to work on two other shrines to go with Colonial Williamsburg. The first would be a "huge figure of Christ . . . towering above everything it surrounds and standing upon the foundations of His teachings." The other shrine would be at Natural Bridge, Virginia, for "here stands a natural bridge out of rock that could be, it seems to me, a mecca for every Christian in this country." Boyce concluded his letter by thanking JDR Jr. for all he had done for the country: "[Y]ou have helped make this country a better place in which to live. May God bless you and your good work always, and may he fill your days with sunshine and happiness which you have so richly deserved."[21]

Interspersed with the large number of congratulatory notes were letters from some local residents asking for financial help. These requests were not surprising considering JDR. Jr.'s notoriety in the peninsula as a result of the restoration. Mrs. Kate Simpson of Newport News, Virginia, wrote in the summer of 1952 to thank JDR Jr. for all he had done for the local area and to request help to pay off some outstanding medical bills. Requesting funds from such a well-known philanthropist was quite a logical connection to make, considering that JDR Jr. had appeared so generous in restoring an old town. Perhaps to make him more partial to her cause, she reported that she "did not smoke, drink or curse" and tried to live a Christian life, all of which closely coincided with his personal beliefs. The Rockefeller organization, however, had a long-standing policy not to honor personal requests for help, because if it became publicly known that such requests were honored, the letters would never stop. Therefore, the standard response was that the Rockefellers contributed to a number of local charities and that the petitioner should seek assistance there.[22]

On 16 January 1953, the *Virginia Gazette* published a retrospective of the past quarter century of the restoration. The *Gazette* noted that "to those of us who live here in Williamsburg and have watched the conscientious and

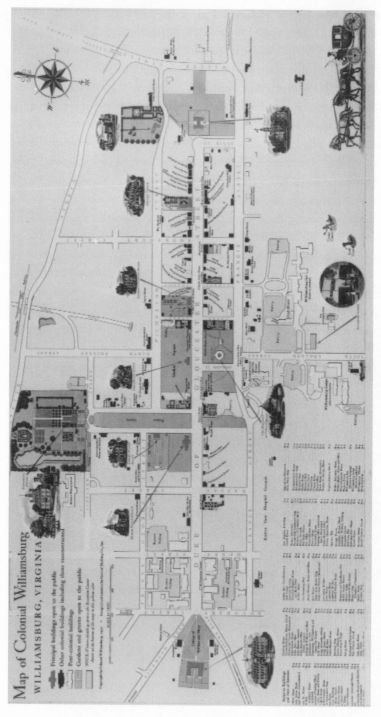

Map of Colonial Williamsburg, ca. 1952 (Courtesy of the Colonial Williamsburg Foundation)

painstaking work of rebuilding the historic part of our city to its original appearance, the ever-evolving 'picture' has been one of great civic interest and pride." In that time, more than six million visitors had traveled to see the restored city and had taken with them a sense of the past. "They find here, too, a remade colonial city, portraying the life and mode of living of our earliest ancestors in the exhibition buildings, so that those great Americans, who by their efforts and struggles made possible the great democracy which is America today, are brought back to memory and live again in our minds." The purpose of the restoration was to impress upon a modern generation the qualities of greatness and leadership exemplified by the colonial leaders who founded the country, "and the lessons portrayed thus inspire all Americans in building a better nation."[23]

The increasing number of popular magazines that profiled Colonial Williamsburg provided the restoration with added free publicity while at the same time giving the public a glimpse of what it meant to America. Articles in *Harper's, American Mercury, Holiday,* and *National Geographic* helped to create popular interest in postwar Colonial Williamsburg. With an American public increasingly concerned about their vacations and the education of their children, Colonial Williamsburg seemed the perfect answer to both problems. Although at this time Colonial Williamsburg perhaps fulfilled its role as a vacation destination better than that as an educational organization, it was laying the ground work for future educational developments.

Beverley M. Bowie's article in the October 1954 issue of *National Geographic* was a good example of postwar descriptive articles on the restoration. Entitled "Williamsburg: Its College and Its Cinderella City," the article thoroughly surveyed the town and its activities, focusing on the craft shops. The *National Geographic* article no doubt helped to awaken interest among a fairly sophisticated readership. Bowie detailed the usual associations of historical figures with the town, concluding his article with an anecdote, told by Kenneth Chorley, of the reaction of one GI who had visited Colonial Williamsburg: "[H]e was a soldier from Fort Eustis down the road. . . . He'd become separated from his buddies, and he was standing all alone in front of the Peale portrait of Washington. Suddenly I heard him mutter 'You got it for us, General. And, by God, we're going to keep it!' And he saluted."[24]

The magazine's readers reacted strongly to Bowie's article. *National Geographic* received over one hundred thousand letters about the piece before the end of that October. As Kenneth Chorley wrote to JDR Jr., "[T]he editors tell us that never in the history of the National Geographic have they received such 'fan mail' about any one article." Such a wave of correspondence unquestionably demonstrated the public's ongoing interest in the restoration and the Americanist beliefs that it promoted. For a country in the middle of the Cold War, with the issues of patriotism and national loyalty ever present, Colonial Williamsburg was a source of encouragement for those who feared the expansion of communism. Many of those who wrote to support Colonial Williamsburg's message probably agreed with philosopher Reinhold Niebuhr, who wrote in 1953 that "we are fated as a generation to live in the insecurity which this universal evil of communism creates for our world." In such a world, Colonial Williamsburg helped to provide a pillar of stability in an otherwise shaky international scene.[25]

In addition to this widely publicized piece, numerous articles concerning the restoration were published across the country during the mid-1950s. The *Virginia Gazette* noted in April 1954 that "subscription lists of a number of national and localized publications which have printed articles on Williamsburg during [the preceding two-month period] approach 38 million." If there were no overlaps in readership, half of the reading public of the United States would have seen an article about the restoration over the previous sixty days. Such a widespread dissemination of material on Colonial Williamsburg indicated that it was truly a national monument. Those who were unable to come to the restored village could read about it and judge its growing influence on American society.[26]

One of the more important articles during this time was Clifford Dowdey's piece in the August 1954 issue of *Holiday*. This was an analytical examination of the restoration that took aim at Colonial Williamsburg's critics. Dowdey also recounted the restoration's Americanist message: "We forget that liberty . . . was more than a word. Its pursuit meant that a war would come . . . to the streets of their town, to the homes of their fellow citizens." In answer to those who had leveled criticism at the project, Dowdey commented that "the concept of Williamsburg is heroic, and only those who do not understand this charge the Project with commercialism." He criticized those who felt that the selling of items in the craft shops and other items in restoration buildings somehow cheapened the project. "These misguided idealists miss the main point of the restoration. If it resulted in an academic collection of hushed buildings where researchers and pastworshipers tiptoed down silent streets and whispered learnedly in empty chambers, then Williamsburg would be one vast museum." He argued,

however, that Colonial Williamsburg was truly a living city, which helped it
to create the ambience of life in the eighteenth century. The people on the
Duke of Gloucester Street were "the modern versions of the crowds that
thronged the old capital on court day." He reminded those who took issue
with the mingling throngs in the restored area that "Williamsburg in its
heyday was . . . a cross section, in flux and ferment, a population whose dynamic interplay created revolutionaries."[27]

Dowdey's reply to Colonial Williamsburg's critics was important because
it helped to demonstrate that the restoration was a living museum that
needed the participation of its visitors. Although for three decades the restored village had been revered as a shrine, its use as a popular tourist site
was beginning. As Colonial Williamsburg opened up to a wider audience,
its mission and its interpretation began to change. No longer did the debate
about the restoration revolve around the question of whether it was a shrine
or a tourist trap; a new role was being created. This change did not occur
overnight; it took a gradual period of a decade or more for it to be fully in
effect. The mid-1950s saw the start of a more sophisticated and less narrow
view of the restoration and its purposes.

Key to this change was the involvement of the individual in the drama of
Colonial Williamsburg. In a report to JDR 3d in March 1954, Arthur Goodfriend summarized his feelings about the future of the restoration. For Colonial Williamsburg to reach its audience effectively, it had to demonstrate
that a living town can imbue the present with the aura of the past. Goodfriend argued that Colonial Williamsburg needed to place its emphasis on
people, both of today and of the past. "Williamsburg can give the people
inspiration only to the degree that Williamsburg, all it is and all it does, is
inspired by the people, and responds to their felt and unfelt need." Colonial
Williamsburg, by speaking more about individuals than about gardens and
buildings, would better promote the ideals of the restoration's founders.[28]

Starting in the mid-1950s, the increasing numbers of visitors broadened
the focus of Colonial Williamsburg. This growth, in addition to the resignation of JDR 3d as chairman of the board and the decreasing influence of JDR
Jr., demonstrated that the restoration was moving into a new role. Annual
visitation had increased nearly ten times in two decades: from thirty-one
thousand in 1934 to more than three hundred thousand in 1953. Higher
postwar wages, greater amounts of leisure time, and improved transportation
were the major reasons for this tenfold increase. As more people walked the
streets and ventured into the buildings, absorbing the Rockefellers' mes-

sage, Colonial Williamsburg became a greater force in American culture. The development of the restoration's research program, geared to the study of colonial social and cultural history, also promised new avenues of interest in the past and the broader interpretation of eighteenth-century life.[29]

In 1954 the *Richmond Times-Dispatch* ran a six-part analytical series on Colonial Williamsburg, providing a study of its influence on the local community. Frank and forthcoming, the series depicted the restoration's struggle for acceptance, its money problems, its out-of-state personnel, and, after a quarter century, its recognition as a member of the community. Such a candid look at one of the most powerful local institutions gave residents a chance to understand their corporate neighbor. In addition, these articles provided a rare opportunity to comprehend the complex nature of public reaction to the Colonial Williamsburg project.[30]

The series revealed that although the restoration initially received a thirty-to-one favorable rating with Williamsburg residents, its popularity dipped a bit when the work on the project began. Some tension existed because the benefactor and many of the early restoration personnel were "Yankees," individuals who, according to local sentiment, lacked an understanding of southern culture. In addition, Kenneth Chorley, the restoration's president, was a controversial figure for some of the townspeople. Chorley exhibited a strong devotion to the Rockefeller family and, as a Northerner, was accused of being unsympathetic to local and southern interests.

Throughout most of his tenure as president of the restoration, Chorley kept his office in New York City, close to JDR Jr.'s offices at Rockefeller Center. Chorley would visit Colonial Williamsburg only on official business, remaining most of the time in the New York area, distant from the day-to-day operations that surrounded the restoration. This remote control certainly did not help matters, as absentee management rubbed both the townspeople and the employees the wrong way. Local residents also complained about the bureaucracy at the restoration. For people who were used to the small town way of doing things, the complexity of the restoration's business office was a new and forbidding entity. But Colonial Williamsburg eventually became aware of these problems and sought to rectify them. In the early 1950s, the restoration hired more local personnel and restructured the running of the restoration to make it more accessible to the community and its employees.[31]

Important, too, was an understanding of the restoration's money problems. Many people believed that Colonial Williamsburg would have access to unlimited resources because it was a Rockefeller-funded operation. But this was not necessarily the case. Although by 1954 the restoration had received a total of $50 million in gifts, cash, and securities, primarily from the Rockefeller family, $35 million of that had already been spent, with a future pledge of $10 million to be added to the reserves. But this apparently large sum was just enough to ensure that the restoration would remain solvent in future years. Heavy annual deficits constantly necessitated the use of capital to pay Colonial Williamsburg's bills. Although many visitors complained about the high cost of visiting the restored town, in reality admission fees never covered the costs incurred by the restoration—a fact of which most of the town's tourists were unaware.[32]

In the quarter of a century that the restoration had been an influential force in Tidewater Virginia, Colonial Williamsburg became a member of the community. There was a greater interaction between the restoration and the local area, especially in the postwar years. Members of the restoration served on local boards and planning commissions, making former outsiders an integral part of the town of Williamsburg. Carlisle Humelsine, who became an executive vice president in 1953 and later president in 1958, hoped to soften the strained relations when he proclaimed that "Colonial Williamsburg is a citizen of Williamsburg." He argued that the restoration needed to put itself forth as a good citizen of the town to achieve a greater acceptance in the community, a statement with which most of the town's residents certainly concurred.[33]

Before coming to Colonial Williamsburg, Humelsine, who was born in Hagerstown, Maryland, and educated at the University of Maryland, worked at the State Department for seven years. He served as either deputy undersecretary or assistant secretary to James F. Byrnes, George C. Marshall, Dean Acheson, and John Foster Dulles. In addition to his duties at Colonial Williamsburg, Humelsine was also associated with the Virginia Department of Conservation, the Virginia Museum of Fine Arts, and the National Geographic Society. His southern background and affiliation with philanthropic societies, as well as his government connections, made Humelsine an excellent candidate to lead the restoration.[34]

Colonial Williamsburg also had a new chairman of the board as the position went to Winthrop Rockefeller, following his older brother's resignation. Winthrop settled in Arkansas in 1953 and began a cattle-breeding farm sixty miles northwest of Little Rock. He also served two terms as the governor of Arkansas from 1967 to 1971, while fulfilling his duties as the chairman of the Board of Trustees.

Colonial Williamsburg's officials realized the need to open the project to a greater number of people and to create an even stronger message describing the restoration's goals. Although not all officials supported the internationalization of the restoration, the younger generation supported the creation of the Williamsburg Award. The award, which included a $10,000 prize, was given to Winston Churchill in 1955 in a lavish ceremony in Drapers' Hall in London and was meant to recognize those who had made a contribution to the preservation of liberty.[35]

In granting the award to Churchill, the restoration sought to praise the former British prime minister for his many years of public service and his fight in the promotion of freedom throughout the world. In his presentation speech, Winthrop Rockefeller sought to demonstrate that the battle for liberty knew no chronological or geographical bounds. Rockefeller noted that although the men who had walked the streets of the colonial city were no longer living, "the lessons taught by the lives of the men of eighteenth-century Williamsburg are timeless. . . . [They] speak across the ages to the perilous present. . . . We today take heart and comfort from the courage and steadfastness of our forebears."[36]

The Williamsburg Award was meant to embody the fact that the beliefs fostered by Colonial Williamsburg were for all people and for all ages. Such a theory greatly expanded the original intentions of JDR Jr., who was uncomfortable with all the international attention being lavished on the restoration. Although he had sought to make Colonial Williamsburg influential in promoting democracy, he generally opposed the increasingly high profile of the restoration. JDR Jr. essentially viewed Colonial Williamsburg as an end, whereas his sons saw it more as a means to an end.[37]

There was a certain irony in choosing a former British prime minister to receive an award that symbolized the American fight against British oppression. Yet the decision demonstrated that in the twentieth century Americans and British fought on the same side to promote a common ideal. The *Christian Science Monitor* noted that although the award was presented on 7 December 1955, "nobody mentioned that it was . . . the fourteenth anniversary of the Pearl Harbor attack—scarcely a day for allied rejoicing. Nobody mentioned that Colonial Williamsburg was once a British town, and that England and the young America had some sharp disagreement in this area." But Churchill claimed that because he was American on his mother's side, he was entitled to enjoy Colonial Williamsburg as much as any American.[38]

On a state visit to the United States in 1957, Britain's Queen Elizabeth

Williamsburg—The Story of a Patriot starring Jack Lord (on the right) at the Information Center (Courtesy of the Colonial Williamsburg Foundation)

II reiterated much of Churchill's sentiment. During a trip to Colonial Williamsburg, the queen spoke of the similarities between her country and the land that was once ruled by the British crown: "Here, at a great period in your history, [the colonists] proclaimed their faith in certain great concepts of freedom, justice, law and self-government." She went on to indicate that "those concepts have had a profound influence on the political development, not only of the United States, but all freedom loving countries." The United States and Britain, allies in the wars against fascism and communism, had much more in common than ever before.[39]

The progress of the restoration also brought up questions of its future role in promoting American ideals well into the future. The production of the film *Williamsburg—The Story of a Patriot* indicated the restoration's focus for the next decade. Filmed in Williamsburg during May 1956, the picture sought to capture political life in colonial Virginia using the restored town as a backdrop. Proposals for a different type of picture, written by James Agee, would have focused on the social aspects of the town and its inhabitants. Agee died before the picture could be put into production, although given the political climate of the 1950s, his script might have been rejected. The restoration then opted for the patriotic theme of the Paramount film, which is shown at Colonial Williamsburg to this day, albeit with a disclaimer about the importance of social history, which is currently the restoration's primary focus.[40]

Williamsburg—The Story of a Patriot details the life of the fictional John Fry, the son of a Virginia planter and a member of the House of Burgesses. When his father dies, John inherits the elder Fry's land and his seat in the House of Burgesses in Williamsburg. Upon arriving in Williamsburg, Fry meets George Washington, George Wythe, and Patrick Henry, and although at first reluctant, he eventually supports the argument for colonial independence. He and his family become caught up in the fervor of revolution as Fry and his son enlist in the militia to fight the British. In telling the story of this fictional patriot, planter, and burgess, Colonial Williamsburg strongly fostered the notion that the importance of the restoration lay in its Americanist message. The sociohistorical aspect of the restoration was not touted as an important issue. In the heat of the Cold War, Colonial Williamsburg needed to produce a film that, in keeping with the Williamsburg Award, promoted the need to foster liberty and the ideals of the restoration's founders.[41]

The film and the new Information Center, both of which premiered in 1957, sought to expand the influence of the restoration's ideology. The new center, which was built on restoration property north of the Governor's Palace, was a modern site that would introduce visitors to the restoration's purpose. Because the center was a considerable distance from the restored area, its appearance would not conflict with the eighteenth-century village. The construction of a motel, originally called the Motor House and later renamed the Williamsburg Woodlands, provided more rooms for visitors, especially the large numbers of families with young children who made up a growing part of the town's patrons. The film, as an introduction to the restoration, became an integral part of visitors' experiences. After the film, visitors climbed aboard buses to be driven to the restoration area, where they could see firsthand the sights to which they had been introduced in the film. The visit to Colonial Williamsburg had become a packaged experience that was carefully regulated by the restoration to portray the themes that they wished to promote.[42]

The start of this new era was a time of reflection on what the restoration had wrought in the local community. Local opposition and discomfort with the influx of visitors soon faded once there was an understanding of what the restoration meant to the country. The new Information Center represented the profound effect that the restoration had on the American public, and the increasing numbers of tourists made it clear that Colonial Williamsburg needed to expand and to modernize its facilities. As Winthrop Rockefeller commented upon the dedication of the new building, "[T]he Information Center is the culminating effort of the Restoration to fulfill this deeply-felt responsibility of making a visit to Williamsburg a moving experience." To deal effectively with the tourists who were arriving at a rate of more than three hundred thousand a year, a number that would more than double in the next decade, Colonial Williamsburg needed to stay current and to make the experience as meaningful for modern visitors as it had been for tourists twenty years before.[43]

Colonial Williamsburg wanted to be a leader in historic preservation, a role that they had assumed in 1926 with the start of the most professional restoration up to that time. The new effort of the restoration was to minimize the influence of crowds, since for one to truly enjoy the historic nature of the restoration, it was necessary to let people feel that they were not being crowded, rushed, or pushed. Winthrop Rockefeller also indicated that the restoration had done much to convince Americans, and foreigners as well, of the importance of the Founding Fathers. He quoted one Canadian family who had come to see the restoration and were enthralled by it. "We are going back to Canada better and happier because we came to Williamsburg and because you have immeasurably strengthened something we have always known, and that is that we, as a people, are truly one in our common origin, in what we represent, and in what we believe. . . . [W]e, too, are very proud of those truly great men who worked for, fought for, and founded democracy in America."[44]

Colonial Williamsburg continued to awe and to inspire well into its thirtieth year. For many who lived in the United States or Canada during the Cold War, Colonial Williamsburg had an important message to convey to a people in need of support for their hopes and dreams. In a period of international turmoil and tension, when the country was torn internally over the fear of communism, the restoration helped to alleviate some of the fears that troubled many people living in the world's democracies.

Among these fears was the spread of communism, especially in Eastern

Europe. The *Virginia Gazette* felt that it was fitting that the "concept and ideals for Jefferson's religious freedom act be emphasized in our own free country and particularly exported to the peoples behind the iron curtain where Communism is fast ending all religious freedom of any kind." Restoration officials believed that Colonial Williamsburg could help oppressed people all over the world express their values and ideals of freedoms—especially religious freedom, which was one of the four main freedoms that Franklin Roosevelt hoped to extend to the postwar world. As the *Gazette* argued, "[F]ree democratic peoples believe that with religious freedom will also come individual freedom, and it is this ideal which urges us to do everything in our power to bring freedom of living and religion to all peoples throughout the world." By keeping alive Thomas Jefferson's beliefs in religious freedom, Colonial Williamsburg was helping to fight the Cold War. If Americans forgot Jefferson's arguments, cold warriors feared that communism would spread. In a war of political ideologies, the promotion of Colonial Williamsburg became one of the United States's greatest assets in the cause of anticommunism.[45]

Yet the question about how a democracy like the United States could fail to grant basic rights to its citizens of color still lingered. Nowhere was this paradox greater than in Colonial Williamsburg, although in the late 1950s there began to be a greater appreciation of the roles of African Americans in the eighteenth-century town. The first concrete indication of this interest was Thad W. Tate's 1957 research report, "The Negro in Eighteenth-Century Williamsburg," which was published as a book in 1965. Although other works on Williamsburg were planned, this work remains the only comprehensive study of African American life in Williamsburg during the colonial era.[46]

Tate discovered that blacks composed approximately half of Williamsburg's colonial population and that they played an essential role in the growth and progress of the town. Although African Americans did not have separately identifiable living quarters, their physical presence needed to be documented by the restoration. If the restoration had opened the interpretation program to black interpreters at this time, Colonial Williamsburg could have done much to provide a more inclusive version of the past. But the restoration in the late 1950s was still haunted by the specter of segregation, and so any advances in this direction were muted by the local social situation.[47]

Some restoration visitors, however, called for a less hypocritical approach to the treatment of African Americans. As Melvin E. Diggs wrote to the restoration in January 1954, "I am wondering (and have been for a long time) why no accommodations by way of an inn or hotel are not made for us colored citizens. Thousands of these visit Williamsburg each year and are disappointed at the lack of needed accommodations. I am hoping that this will be given careful consideration by Colonial Williamsburg and this condition will be remedied in the near future."[48]

Similar sentiments were expressed by Marjorie B. Robinson in a letter to JDR Jr. in May of that same year. Robinson indicated that although she and her friends were "deeply moved" by the restoration, she was disappointed that Colonial Williamsburg had failed in its role to promote the ideals that were expressed in all facets of the restoration. Specific to her complaint was the "lettering on the door of the Women's Rest Room which reads: Ladies white." She understood that "segregation of Negroes, though surely passing, will be practiced for many years to come in the South. . . . [But I] feel an obligation to try to find inspiration for the future in the best of this country's past—in our American heritage striving for freedom."[49]

There was a fair amount of local discussion about segregation and its role in the Virginia of the future, especially after the *Brown v. Board of Education* ruling by the Supreme Court, which in 1954 reversed the 1896 *Plessy v. Ferguson* decision and eventually resulted in the desegregation of public schools. In recognition of this eventual change in social structure, the *Virginia Gazette* published an article on 9 April 1955 devoted to this topic. Although many Virginians believed that the eventual end of segregation was a foregone conclusion, the main question remaining was how quickly these changes were to take place. Many Southerners, accustomed to the old way of doing things, would be reluctant to accept wholesale changes right away. Greater acceptance of black-white equality would come only after a period of adjustment.[50]

In general, the restoration's reply to letters about segregation was similar to the one that Kenneth Chorley gave in 1953. In a letter to Broadus Mitchell, Chorley argued that the restoration felt that it was making strides in this area but that it needed to move slowly. He did note that "from the time our first exhibition building was opened in 1932, Negroes have been welcomed, both in all-Negro and mixed groups. . . . We are, to the best of our judgement, doing all that we can in this situation. We have felt that by pushing too fast too far we might only aggravate a prejudice we want to see disappear."[51]

But not all of those who wrote criticized the restoration. Many of them were enchanted by the town and its atmosphere. One of these was Carol G. Williams, who visited the town in September 1954 and felt that the "Restoration makes the 18th century live again, and everywhere we were impressed not only by the authenticity, but by the cleanliness [and] the courtesy. . . . It was a thoroughly delightful experience." Mrs. Samuel H. Oakley expressed similar views in her letter of October 1954. She felt it was a "priceless privilege" to walk down the restoration's preserved streets. Oakley argued that the restoration's greatest accomplishment was that "it will help our children to learn upon what foundations and through what trials our country was built—and encourage them to maintain the ideas of those men whose words and deeds still live gloriously."[52]

Some correspondents, however, were disappointed in the presentation of the restoration and the staff employed to aid the visitors. N. C. Morris complained to restoration official Thomas McCaskey that "the persons who took charge of the groups showed very little or no enthusiasm in their work." For Morris, these workers should have been proud and excited to demonstrate the accomplishments of the restoration. C. Russell Doyle made a similar complaint to Kenneth Chorley a few years later, indicating that on his last visit "I found the beauty of the place as in the past, but the spirit and atmosphere seemed to be lacking. Some of the staff are apparently becoming bored with telling the story of Williamsburg." Such complaints may have been the result of increased tourist traffic, especially during the summer months. Dissatisfaction such as this led some travelers to wonder if Colonial Williamsburg was mainly a tourist trap.[53]

With both its supporters and its critics, Colonial Williamsburg moved into a volatile political situation from which there was no clearly marked road of escape. In an attempt to please two masters, the restoration ultimately pleased neither. Economics and the fact that the restoration was located in Virginia dictated that moves toward integration be made slowly. Should the restoration offend the client base that it was most trying to attract, forcing the project into bankruptcy, any future efforts to demonstrate the lives of African Americans would be for nought. Thus Colonial Williamsburg chose the middle road, subjecting itself to criticism from all sides, but ensuring financial viability for the years to come.

At the time when there were debates about the future course of the restoration, Colonial Williamsburg still served as a mecca for foreign travelers coming to the United States. Trips to the restoration also often featured journeys to the two other local national landmarks: Jamestown and Yorktown. A typical VIP tour in the late 1950s would have followed this itinerary. The tour would begin on Jamestown Island, site of the first permanent British settlement in the New World. If time permitted, the visitor would be shown a bit of the wilderness that had overtaken Jamestown Island and might be taken through the new Visitors Center, with its historic displays and dioramas. Next the visitor would stop at the Jamestown Festival Park. The most striking display there was the accurately reconstructed original village of Jamestown, a stockaded community of mud and thatched huts showing the primitive living conditions. From the seventeenth-century Jamestown stockade, the visitor would return to Colonial Williamsburg to see the progress of 150 years and the "spot where many of the democratic ideas of the Revolution were forged." If possible, the visitor would also be driven to the battlefields around Yorktown where the final major battle of the American Revolution was fought in 1781.[54]

After such a tour, these dignitaries would have seen some of the landmarks of the Colonial National Monument, which were promoted as icons of the era and brought together Americans and foreigners alike in a search for a better understanding of the American past. The proximity of these three important sites within a few miles of each other, connected by the Colonial Parkway, made the Tidewater the perfect spot for a crash course in Americanism. Obviously, Colonial Williamsburg and the Colonial National Monument fit well into the State Department's agenda for indoctrinating foreign officials.

In addition to dignitaries, Colonial Williamsburg also wanted to lure tourists, both native and foreign, to its winter events. To encourage people to visit in the off-season, the restoration began for the first time to offer "a series of packaged weekends, including special rates and behind-the-scenes exhibits and events normally unavailable to the in-season visitor." Such events provided an up-close look at some of the craft shops, private dwellings not usually open to the public, and the Colonial Williamsburg Archaeological Laboratory. These programs were designed to elicit greater interest in Colonial Williamsburg and to provide a special opportunity to those who felt that the summer tours did not give them enough time to adequately study the restoration.[55]

Another sign of the increasing prominence of the restoration and its national role came in the recognition from a noted historical scholar, Daniel Boorstin. At the time an associate professor of history at the University of

A postwar couple views the front of the Raleigh Tavern
with a guide in colonial dress, ca. 1955 (Courtesy of the
Colonial Williamsburg Foundation)

Chicago, Boorstin wrote about the restoration in the January 1958 issue of
Commentary. Although Colonial Williamsburg had been received poorly by
many of his fellow historians, Boorstin could not support their views. He
thought that Colonial Williamsburg was far more significant than his colleagues did and argued that the restoration represented what "distinguished
our national past from that of people in other parts of the world." Boorstin
was promoting a belief in American exceptionalism, the idea that the
United States, due to its emphasis on democracy, was inherently superior
to Europe. He went on to describe the democratic nature of the restoration,
noting that it was unlike the typical European history museum, which "is
a pretty esoteric place." Colonial Williamsburg, he argued, was superior to
its European counterparts because it was inherently geared more toward
the common people and their experiences in the country, as opposed to traditional European museums, which primarily displayed the lives of the
monarchy and aristocracy to the detriment of average citizens.[56]

Because Colonial Williamsburg exuded this democratic air, Boorstin felt that the restoration served as an excellent example of American political ideology. In stressing the continuity of the past and present in American culture, Colonial Williamsburg served as "an American kind of sacred document." Although finding much to praise in the restoration effort, Boorstin found a few points to criticize as well: the tendency to overhomogenize the past and the temptation to make it too pretty and too relevant. No doubt, Colonial Williamsburg was guilty on these points. In attempting to create a perfect vision of the past, the restoration had sacrificed historic reality.[57]

Yet, as Boorstin argued, the tendency of Americans to re-create their past is understandable, since few historic relics remain. Due to the town's development over the years, much of the historic area in Williamsburg actually had to be reconstructed, not merely restored, thereby creating a false image of the eighteenth century. The restoration tended to de-emphasize the fact that most of the structures that visitors saw were, in fact, re-creations.[58]

In conclusion, Boorstin blandly criticized the American penchant for erasing the past just to improve it. Such was the case with Colonial Williamsburg. In re-creating the eighteenth century, the restoration's founders sought to make the past better than it actually was. He argued that for a country that desires a model future, the United States is quick to deny any errors in its past. Thus, "a house is removed to make way for a road; it is reconstructed to fit in the modern improvements: the two-car garage, the television room, or the air-conditioning." In this way, the nation need not be bothered by incongruities in its history. Rather, Colonial Williamsburg demonstrated how one could improve on the past and use it to sell an important message to a later generation of Americans who, just as they were ready to purchase the manifestations of modern consumerism, were equally prepared to "buy" a sanitized version of the American past.[59]

Yet the restoration's pristine nature allowed it to be accepted and touted as an educational landmark precisely because it kept certain aspects of colonial life in abeyance. By keeping the Revolutionary era one of beautiful architecture, tree-lined streets, famous men, and quaint customs, the people of the twentieth century could not help but admire its attributes. Ultimately, Colonial Williamsburg filled a growing void in twentieth-century life. In its presentation of a culture lost in the rush for progress, industrial might, and material affluence, Colonial Williamsburg became a respite from the chores of daily living and the chance to wallow in the sanctity of the past. In Colonial Williamsburg, Americans could be proud of their country's past and hopeful for its future, knowing that what many Americans in the mid-twentieth century viewed as the country's principal qualities were being permanently enshrined by what many locals called the Rockefeller restoration.

The retirement of Kenneth Chorley in 1958 and the death of JDR Jr. in 1960 demonstrated that a new generation was in charge of the restoration. Huge changes had occurred during the three and a half decades that Williamsburg had been host to America's most famous monument to historic preservation. These years forever changed Americans' perception of themselves and their country. As the most prominent physical representation of the nation's values, Colonial Williamsburg played a vital role in this transformation. The great national and international recognition that the restoration received during this period was undoubtedly surprising to those who had witnessed its creation. Colonial Williamsburg had exceeded the expectations of even its strongest supporters.

Yet in the coming years the restoration would be forced to change its message as events at home and abroad would once again alter Colonial Williamsburg's role. As the restoration matured, social and political forces would inexorably move the United States and the restoration to confront their failure to adequately address the history of women and African Americans. As the realization of this fact took hold, the facade of Colonial Williamsburg's presentation would slowly begin to crack. A truer representation of the past at Colonial Williamsburg would inevitably have to unfold. A more astute and diverse audience would not permit such a simplified, Americanist presentation to remain the guiding force of the restoration. If Colonial Williamsburg wanted to be successful in the more complex, critical society of the last third of the twentieth century, it needed to change with the times. This change would create a restoration that was more in keeping with the America that saw a virtue in the diversity of its citizens rather than one that ignored their differences and argued for their uniformity. The gradual transition to the modern presentation would not be an easy one, however. The country would go through a painful metamorphosis to achieve these new freedoms. In its own way, Colonial Williamsburg would also need to change and work to balance its previously one-sided presentation of the past.

6

Achieving Maturity

A s Colonial Williamsburg moved into the 1960s, it reached its maturity, finalizing the major restorations and reconstructions that the founders had envisioned almost forty years earlier. The project was poised to represent an eighteenth-century town more completely than ever before. Yet other historical re-creations slowly pushed Colonial Williamsburg toward providing a broader interpretation of the colonial era in Virginia. Many of these newer sites portrayed the lives of average citizens and not simply the elite. In addition, the undercurrents of change in American society in the 1960s began to be felt within the town. The growth of the civil rights movement not only dictated a change in governmental policy toward African Americans but also meant that all aspects of American society had to begin to include groups that had been neglected for so long in the American experience. The Vietnam War and Watergate caused some Americans to question their country's traditional beliefs, its political institutions, and the presentation of its history. Nevertheless, many white visitors still did not wish to see a presentation of African American history or witness a stronger presence of blacks in the historic area. Yet a failure to bring Colonial Williamsburg up to date with changing national and international events meant that it risked obsolescence. The restoration's location in Virginia, a segregated state whose capital had been the capital of the Confederacy, necessarily complicated any attempts that might be made to alter its presentation of the country's colonial past to reflect the contributions of nonwhites.

Today most white Americans have gradually accepted the importance of African Americans in the nation's history. Yet the situation at the start of the 1960s was not nearly as welcoming. African Americans still struggled for basic human rights in the South and faced great opposition to relatively minor changes, such as the integration of lunch counters, waiting rooms, restrooms, and water fountains. Would people who were reluctant to eat a sandwich next to a person of color want to hear that person's history presented on an equal basis with that of the white Founding Fathers? This key dilemma facing the restoration would force a new approach to handling the delicate issues of slavery and the presentation of African American history.

Colonial Williamsburg would also have to deal with possible discord between town residents and restoration officials. Forceful moves to integrate the restoration could have been attributed to a "Yankee-ization" of the South: forcing northern ideas on a proud people. Therefore, any moves to open the restoration to the presentation of African American history needed to be done slowly and with great tact and planning. Changing people's minds about how the past should be presented would be the hardest job of the restoration. Most of the basic problems such as altering the program, creating new scholarship, and hiring African American interpreters could be remedied. The main difficulty was removing the block in the minds of many white Americans that prohibited them from accepting former slaves as equals whose backgrounds and histories deserved as much attention as those of their former masters. An integral part of this process would be to raise the respect given to African Americans as a whole, which would help visitors appreciate the importance of black history.

In addition, international affairs were still an important issue for the restoration during this period of the Cold War. The strength of the Soviet Union would become clearer with the installation of nuclear missiles in Cuba following the failed invasion at the Bay of Pigs in 1961, which led to the showdown of the Cuban missile crisis of 1962. These events heightened the tensions of the Cold War and drove home the restoration's message. The film *Williamsburg—The Story of a Patriot* reinforced this notion of the restoration's promotion of democratic principles. Although the restoration's formal role as an official indoctrination point for American servicemen had ceased to exist, local soldiers and sailors continued to make unofficial visits to the restoration.

Colonial Williamsburg also continued to be a stop on the itineraries of foreign visitors who came to see the Rockefeller vision of the past that had garnered so much attention. One such visitor whose view of the world of the 1960s contrasted with Colonial Williamsburg's message was Sir Patrick Dean, the British ambassador to the United States. Dean made his remarks during the "Prelude to Independence" celebration that occurred annually between 15 May and 4 July. He believed that the view of a "cold war Iron Curtain concept of the world society" was inherently damaging. Dean argued that this perspective promoted the belief that one day there would be a victory in the Cold War, with one side surrendering to the other. Such an idea, he argued, damaged hope for coexistence. Dean's position conflicted with Colonial Williamsburg's notion of world affairs—one that heralded the cause of democracy and the need to fight against unrepresentative systems of government. Although Dean used Colonial Williamsburg as the platform for his idea, his remarks probably did not sway anyone in the restoration away from what they felt was the project's traditional role in supporting democracy and representative government.[1]

While the rest of the country suffered through unsettled times during the 1960s, as centuries of American racial intolerance prompted riots across the nation, events in Colonial Williamsburg remained generally calm. There were hints of the unrest, which was commonplace throughout the South and the country in that decade, but the town and its environs did not suffer from the overt divisiveness that plagued many other areas. People in the community, both black and white, knew that their prosperity depended on the success of Colonial Williamsburg. As an attraction that brought up to one million people a year to the historic area and other local sites, the restoration was an important employer on the peninsula, and its decline would bring irreparable economic harm to the region.

In the early 1960s Americans were still enjoying the fruits of postwar prosperity, and the restoration actively sought to promote itself as an important ingredient in the advancement of Americanism during this period. Edward P. Alexander, a vice president of the restoration and its director of interpretation, promulgated these views in a *New York Times* article in 1962. Colonial Williamsburg's influence was still widespread at this time, ranging from collectors of colonial antiques to supporters of the restoration of old buildings. The restoration's development had encouraged these activities, as well as a greater appreciation for colonial America's material culture.[2]

A common theme echoed by visitors since the late 1940s was the fear that Colonial Williamsburg's increased growth and popularity would result in its further commercialization. Some people, especially those who lived in the vicinity, had made a habit of visiting the restoration at least once a year. For them, Colonial Williamsburg was a beautiful and tranquil place that gave them a break from everyday life. Many of these visitors had been coming to visit the town since the end of World War II and had noticed the growth in popularity of this famous landmark. For many of them, the intimacy of the restoration had suffered a decline. More people, more cars, and more noise would necessarily interfere with their view of what the past should have been like. For all these reasons, growing popularity and commercialization should be decried, they argued.

Yet easier access to the restoration meant that more people would have the chance to see the project and to understand why it was so important to so many visitors. Colonial Williamsburg was reluctant to back away from its Americanist presentation of the past. Visitors of this period, who were predominantly white, often viewed the past in a traditional way and usually appreciated presentations that highlighted the roles of the Founding Fathers, as Jill Allen Mons indicated in a letter to Colonial Williamsburg. Mons wrote that her family visited Colonial Williamsburg and "more than the hundreds of lovely flowers and the beautifully restored buildings, we treasure the memory of the atmosphere of *Americanism*" [emphasis in original]. She and her family saw *The Story of a Patriot* three times and were deeply moved by it. In addition, the teachings of Colonial Williamsburg and its emphasis on liberty were important to Mons, who wrote that "it thrills me more than anything to know that somewhere the spirit of liberty still flourishes. Thank you and God Bless you!"[3]

Other visitors were impressed with the extent of the restoration and how geographically inclusive it was becoming. Although many tourists might have heard of Colonial Williamsburg, they did not know exactly what the restoration looked like until they visited it themselves. Such was the experience of John H. Eden Jr. when he and his family journeyed to Colonial Williamsburg in the summer of 1960. Eden wrote about his surprise at all that the restoration had accomplished in the past three and a half decades. "We are at a loss for words to convey our feelings upon a recent visit to Williamsburg and to express our appreciation—as Americans—for all that has been done for us." He also wrote that the restoration surprised them since "this was our first visit and . . . we had not realized the tremendous amount of work accomplished for the preservation and public presentation of our great American heritage." The restoration needed to be experienced to be fully understood because pictures and text alone could not demonstrate its scope.[4]

Greater crowds and the increasing numbers of hotels, motels, and restaurants in the town attested to its status as a popular tourist destination. Yet many visitors wanted to ensure that the growing popularity of the town did not turn it into a tourist trap. Such sentiments were expressed by Mrs. James L. Oliver and Mrs. E. O. Reynolds who liked the atmosphere of the restoration in 1960. But as Oliver wrote, "We enjoyed every minute of our pleasant and comfortable stay. . . . Just don't let it get any more commercial than it is now, however." Of course, the restoration had to walk a fine line between popularity and commercialization. Restoration officials certainly wanted their Americanist message to be spread nationally, and they desired large numbers of visitors to come to Colonial Williamsburg, but not at the expense of destroying the town's colonial ambiance.[5]

As the wealth of the American middle class increased in the early 1960s, many Americans traveled more both within the country and abroad. Naturally, many of these new tourists wanted to compare the places they had visited. Because of Colonial Williamsburg's high profile as the nation's first full-scale historic restoration project, and because of the large amounts of Rockefeller money invested in the town, many visitors wanted to see how the restoration measured up to other historic shrines and monuments. Carl A. Albrecht's experiences may have been typical of many Americans who were looking to examine the country's history. He wrote to Colonial Williamsburg: "Our whole family has traveled a great deal in the United States and abroad but . . . we have never experienced such a wonderful atmosphere as we have in Williamsburg." But Albrecht saw his trip to Colonial Williamsburg as more than merely a family vacation. He took away a deeper meaning from the restoration, which prompted him to contrast the present-day political scene and that of the eighteenth century. He wrote that "to live history over again is indeed a unique experience. . . . I only wish . . . the inspiration which one receives from Williamsburg could also reflect on our present day political leaders." He felt that a trip to Colonial Williamsburg would be a good thing for those in power in Washington, a sentiment that was shared by a large number of congressmen who made the journey south to the restored capital.[6]

Many visitors also felt that Colonial Williamsburg could serve as an inspirational site for themselves, as well as for the nation's politicians. Without doubt, much of the influence of the restoration came from these visitors' desire to see colonial Virginia the way it was portrayed by the project. As T. Jasper Lowe indicated to Chairman of the Board Winthrop Rockefeller, Lowe's family took away a strong sense of the American past. "You would have been happy to hear my young teenage daughters express their enthusiasm and . . . Mrs. Lowe and I were spiritually renewed and pledged ourselves to a higher quality of citizenship." For the Lowes, and doubtless many others, Colonial Williamsburg was more than just another tourist site; it engendered an enthusiasm and a spiritual awakening in the early 1960s, just as it had three decades earlier. In addition, through a better appreciation of the colonial past, many visitors claimed that Colonial Williamsburg could make one a better American and therefore a more capable participant in the battle against beliefs that threatened to undermine core American values.[7]

But not all tourists were unqualified in their praise for the restoration. Some visitors, such as Marvin Frankel, found Colonial Williamsburg to be only a partial portrayal of life in the past. In his letter to Colonial Williamsburg in April 1961, Frankel said that the restoration seemed to be one-sided in its presentation of life in colonial Virginia. "It seems . . . to reflect the period only very partially in that what is restored represents the houses and domestic arrangements only of the very rich." Frankel understood that it was probably easier to re-create the lifestyles of the wealthy and prominent, but "if it is possible, future efforts should look to portrayal of other levels of 18th century Williamsburg society." He was prescient in his comments, as this was the direction in which Colonial Williamsburg would eventually move, although not for at least another fifteen years.[8]

Nevertheless, the vast majority of those who visited the restoration in this period expressed little desire for change. According to a poll conducted by Dr. Raymond Franzen of New York City, 99 percent of Colonial Williamsburg's visitors would recommend a visit to the restoration to their friends. The survey sought information in two major areas: the knowledge of the past gained by the visitors and any satisfactions or dissatisfactions expressed by tourists. Most Colonial Williamsburg visitors, the survey found, were between thirty and fifty years of age and earned between $6,000 and $12,000 a year. Ninety-four percent said they considered Colonial Williamsburg an important experience where history was brought to life. Since most Americans of the period were still deeply sensitive to portrayals of their country's past and were more interested in the lives of prominent individuals than in the lives of workers, servants, and slaves, few visitors complained about

Costumed interpreters dancing in the ballroom of the Governor's Palace, a part of the traditional portrayal of the life of wealthy Virginians (Courtesy of the Colonial Williamsburg Foundation)

the lack of balance in the restoration. And Colonial Williamsburg sought to ensure that their "guests" were happy with what they saw. The notion of forcing a sociohistorical education down the throats of visitors was not popular with restoration officials. In this way, Colonial Williamsburg's slow move to alter its presentation of the past drew support from both its officials and the majority of its visitors.[9]

The 1960 excavation of the Hay family cabinet shop demonstrated the restoration's continuing interest in developing its presentation of the town. This research yielded important information about the craftsman's workshop, including tools, gun fittings, and pieces of furniture. This site was particularly well preserved, and it proved to be invaluable to researchers trying to gain a better understanding of the lives of colonial craftsmen. In this way, Colonial Williamsburg gained further insight and appreciation of its earlier inhabitants and also could more effectively counter arguments that the restoration was a "fake."[10]

Newspaper articles also argued for Colonial Williamsburg's authenticity. The free publicity for the restoration that was provided by a *New York Times* article on the restoration in April 1961 was beneficial for the project's future. This piece by Herbert Rosenthal provided an overview of what a visitor might expect in touring the restored village. In addition, Rosenthal highlighted the areas of authenticity of the project, making the point that Colonial Williamsburg was not a fantasy but a serious historical restoration and reconstruction project. He also described the various attractions for families, such as baby-sitting services provided during the evening so that parents "may make a candlelight tour of the Capital or a special night visit to the craftshops." Yet informing the public about Colonial Williamsburg's attractions was not the sole purpose of Rosenthal's article. He also wished to promote an Americanist agenda. In his conclusion, Rosenthal wrote that "all visitors come away more vividly appreciative of the contributions of early Americans to the ideals of their country."[11]

This free publicity, combined with a salute to Americanism, was a potent means of acquiring visitors for the restoration. Colonial Williamsburg had strong allies in its effort to foster patriotic sentiments in the American people. Many visitors probably felt that positive comments in such newspapers as the *New York Times* meant that Colonial Williamsburg was truly worth visiting. The association with the Rockefeller family doubtless created further intrigue as well. The proximity of the restoration to other areas of interest, such as Mount Vernon and Monticello, also made it a logical addition to the agenda of those who planned to take a vacation in the richly historic area surrounding Williamsburg. For these visitors, many of whom wanted to take "patriotic" summer tours, the image of the role that Colonial Williamsburg played in the nation's history was already firmly cemented in their minds. Therefore, attempts to alter the town's presentation to a more sociohistorical format could have left many of these people gravely disappointed.

Other visitors, however, objected to the education that Colonial Williamsburg was providing. Long lines and crowds lessened the experience for some, while others found that certain aspects of the restoration tended to overemphasize patriotic themes and ideas. As Martin L. Dolan wrote in October 1962, "[T]he only thing that . . . rubbed me the wrong way was a certain too strong Americanism or super-patriotism." Dolan said that he "snickered" at some of the flag-waving in the films at Colonial Williamsburg. Not surprisingly, others such as Robert C. Krantz did not like being treated like a "school-child" and informed Nelson Rockefeller (who had little to do with the restoration) that the workers at Colonial Williamsburg apparently thought that he was a "sheep." He protested about being herded around without having the opportunity to spend the time to see the things he wished.[12]

Although some employees might have lessened the appeal of the restoration to a certain degree, a larger question of authenticity continued to haunt the efforts of the project to re-create the past in a way that was enjoyable and educational. More and more, visitors began to realize that the restoration was continually downplaying aspects of the past that were not as comfortably re-created. In one of the more critical letters on file, Aaron W. Berg wrote to Edward P. Alexander to question the lack of effort in recreating "the more seamy and unattractive facets of life in Williamsburg during the period depicted." Berg wanted to see the "other-side-of-the-track Williamsburg," one that was not being presented by the restoration. By claiming that the project was "too set, too stagey, too onesided," Berg expressed a dissatisfaction with the restoration's presentation that many scholars would echo in the future. Alexander's reply to Berg was a standard response given by Colonial Williamsburg to such criticism; he wrote essentially that it was impossible to accurately re-create all aspects of the past to everyone's satisfaction. Yet in his letter Alexander clearly skirted the issue of displaying the "other-side-of-the-track" part of the city, probably because that kind of display could offend too many of the town's visitors.[13]

Another problem of authenticity concerned the provisioning of the local taverns, the Governor's Palace, as well as the local homes. There were no butchers or farmers re-created in Colonial Williamsburg, so where did the meats, grains, fruits, and vegetables come from? This question was not anticipated early in the project, when buildings were restored for their beauty and educational value. Yet if one was meant to believe that Colonial Williamsburg was more than a museum—indeed, an actual colonial-era town—these parts needed to be included. Of course, attempting to do so would be expensive and would use much of the limited space that was available from the land purchases. Anne H. Cutler commented on this obvious discrepancy in 1963 in a letter to the restoration's president Carlisle Humelsine, writing that "I love Williamsburg as you do and we both want people to see the best it has to offer." Cutler was also critical of the town's attempt at "childishly distorting the truth" about the past to win the interest of its patrons. She supported the notion of promoting Americanist ideals, but in such a way that "the lesson learned will not only be a useful and pleasant experience but also thought-provoking and a source of inspiration to present and future Americans."[14]

Racial issues were another feature of Colonial Williamsburg about which
many visitors felt compelled to comment. As had been the case for decades,
African Americans were generally confined to employment as waiters, bell-
hops, maids, and maintenance workers. Supervisory roles, guides, interpreters, and virtually all other positions were held by white employees. For
northern visitors, such discrepancies in employment may have seemed discriminatory. One visitor, Marian G. Hittner, wrote to Chairman of the Board
Winthrop Rockefeller in 1963 to voice such a complaint. "A tour of Colonial Williamsburg the day after our arrival served to demonstrate such severe evidence of discrimination in employment that we would have left immediately, had my son not become ill." Restoration officials certainly were
not trying to upset anyone to the degree that Hittner was affected, but they
had to bear in mind the large number of visitors they received from southern states. In fact, one such visitor was equally upset that the restoration
had adopted integration in its hotels and restaurants. E. L. Rose wrote to
Carlisle Humelsine in early 1964 to complain about this new policy. Even
though the Rose family had previously enjoyed Colonial Williamsburg, "we
no longer will be able to do so because of your complete integration. . . .
From now on we will not be a friend or booster of your project." As these
comments demonstrate, Colonial Williamsburg needed to take careful steps
toward progress, counting both the pluses and minuses of that move.[15]

As the restoration became better known, and therefore more closely analyzed, it began to receive more critical reviews. The harshest criticism to
date was published on 22 September 1963 in the *New York Times* by Ada
Louise Huxtable. Huxtable demonstrated no compassion in her critique of
the restoration, which she called a "dangerous bore." It was boring because
it failed to accurately re-create the life of an eighteenth-century town and
dangerous because it "fostered an unforgivable fuzziness between the values of the real and the imitation in the popular mind." Huxtable particularly complained about Colonial Williamsburg's process of restoring and rebuilding sites that were completely destroyed or severely damaged. In her
view, this perverted the role of true historic restoration and preservation.
Rockefeller money that could have been spent to preserve the architectural
heritage of other cities was not available because so much of it was funneled
into the restoration's rebuilding scheme. In addition, guides often blurred
the distinction between what was real and what was fake, which item was
a period piece and which was a reproduction. To further her point, Huxtable

described the tearing down of a nineteenth-century landmark to build a re-production of the Williamsburg Inn, which is a twentieth-century structure built in the Regency style. In essence, Huxtable took Colonial Williamsburg to task, arguing that it had done more harm than good and had created a false understanding of what a good historical restoration should be.[16]

Many of Huxtable's arguments rang true. Guides often failed to explain that most of the structures were rebuilt—especially some of the most important buildings such as the Capitol, the Governor's Palace, and the Raleigh Tavern. Part of the problem with Colonial Williamsburg was that it took time and interest away from other worthy sites where more of the original buildings were maintained. But few other places could offer the chance to re-create a whole town in the way that Colonial Williamsburg did. That opportunity had initially drawn JDR Jr. to the project and had encouraged him to start the process. Although Colonial Williamsburg may have set the preservation movement back to a certain degree, it also strengthened it because people had begun to pay more attention to earlier structures and the value of saving them.

Public reactions to Huxtable's comments were printed on 13 October 1963 in the *New York Times*. Several of those who wrote were museum specialists or worked with art or antiques. Her supporters were pleased with her candor and well-argued criticism of the restoration and its failings. Paul Perrot, director of the Corning Museum of Glass, wrote, "Mrs. Huxtable's article is the kind of thing we need more of, and it is good to know that she has a regular nationwide platform." Yet not all agreed. Thomas G. Morgansen argued that "the very name of this magnificent project, so justly admired, enjoyed and cherished by the vast majority visiting it, completely refutes the Huxtable thesis." More readers wrote to support Huxtable than to oppose her, demonstrating a quiet dislike of Colonial Williamsburg that had not previously come to the fore in such a prominent public forum. Although such criticisms began to tarnish Colonial Williamsburg's reputation and forced it to come to grips with its presentation of the past, another decade would pass before major changes were made.[17]

Most of those who took the time to write to the restoration in the early 1960s had positive views to relate. For the restoration's supporters, its ideological message was still strong and vibrant. Florence Strand wrote to support the restoration's attempt to promote the importance of the Founding Fathers. "The inspiring picture of Patrick Henry daring to risk his material future for the sake of an ideal is an idea that is almost lost in our present approach to American history," she wrote. Winifred B. Clayton echoed similar sentiments: "In these days when patriotism is so often ridiculed, it is refreshing to see a movie in which a Patriot such as Patrick Henry is treated as a true hero." Many wrote of the inspirational qualities of *The Story of a Patriot* and its power to move them. With such strong, positive voices writing to the restoration, officials there undoubtedly must have felt that the project was following the proper path in its portrayal of the past and American ideals.[18]

To further promote the ideology of the restoration and to bring its work to a wider audience, Colonial Williamsburg arranged to rent or to sell eight films and five filmstrips produced by the restoration, including *The Story of a Patriot*, to be distributed nationally by Modern Learning Aids, Inc. The agreement made between Edward P. Alexander and William M. MacCallum, vice president of Modern Learning Aids, would allow the distribution of the thirteen titles to schools, clubs, or other groups for educational purposes. The distributor stocked the films in six centers across the country, including New York City, Washington, D.C., San Francisco, and Atlanta, which allowed for easy shipping of the films to those who requested them. This arrangement was an excellent way for the restoration to get its message out. Aside from *The Story of a Patriot*, most of the films centered on the process of the restoration, but they also included themes of national loyalty and the importance of the Founding Fathers, as well as the role of the restoration in promoting an appreciation of American values.[19]

In November 1963, the purchase of Carter's Grove Plantation from the McCrea estate by the Sealantic Fund, Inc., a Rockefeller-supported philanthropic organization, opened up new territory for the restoration. Kenneth Chorley had mentioned the possibility of acquiring the mansion in the 1957 annual report, but no action could be taken until Mrs. McCrea's death. The main house at Carter's Grove was originally built between 1750 and 1753 by Carter Burwell, grandson of Robert "King" Carter, the wealthiest man in colonial Virginia. After leaving the control of the Burwell family in 1838, the property passed through a variety of owners before being purchased by Archibald and Mary McCrea in 1927. Mary McCrea, a Burwell descendant, saw the opportunity to restore this house as her contribution to the future. The interior was decorated in the American revival style of the 1930s, and the two outbuildings on either side of the main house were connected to the larger dwelling. Mrs. McCrea's death in 1960 paved the way for the purchase by Sealantic and its subsequent debut to the public on 14 April 1964. The house was opened under a special contract with Colonial Williamsburg, and it became the property of the restoration in 1970. The purpose of the purchase was to show visitors a great colonial mansion of the eighteenth century, demonstrating to them both the town and country aspects of eighteenth-century life. Yet unbeknownst to the restoration, the grounds of the plantation contained an important archaeological site. In 1969 the restoration hired English archaeologist Ivor Noël Hume to discover remnants of no longer extant buildings that may have been on Carter's Grove Plantation. Although some remnants of these buildings and fences were found, the most important discovery was Wolstenholme Towne, the settlement of Martin's Hundred, a seventeenth-century immigrant group that was largely destroyed by the massacre of 1622.[20]

The expansion of the work at Carter's Grove not only yielded the long forgotten seventeenth-century settlement but also gave Colonial Williamsburg the opportunity to introduce slave quarters as well as discussions and interpretations of plantation slave life that could not be conducted in the restored town. Work in this area did not begin until the 1980s, but the acquisition of Carter's Grove was an important step in the direction of a more inclusive presentation of eighteenth-century life, as well as that of the early settlements of Virginia. In addition, the interior of the McCrea mansion was an excellent example of the colonial revival style of the 1930s and illustrated the trend that the Colonial Williamsburg restoration had fostered and made famous. In this way, Carter's Grove and Colonial Williamsburg had a deeper relationship than was obvious on the surface. Aside from their related histories and locales, the McCrea mansion paid tribute to the ideal that Colonial Williamsburg tried to promote, and in that sense it too was a monument to the restoration and its ideals.[21]

In addition to the opening of Carter's Grove, the spring of 1964 saw the start of a large archaeological project on more than sixteen acres on either side of Francis Street on the site of the old Public Hospital—one of the first mental hospitals in the country. Also included in the area were the Travis House, which was extant, and the Custis tract, which had contained a large six-chimney house that had burned in the early nineteenth century. Due to the lack of information about the house on the Custis tract, the restoration hoped that the archaeological digs would provide them with useful data on that building's structure, as well as further information about the Public Hospital, about which much was already known. The Custis tract would also reveal more of George Washington's history at Williamsburg, since it was here that he had met Martha Custis, the widow of Daniel Parke Custis, who had inherited the house from his father. In a speech to the Sons of the Revolution in Richmond in 1962, Winthrop Rockefeller had spoken of Washington's "very human qualities, especially as shown in his youth." Colonial Williamsburg hoped to resurrect these qualities and the less publicized part of Washington's life with the Custis House.[22]

In addition, the reconstruction of the Hay Cabinetmakers Shop on Nicholson Street was nearing completion and the Prentis Store on Duke of Gloucester Street was scheduled for improvements to make it more closely resemble the original structure. One of the last major buildings to be restored in the historic area was the Robert Carter Nicholas house. The site on Francis Street was occupied by a modern court building, which was to be removed within two years to allow the reconstruction of the Nicholas house. The vision of forty years ago was finally coming into focus to create the restoration that the founders had envisioned. The Rockefeller Brothers Fund granted the project $2 million to help complete the restoration of these buildings and to fulfill JDR Jr.'s dream. Restoration officials hoped that after receiving more than $70 million in Rockefeller money Colonial Williamsburg would become a self-supporting organization.[23]

To support the further internationalization of Colonial Williamsburg and to promote its mission, the soundtrack of the film *Williamsburg—The Story of a Patriot* was translated into seven foreign languages. One row of thirty-one seats in the theater at the Information Center was set aside for those who wished to hear the track in either German, French, Spanish, Italian, Russian, Portuguese, or Japanese. Although there was no attempt to correlate these translations with the lip movements of the screen actors, the translations were geared to be simultaneous. Essentially the service functioned as a personal translator for each guest, especially as the tracks were recorded by translators from the State Department. For a group showing, the translation could be broadcast through the external speakers, covering up the English soundtrack. This new addition was integral to the restoration's desire to be more inclusive and to welcome visitors from abroad, and it probably encouraged Americans who had foreign visitors to take them to Colonial Williamsburg to see the sights as well as the film.[24]

By the mid-1960s, Colonial Williamsburg was finally beginning to complete its restoration process as well as attempting to enrich the experience for its visitors. The restoration also made its first foray into the broadening

The facade of the George Wythe House (Courtesy of the Colonial Williamsburg Foundation)

of the educational program to include information about African Americans. The first scholarly attempt at discussing a long-neglected aspect of the past was the repeating recorded message placed in the Wythe House laundry in 1965. This passive form of information allowed visitors, if they wished, to push a button and hear an account of the work of the slaves in the laundry. Nevertheless, someone tampered with the apparatus and prevented tourists from hearing the information. Although the culprit was never discovered, Colonial Williamsburg officials John Harbour and Edward Spencer felt certain that members of the janitorial staff had committed the mischief.[25]

Clearly, some people in the restoration were opposed to the introduction of black history at Colonial Williamsburg. Their sentiments probably mirrored those of some visitors who would not have been at all interested in listening to an account of the lives of slaves. Publication projects centering on the lives of certain free and enslaved African Americans also fell through for reasons that are not clear. The restoration waited until there was a greater acceptance of the role of blacks in American history before they presented a program that was consistent with the importance of African American history in Virginia.[26]

By 1966 large numbers of Americans were still as eager to embrace the restoration as they had been during the previous four decades. Colonial Williamsburg had played host to more than thirteen million visitors by the spring of that year, with an annual visitation rate of close to one million each year, including local residents, cross-country travelers, and foreign dignitaries. Colonial Williamsburg attracted a wide variety of guests, from the very young to the elderly. More than $70 million had been spent since the initial purchases by JDR Jr. forty years ago. The project, which at one time was estimated to cost $5 million to complete, had cost more than twelve times as much. Even though Colonial Williamsburg had changed quite dramatically over this period, the continuity of responses to the restoration during this time reflected an interesting similarity in how Americans had viewed Colonial Williamsburg through the decades. Problems of different magnitudes and intensities plagued the country from the 1930s through the 1970s, but visitors found solace in the restoration during all of these periods. Credit for this is certainly due to project officials who successfully promoted the restoration during this time. Nevertheless, Colonial Williamsburg's failure in the late 1960s and early 1970s to adequately address African American issues would be a stumbling block to obtaining support from all of its patrons.[27]

Yet the restoration slowly tried to integrate African American history into the project. This integration was done most notably in the guidebook to the exhibition buildings. In the guidebook published in 1968, one paragraph was accorded to black life in a city in which in colonial times half of the population was of African descent. This description served to inform visitors of the basic lives of slaves, the differences between city and country life, and the difficulty in discovering details about slaves because of the paucity of sources. Since guidebooks from earlier decades made no mention of black life, this addition was an advancement, although quite a modest one.[28]

Most of Colonial Williamsburg's presentation, however, had not been altered to show a greater sensitivity to African Americans. A short sequence in *The Story of a Patriot* demonstrated the racism inherent in the film. Homer L. Pettengill wrote to the restoration in April 1968 to complain about a scene that has since been removed. Pettengill, and doubtless other visitors

as well, objected to "one sequence [which] shows a negro servant testing
the drunkenness of a tavern patron. [He] waves his hand in front of the
white man's face, and finding him drunk, steals his money." This short
piece was most likely meant to be humorous, and had the servant been
white it might have been interpreted in that vein. Because the servant was
black, however, it appeared to certain members of the audience that this
was a comment about the supposed dishonesty of African Americans. As
Pettengill commented, "[I]t is a portrayal of a stereotype that I find offensive and in very poor taste anytime, including 1968." By the late 1960s,
more than seven million viewers had seen *The Story of a Patriot* in more than
eight-five thousand showings. Its Cold War theme—the striving of Americans for independence against a cruel foreign master—still resonated with
the audience. Although white Americans' views of blacks had slowly begun
to change by this time, their patriotic sentiments had not. Although the Tet
Offensive in January 1968 had begun to erode the sense of American in-
vincibility, most of those who came to Colonial Williamsburg through the
1960s probably still supported its traditional Americanist interpretation of
the past.[29]

The year 1968 also saw the growth of the restoration as four new exhibition sites opened on 1 July. In preparation over the previous two years, this
was the largest unveiling of new exhibitions since the beginning in 1934.
The four buildings were the home of wealthy political leader Peyton Ran-
dolph (notable for having the only known oak-paneled room in eighteenth-
century America), the home and shop of silversmith James Geddy, Henry
Wetherburn's tavern, and the newly restored Wren Building of the College
of William and Mary. The restoration hoped that, in addition to their value
as further examples of colonial life, these new buildings would help alleviate the crowding, which had become particularly bad during the summer.
The restoration also created a new type of combination ticket that would
allow people to see seven major buildings at a cost of $3.50 for adults, with
discounts for students, military personnel, and children. Visitors could see
the Capitol, the Governor's Palace, and the Wren Building and then choose
to visit four more sites. This ticket would give visitors the freedom to tai-
lor their tours, and the restoration assumed that not everybody wanted to
see the same thing, which would alleviate some of the overcrowding.[30]

By the late 1960s and early 1970s, visitors became more vocal in their
criticism of the restoration's failure to deal properly with African American
issues at Colonial Williamsburg. Several letters during this period pointed

out frankly and openly the project's failure to adequately address these points. Mr. and Mrs. T. J. Kent Jr. disliked the apparent inequality in hiring, which had been in place for four decades at Colonial Williamsburg. "We *would* [emphasis in original] like to make the following suggestion—that your staff be racially integrated from top to bottom." The Kents echoed sentiments expressed by other writers in condemning what they saw as overt discrimination against blacks in the hiring process. Racial issues were a major news item in the late 1960s, and as the Kents indicated, they appreciated the importance of equity in hiring, "especially in the year 1969 when probably our biggest domestic problem in America is to achieve racial equality."[31]

Another visitor during the same time period, Ann Agran, found another problem with Colonial Williamsburg. Although she enjoyed her trip, she also wanted to let the restoration know that "there was a serious gap in its historical reality." Agran was opposed to the presentation of the life of only one "social class." She commented, "Nowhere was there any discussion about the cultural borrowing from African tribal life or customs. . . . The contributions of the black population have been largely omitted." The lack of such material, which was overlooked for decades, was becoming readily apparent. Nor did the staff try to make up for this shortfall. As Agran noted, "[A]ny questions asked about [the African] aspect of the life are met by the hostess by obvious discomfort and embarrassment." Colonial Williamsburg's desire to be an educational institution was not fulfilled by such an obvious lack of emphasis on the role of half of the town's colonial population. For adults, who had the opportunity for other sources of education and were less impressionable, this problem was not necessarily damaging. But as Agran noted, "[T]he negro child touring this exhibit is once more deprived of learning about the cultural contribution made by his forefathers!"[32]

Criticism of Colonial Williamsburg's lack of a discussion of slavery, which began slowly in the late 1960s, grew to a good-sized wave by the 1970s. More and more visitors, black and white, began to write to the restoration complaining of an obvious lack of balance in the presentation of Williamsburg's past. As Mr. and Mrs. F. H. Bonaparte mentioned in their December 1971 letter, "[A]s before there is a great feeling of alienation because of the almost total absence of the story of the significant part black people played in weaving the historical fabric presented to those of us who visit here." The Bonapartes, who were African American, were opposed to the failure of the restoration to document the role played by blacks in the Revolutionary War. As they noted, "[T]he opportunity you have to correct many blatantly false historical concepts is excitingly infinite. We would encourage you to do so." They, too, were worried about the effect that Colonial Williamsburg might have on children's perceptions of themselves and their past. Although the restoration had the ability to promote patriotism and a love of country, it also had the chance to damage people's self-esteem and their understanding of the past. "Your corporation cannot allow the perpetuation of these false concepts. Historical correction is mandatory for our children's and your children's sakes," they added.[33]

Some visitors also began to question *The Story of a Patriot* and the overly patriotic themes of the film. As the controversy over American participation in the Vietnam War reached a crescendo in the early 1970s, it was not surprising to find a less willing acceptance of the Americanist themes that had worked well in previous decades. M. K. Walker indicated his sentiments in a letter in the spring of 1971. "Although I have looked forward to seeing Williamsburg for years, my entire trip was ruined by the boring, terribly poorly presented, super patriotic movie suggested by your information center." The film's message had not changed, but clearly popular sentiment about notions of patriotism had begun to change.[34]

In addition, critiques of the restoration by museum professionals began to arise, as S. K. Stevens's comments to Carlisle Humelsine illustrate. Stevens was employed by the Pennsylvania Historical and Museum Commission and demonstrated little empathy for his colleagues at the restoration. He commented, "I believe you might be surprised at the number of professional people who share my critical view of Colonial Williamsburg. Let me . . . say that I think it is very fine for what it is, but it is not really a synthetic restoration and really a re-creation." Stevens's point was, of course, correct. The initial aim of the restoration had been to re-create the town in such a way as to inspire its visitors. He questioned the reality of the restoration and its ability to truly teach the past: "Is it not true that so called 'restored' Williamsburg and the presentation of it is quite a bit removed from the reality of what the town was at the time of the Revolution?" No doubt Stevens was right on target with such criticism, and the project had to make a stronger attempt to portray the past accurately to ameliorate some of these problems.[35]

The restoration was going through a difficult financial period during this time, however. Its previous division into two entities, Colonial Williamsburg, Inc., and Williamsburg Restoration, Inc., ended in 1969. The Internal Revenue Service demanded an amalgamation of the two branches, which led to the creation of the Colonial Williamsburg Foundation, the current title for the restoration. The combined operating deficit for the restoration rose dramatically from $314,000 in 1966 to $878,000 in 1969 and to $1,812,000 in 1970. These losses were offset by the Rockefeller endowment, which allowed the project to continue operating without seeking outside funding. But just as the criticism of its operations was heating up, the restoration was in an increasingly difficult financial situation. The production of a replacement film for *The Story of a Patriot* was not possible, and it would not be easy to dramatically shift the orientation of the town.[36]

Unlike other historical museums or re-creations that were gated, Colonial Williamsburg let anyone walk down the streets of the restored town. This open policy meant the possible loss of thousands of dollars in revenue if these individuals failed to buy admission tickets. At the same time, the restoration did not want to offend potential visitors by being overly rigid in enforcing entrance policies. To help boost revenue, work was under way to build two stores where visitors could purchase items made in the craft shops. The Tarpley's and Prentis Stores on the Duke of Gloucester Street opened in 1973. These shops provided more income for the restoration and gave visitors a chance to take home inexpensive replicas of products made in the colonial area.[37]

Along with the growing financial concerns, Colonial Williamsburg also faced a change in leadership in 1973 when Winthrop Rockefeller died of cancer on 22 February after nearly twenty years at the helm of the restoration. His death led to the end of direct Rockefeller influence on the operation, placing authority in the hands of those with ties to the region. Rockefeller's successor was Associate Supreme Court Justice Lewis Powell, who was elected on 19 May. Powell had been a member of the restoration's board since 1954 and had served as general counsel to the restoration from 1956 until his elevation to the Supreme Court in 1971. Powell's duties on the Court, however, would severely restrict his participation in the affairs of the restoration, and so the president, Carlisle Humelsine, would be considered the chief executive officer. One year after the death of Winthrop Rockefeller, former president Kenneth Chorley died in the spring of 1974 at the age of eighty. Thus, within a short span, two individuals who had represented the Rockefeller ties to the restoration had passed away. Colonial Williamsburg now was poised to become less of a Rockefeller enterprise and more of a locally controlled entity, as both Powell and Humelsine were Southerners. This change would help lessen the perception of outside control of the restoration and better equip it to handle the future delicate transition to a social history museum.[38]

Yet many people still had positive sentiments about traditional Colonial Williamsburg and what it had to offer. Sarah L. Fry's letter expressed the common sentiments of those who supported the restoration. "My fourteen year old son, who has never been the best history student said, 'Mother if everyone could study history this way there would be no failing students.'" She added about herself, "I feel refreshed of mind, body [and] spirit." Although Colonial Williamsburg could still enliven its visitors' interest in the past, the problem was the unbalanced nature of its presentation and its remaining Americanist ideology. But many tourists lauded the restoration for maintaining such values. Francis J. Fazzano was especially pleased with a particular hostess, Mrs. Mann, who "in simple and intelligent language recounted the history of Williamsburg so eloquently that I think I learned more about that history than I ever did in my years of schooling." Mann also included part of her personal life, which Fazzano and his wife found particularly touching: "She brought into her comments the story of her son who was killed in Vietnam, and it so impressed me and my wife that, quite frankly, it brought tears to our eyes." In this way, Colonial Williamsburg still acted as a monument to national ideals in times of hardship.[39]

To ensure that Colonial Williamsburg brought in as much money as possible from its visitors, the restoration began a plan in January 1973 that would limit access to certain parts of the restoration solely to paying customers. In the past, visitors could ride the buses and visit the craft shops for free, but now there would be a general admission charge of $4.50 for adults and $3 for children between six and twelve. Individual tickets would no longer exist, replaced instead by the general charge. But in keeping with the restoration's continuing interest in promoting its Americanist beliefs, *The Story of a Patriot* could still be seen free of charge at the Information Center. Of course, one did not need to see the film to understand the restoration, as was commonly claimed. Rather, the film served as an indoctrination into Colonial Williamsburg's ideological beliefs as opposed to an introduction to eighteenth-century life. The switch to the general admission charge was primarily a way to help make up Colonial Williamsburg's $4 million deficit. Although funds from the endowment were available, the restoration tried, whenever possible, to make up financial shortfalls from its visitors instead of touching the Rockefeller money. In an article from 1972 that detailed the changes at Colonial Williamsburg, the *New York Times* kept up its general support of the restoration. But the paper also noted criticism from those who saw Colonial Williamsburg as "little more than Disneyland two centuries removed." Nevertheless, the piece concluded on a positive note, indicating that the "restoration includes most of the 18th-century capital of Virginia and invokes the spirit of George Washington, Thomas Jefferson and Patrick Henry. . . . That is a hard combination to beat, even at higher prices."[40]

Yet the *New York Times* made its own contribution to the Williamsburg-Disney connection in a piece written by Dick Schaap for the Sunday Travel and Resorts Section on 28 September 1975. Schaap and his family made a back-to-back trip to Colonial Williamsburg and Disney World in Orlando, Florida. He wrote that his children were lured by *The Story of a Patriot* to think of Colonial Williamsburg strictly in its traditional terms, with emphasis on Washington, Jefferson, and Henry. Yet the history lesson was quickly forgotten when the family traveled to Disney World. His article compared a serious attempt at historical restoration and reconstruction with a purposely created fantasy land. The excessive cleanliness and pristine nature of Colonial Williamsburg tended to give it the air of an amusement park, and Disney's portrayal of history was often similar—idealistic without any dirt, grime, or fuss. In addition, the lack of any discussion of slavery at Colonial Williamsburg contributed to this overly pristine image. Only when Colonial Williamsburg came to grips with its true past could it properly overcome this barrier and clearly differentiate itself in the minds of its visitors.[41]

Colonial Williamsburg also had to deal with the rise of competing recreations and restorations of historical villages. Many of these sites learned from Colonial Williamsburg's mistakes and benefited from them. Old Sturbridge Village and Plimoth Plantation, both in Massachusetts, sought to recreate life during the early nineteenth and seventeenth centuries, respectively. Old Sturbridge Village, which opened in 1946, re-created a New England community at the start of the 1800s. The village had costumed interpreters who carried on the daily activities of farmers, townspeople, artisans, blacksmiths, and millers. Their orientation was geared to presenting the daily events of family life at the time. Plimoth Plantation, which opened in 1957, was a re-creation of the 1627 Pilgrim village. Costumed interpreters portrayed famous Pilgrims such as William Bradford, John and Priscilla Alden, and Myles Standish. The interpreters reenacted the daily life of the plantation: baking bread, shearing sheep, and salting fish. They also "back-bred" livestock to re-create some of the animals that the Pilgrims had: lineback cattle, a Dartmoor pony, and several older breeds of chicken. Unlike Colonial Williamsburg, both Old Sturbridge Village and Plimoth Plantation were begun as social history museums with the primary purpose of demonstrating the lifestyles of average people. Colonial Williamsburg, which was still encumbered by its Americanist agenda, had trouble competing in this area.[42]

Some visitors who had visited those museums before coming to Colonial Williamsburg were less than impressed with what the restoration had to offer. In her letter of November 1972, Rita Jaros expressed her displeasure at the failure of Colonial Williamsburg to measure up to these other museums. "To see the Sturbridge blacksmith demonstrate the creation of one solitary nail was an enlightening experience that I shall never forget." But she found Colonial Williamsburg to be too rehearsed and commercial. "At Williamsburg everyone was too busy saying note pieces and then selling something," she claimed. The lack of veracity in Colonial Williamsburg's presentation also bothered Jaros. Echoing a theme that had become common since the late 1960s, she complained of the lack of discussion about slavery. "At *no* time in *no* place by *no* person [emphasis in original] was the word or concept of slavery discussed, mentioned or hinted at." In a scathing rebuke of the restoration, she clearly pointed out its failings in dealing with one of the most difficult portions of American history. "It seems incredible that a whole society, . . . based on slavery, never showed evidences of slavery. . . . Certainly our history of slavery is an unpleasant one . . . but deal with it we must, or we are as guilty as a German reconstruction of the 1940s would be without mention[ing] the 'final solution.'"[43]

Museums such as Plimoth Plantation were moving into the vanguard of what has come to be called "living history." Although Colonial Williamsburg was the initial leader in historical restoration and reconstruction, it began to fall behind these other presentations in certain areas. Of course, one issue that northern living history museums generally did not have to contend with was the role of slavery. Although slavery did exist in pockets in the North into the nineteenth century, it was a minor part of the society—certainly not as important an institution as it was in the South. In this way, northern museums were fortunate that they detailed societies that did not have as diversified class or racial divisions as Williamsburg did.

Comparisons with these other projects and the dissatisfaction with Colonial Williamsburg's portrayal of slavery continued into the mid-1970s. Vincent J. Mara agreed with Rita Jaros that Old Sturbridge Village offered a superior experience to Colonial Williamsburg. Mara found Sturbridge to be much more accessible and equal in "educational impact" to Colonial Williamsburg. Mary Mullaney questioned the lack of information on slaves, asking if "all the studies of Americans in those times left no information about slaves and how they lived and where?" The truth of the matter, of course, was that since 1957 Colonial Williamsburg had possessed that information from Thad W. Tate's research report and later book. Although the restoration claimed in its guidebook that there was a lack of sources on African American history, this was clearly a ruse. Fearful of offending its white southern visitors and unwilling or unable to spend the money, Colonial Williamsburg chose to overlook this obvious failing.[44]

Colonial Williamsburg's fiftieth anniversary year of 1976 brought no relief from the criticism of the restoration. Many who visited for the first time had high expectations, which often were not fulfilled. Most complaints dealt with high prices and discourteous staff people, problems that were exacerbated by the dual celebration of the country's two hundredth birthday and Colonial Williamsburg's fiftieth. Sallie Mathews expressed a sentiment common to many visitors who came during the bicentennial year: "[S]uch commercialism was very disheartening and seemed out of place . . . [and] our celebration of the bicentennial turned out to be a disappointment." Although Colonial Williamsburg was not alone in promoting itself commercially, those visitors who expected a more intellectually stimulating experience may have been disappointed.[45]

Others felt more satisfied when they visited Colonial Williamsburg's greatest competitor, Henry Ford's Greenfield Village in Dearborn, Michigan. Greenfield Village consistently outdrew Colonial Williamsburg in visitors, averaging about 1.5 million paying customers a year, although it offered little of an educational experience. Ford's plan was to bring to one spot outside of Detroit certain American landmarks, such as the Wright brothers' bicycle shop from Dayton, Ohio, and Thomas Edison's laboratory from Menlo Park, New Jersey, along with a variety of homes, shops, schools, mills, and stores. Of the almost one hundred buildings in all, most were open to visitors. However, the village did not try to present a unified picture of the past as did Colonial Williamsburg. Greenfield Village was just a hodgepodge of buildings; some were authentic historic structures, and others were re-creations. In many ways, such criticism of Colonial Williamsburg was ironic; although the restoration had its flaws, it was certainly a far more serious attempt at historic restoration than Greenfield Village ever was. Yet Mrs. Charles R. Berlucci was not inclined to agree. "As for Colonial

Williamsburg . . . it is beautiful but far overrated and far . . . overpriced. . . . This is not only my feeling but [that] of countless others we encountered during our five days there." Berlucci was pleased that she and her family had easy access to Greenfield Village, however, because she felt there her sons "have grown up understanding the early American Arts and Craft."[46]

In reality, Colonial Williamsburg was doing its best to accommodate the growing numbers of people who wished to see the buildings at an economical price. A $7 three-day general ticket allowed visitors free access to all the exhibits except for the Governor's Palace, which cost an extra $2. The restoration also offered a $5 one-day ticket and a $10 week-long ticket. Yet even with about one million visitors a year, Colonial Williamsburg could not stay in the black, and it was often forced to dip into its $3.7 million yearly endowment income to subsidize the work of the restoration. To help ease crowding, the restoration attempted to put together more outdoor activities, taking advantage of the gardens and greens to provide visitors with programs outside the buildings.[47]

Well into the bicentennial year, the issue of slavery remained an important one for visitors who complained about Colonial Williamsburg's failure to demonstrate much progress in this vital area. Avrom Fischer noted in his letter of August 1976 that "[t]he single worst aspect was the almost total absence of any reference to slavery." Fischer felt that the failure of Colonial Williamsburg to discuss slavery made it difficult for young people to comprehend the roots of the racial problems that beset the country in the 1960s and 1970s. How were they to understand the inequalities of modern life if the restoration did not mention slavery and its effect on modern-day Americans? Fischer felt the restoration needed to explain the lives of slaves because that information would "educate us all and could give Black Americans a feeling of their heritage in Williamsburg." Fischer was not opposed to the Americanist ideal of the restoration, however. Even with its faults, he was pleased with the overall goal of Colonial Williamsburg: "I believe the great heroes of our [Revolution were] heroes to all men because of the purity of their dreams, regardless of how their lives may appear."[48]

Finally, of all those who criticized Colonial Williamsburg's failure to deal adequately with the slavery issue, Gladys Vanderbilt perhaps said it the best. She attempted to understand the issues facing Colonial Williamsburg yet argued for the inclusion of more references to slavery. "It is quite understandable that those involved in the restoration were reticent to admit that their forebears could not have accomplished such a feat of conquering the wilderness without the free labor available to them." On the other hand, the truth was that they had considerable help that needed to be recognized; "since a group of people were forced to labor under great stress . . . deprivation, and most of all, loss of human dignity, at least some of the restored area should be designated to exhibit their contributions."[49]

Without question, the restoration's officials were aware of many people's view of the failure of Colonial Williamsburg to adequately handle the issue of slavery. The combination of voices had grown to such a roar by the mid-1970s that the restoration could rightly deduce that it was time for a change, no matter what were the opinions of a few restoration workers or certain members of the public. Setting this change into motion would mean a fundamental shift in the restoration's priorities, however. Such a change would open a new era for the restoration, one in which it made a clean break with the past and moved into the ranks of more accurate social history museums.

In an article in November 1976, the *New York Times* analyzed Colonial Williamsburg's growth over fifty years. The *Times* voiced a common criticism—the excessively pristine nature of Colonial Williamsburg and its tendency for oversimplification. "Williamsburg does not have the flaw of vulgarity; . . . it feels somewhat like a house in Greenwich [Connecticut], just a bit too neat and prim and tasteful to be altogether convincing. The fact that its two major buildings, the Governor's Palace and the Capitol, are both twentieth century re-creations does not help in this regard." Yet without these buildings Colonial Williamsburg would not be Colonial Williamsburg; these edifices served as cornerstones of the Americanist message: the power of the people triumphing over the tyranny of the king. In reality, the restoration was not a true model of historical preservation because over three-quarters of the town had been rebuilt. But critics were wrong to compare Colonial Williamsburg with Disneyland. Disneyland was a fanciful place that had never existed. Williamsburg in the eighteenth century was a real town with real people, and all the restored or rebuilt buildings were externally as close to their eighteenth-century form as possible. In addition, Colonial Williamsburg had held a significant place in many people's hearts as an inspirational shrine and a monument to the glories of the struggle for independence. Nevertheless, the restoration had an inherent quaintness that could not be removed. This quality resulted from its origins—an idealized dream about what American life could be like. Although Colonial Williamsburg would inevitably remain a victim of its past, it could pass on its knowledge to other historic sites in the hope that they could benefit from the restoration's mistakes.[50]

Much like the nation, Colonial Williamsburg passed 1976 with less fanfare than expected. The internal divisions over the Vietnam War and Watergate created a malaise that enveloped the country during the decade. By the mid-1970s, Americans were more cynical and less receptive to shrines like Colonial Williamsburg than they had been in the past. The idea of a perfect nation that represented a beacon to the world was no longer valid. Rival museums demonstrated Colonial Williamsburg's failings, and many visitors wanted to know more about the average people who lived in the past, not just about the lives of a few famous men. Washington, Jefferson, and Henry would still exist in Colonial Williamsburg's panoply of secular gods, but visitors had become less easy to please by the late 1970s. To have interpreters simply speak of these figures in worshipful tones would no longer suffice. Both national and international events forced Colonial Williamsburg to change. Comparisons with places like Disneyland and Disney World also damaged the restoration's self-esteem. In letters to the restoration, visitors called more and more frequently for a greater authenticity. If Colonial Williamsburg wanted to live up to its promise of being in the forefront of history museums, it needed to distance itself from its Americanist past. In order to succeed, Colonial Williamsburg had to change with the times.

This change, however, would necessarily be built upon the previous fifty years of work. The restoration would create a presentation that embodied ideals of both periods: the traditional view and the more modern social interpretation. Although Colonial Williamsburg became emblematic of the distinct shift in historical interpretation in the 1970s, the restoration would still have aspects that would inevitably harken back to its founding principles. Just as Americans tried to understand the complexity of their past to achieve a more accurate rendering, so too would Colonial Williamsburg be forced to engage in a similar process. This reinterpretation of the past would unquestionably please those who felt that social aspects had been neglected while it angered others who deemed such interpretations to be without serious merit.

7

New Challenges

By the late 1970s, Colonial Williamsburg, the town that had served so long as a shrine to American ideals, finally turned to its new role as a social history museum. This new focus was geared to creating a more complete picture of eighteenth-century life in the Tidewater region of Virginia. This transition was motivated by restoration president Carlisle Humelsine who, starting in 1977, tried to assess what Colonial Williamsburg's future educational mission should be. He also needed to ensure the financial viability of the restoration since the project had accumulated a $4 million operating deficit in 1976. Clearly, no single individual could finance the work of the restoration in its second half century, so Humelsine appealed, via an article in the *New York Times*, for charitable contributions from the general public to help the organization meet its financial needs. The restoration also introduced a new ticket policy: $7 for adults and $3 for children for the first day of their visit to the restoration, with subsequent days costing $3 and $1.50, respectively. As before, there was also a separate charge for visiting the Governor's Palace—$2 for adults and $1 for children. This increase in revenue was needed to help offset rising expenditures, such as yearly maintenance costs that exceeded $2.3 million per year.[1]

Humelsine also brought together a group of young scholars—including Harvard Ph.D. Cary Carson—whose job was to devise a plan of interpretation for the coming decades. Motivated by a weak job market for professors in the 1970s, historians with doctoral degrees began to move out of academia in sizable numbers to work for public history organizations, in addition to positions in business and industry. As a result, Colonial Williamsburg was able to avail itself of the help of these professional historians in reshaping its presentation of life in colonial southeastern Virginia. These historians decided to move the restoration toward its new role as a social history museum. An important result of this undertaking was Carson's work "Teaching History at Colonial Williamsburg," which brought forth a new presentation of the town's history called "Becoming Americans," along with the more traditional political interpretation, which was to be called "Choosing Revolution." Under this plan, the restoration would focus on the transformation of both white and black residents from British subjects to American citizens. The interrelationship of these two cultures would provide a framework for programs about the economic, social, and cultural aspects of life in colonial Virginia within the context of the political changes taking place at the time. This idea would combine Colonial Williamsburg's traditional political presentation with a broader look at the people who made up the general population of the actual colonial Williamsburg. Such a presentation would be more balanced and would highlight the contributions made to American society by all groups. These changes demonstrated the restoration's understanding that "millions [of] visitors over the years have come to regard Colonial Williamsburg as one of the nation's ultimate authorities on American history." In working to update the restoration's presentations, these young scholars viewed themselves as teachers who were transforming the restoration into their classrooms and its visitors into their students. The transition from an Americanist monument that presented a one-sided view of the past to an educational institution with a broader interpretation of historical events would solve some of the restoration's problems but would also introduce new ones.[2]

This new program became the cornerstone of the future work of Colonial Williamsburg, marking a transition from the traditional interpretation to the modern view of the town and its people. Such an alteration would be a long and never-ending process. In social history one had to take into account the varying lifestyles of different classes, researching them in detail to create an interpretation of the past that was as correct as possible. This research required considerably more time and energy than merely promoting an Americanist idealization of the period. Thus the restoration realized that it had to examine previously underrepresented groups to understand the intricacies of their lives. The lives of slaves within their own world of the slave quarters, as well as the lives of women outside of the public view, needed to be explored.[3]

The restoration was also working to develop a picture of southeastern Virginia before the founding of Williamsburg through the archaeological excavations of Wolstenholme Towne, the seventeenth-century settlement on the banks of the James River on the property of the Carter's Grove Plantation. This addition to the restoration's presentation forged a link with nearby Jamestown. Visitors could get a sense of the continuity of European settlement on the peninsula through the end of the eighteenth century. Wolstenholme Towne was re-created by placing posts back in the original postholes to reveal the outside boundaries of the town's structures. First opened to visitors in the summer of 1979, the four-acre site added to the restoration's attempts to broaden its presentation of the region's history and to move past its original role.[4]

Yet the content of past programs would inevitably remain a part of the restoration's newer presentation. Scholars found it easier to build on the existing structure than to revamp it completely, and the political history of eighteenth-century Williamsburg would continue to be an integral part of the modern interpretation of the restoration. But the restoration needed to introduce more average people into the community. The question remained as to the best way to accomplish this goal. Hiring two thousand townspeople, all dressed in colonial garb, to mill around day in and day out from the early morning to late at night to create a semblance of the town's life during the eighteenth century would not be practical either economically or logistically. As a result, visitors would necessarily be asked to subscribe to make-believe, something that they were already doing, but in a slightly different way. Colonial Williamsburg would also need to convey in clearer terms what these average people's lives were like and how they influenced daily affairs in the town. The trade shops, on a selective basis, were already presenting the lives of some average citizens, but the program needed to expand to include the roles of women and African Americans. The restoration also needed to convey the culture that African Americans had developed independent of their masters, since although slaves were economically and socially subjugated, they still were able to forge their own society. The relationships between whites and blacks were more diverse than was generally supposed to be the case, and the restoration needed to develop its programs to demonstrate this.[5]

An African American interpreter with a visitor (Courtesy of the Colonial Williamsburg Foundation)

An important development was the incorporation of more African American interpreters into the programs to give visitors a sense that there was a black presence in the eighteenth-century town. At least 50 percent of the interpreters needed to be black to show accurately their proportion to white residents. Although this goal was not easily obtainable, any strides made in that direction would promote the authenticity of the restoration. Nevertheless, there was no organized program of black interpretation at Colonial Williamsburg until 1979 when three African American reenactors were hired to portray a variety of roles, including a recently arrived slave, a scullery maid, an apprentice cooper, and a free black barber. Work was not easy for these interpreters, who received chilly receptions from some white patrons, as well as a number of black restoration employees. Despite some problems, visitors finally were able to hear the other side of the story, at least to a certain degree. Naturally, any visitors who were not interested could also avoid these presentations. In essence, tourists could visit Colonial Williamsburg without understanding the more complex nature of its society if they so desired. In this way, the restoration again strove not to offend those visitors who preferred to remain ignorant of certain aspects of the town's history.[6]

One of the first ways that the restoration demonstrated its commitment to presenting the past more accurately was the refurbishment of the Governor's Palace. In reassessing the information about the palace, and using, in particular, the inventory taken at the death of Lord Botetourt, who had been the royal governor of Virginia from 1768 to 1770, researchers decided that the furnishings installed during the 1930s were too ornate. The result was a downscaling of the interior, along with the creation of a new interpretation of the building's occupants. The restoration acquired new pieces of furniture and crafted reproductions from documented prototypes. Yet problems still existed with this new attempt at portraying the past. In a strongly critical article entitled "'Slumbering on Its Old Foundations': Interpretation at Colonial Williamsburg," Carroll Van West and Mary Hoffschwelle attacked Colonial Williamsburg's poorly diversified presentation of the history of colonial Virginia. They argued that "the re-creation of America's colonial experience at Colonial Williamsburg remains narrow and misleading." Even though the refurbishment of the Governor's Palace was an attempt to present a more accurate view of the past, it did not live up to its promise. The newer interpretation did not seriously depart from Colonial Williamsburg's previous presentation of the building and its people, the authors argued. Instead, the interpretation relied too heavily on traditional notions of the past, which focused on the colonial elite. The presentation emphasized the role of the royal governor and paid too little attention to the differences between his white English staff and the African American slaves from the colony.[7]

The new interpretation also made little attempt to portray the role of women, beyond that of an upper-class woman. The lives of female slaves could have been documented and interpreted, but this was not done to a significant degree. Thus, the so-called new interpretation of the palace, although somewhat better than the old one, did not adequately address the issues that the restoration was trying to promote. The restoration still placed too much emphasis on the romantic aspects of life, with a few anecdotes about everyday living, rather than making a full-scale attempt at a social interpretation of the palace and its people. West and Hoffschwelle concluded, therefore, that the Governor's Palace, like Colonial Williamsburg's other sites, remained focused on the presentation of great men and their actions.[8]

Edward B. Fiske also highlighted the transformation of the palace in an article that he wrote for the *New York Times* in July 1982. Fiske discussed the palace's newly toned-down nature, prime examples of which were the venetian blinds that replaced many of the more lavish curtains that had framed the windows of the governor's residence. In addition, the bright blue wallpaper in the ballroom, as well as some of the prints in the bedrooms, were not what many visitors expected to see in the home of the colonial elite. Fiske thought the newer approach to the palace's interpretation, which asked the visitors to participate in the life of the eighteenth-century town, was better suited to children than adults. Grown-ups, he felt, were "well advised to sign up for one of the conventional tours at noontime." Although not everything at the palace was to his liking, Fiske commented favorably on the craft shops and the "restored historical houses" in which visitors could stay to make their trip more "authentic."[9]

Another major event again placed Colonial Williamsburg in the international spotlight: the annual meeting of the world's leading economic powers held in the restored village in 1983. President Ronald Reagan, the host of the ninth annual economic summit of major industrialized nations, chose the town more for its traditional presentation of American life than for its growing commitment to social history. The weekend of the summit in May 1983 was also the first time that the restoration had ever closed its doors to the public. This action was not warmly greeted by all in the local community, many of whom wished to feel free to stroll down the Duke of Gloucester Street and through any other part of the restored village. In addition to the leaders of the world's largest industrialized countries, more than three thousand journalists inundated the town to cover the event. The restoration's decision to close over the weekend to host the prominent visitors cost approximately $500,000 in lost revenues. Officials hoped, however, that the added publicity from the event would raise the public's interest in the town and perhaps encourage greater visitation during the upcoming summer months.[10]

Showing that times had not changed much since the 1950s, the *New York Times* reported that "Williamsburg remains the landmark to which the Federal Government shuttles its visitors from abroad." The article went on to compare the restoration yet again with a theme park, arguing that "it is officialdom's Disneyland, an attraction for foreign visitors of distinction." It appeared, therefore, that Colonial Williamsburg had not succeeded in shaking off its old image. As historian Henry Steele Commager said of Colonial Williamsburg, "[I]t's a national shrine and a very natural place to go. . . . You don't have to go to Kansas or Nebraska, . . . you just drive down from Washington. It's our equivalent of Cambridge or Oxford." This assertion was a rather unusual comparison to make between Colonial Williamsburg and two ancient university towns, but it reinforced the fact that Colonial Williamsburg was still held in high regard as a place that held the key to American history. Certainly for the Reagan administration, which sought to harken back to the country's prior glories, the traditional Colonial Williamsburg, a monument to freedom during the height of the Cold War, served an important purpose. For the nearly 150 world leaders who had visited Colonial Williamsburg since the end of World War II, the restoration presented the glory of the country's past much like an American version of Versailles, the site of the previous year's economic summit. Even into the early 1980s, Colonial Williamsburg remained a shrine for some, as well as a place where foreigners could be brought to help them understand American principles and ideals.[11]

Colonial Williamsburg again made news in 1985 with the opening of the DeWitt Wallace Decorative Arts Gallery. The gallery was constructed to display eight thousand antiques of British and American origins dating from the seventeenth through the nineteenth centuries. The museum was housed underneath the Public Hospital, which was a reconstruction of the first institution for the treatment of the mentally ill in America. In the 26,000-square-foot below-ground gallery, visitors had access to parts of the restoration's collection of antiques that previously had been hidden from public view. The exhibits included ceramic, glass, silver, and pewter objects, as well as scientific instruments, textiles, and prints. A number of speciality wares, including samplers, thimbles, watches, nutcrackers, dinner bells, and pipe tampers, were also on display. Named after DeWitt Wallace, who was the founder of *Reader's Digest*, the gallery was built with a $14 million donation that covered most of the cost of the $17 million construction. This private bequest made Wallace the second largest benefactor to Colonial Williamsburg outside of the Rockefeller family.[12]

Above ground, the restoration was making strides in implementing its broader approach to African American history, as well as working to escape its pristine presentation of the past. Instead of using paints to cover the exterior of many surfaces, the restoration was using whitewash, a less expensive and more realistic cover, or in some cases leaving the surfaces bare. This was particularly true of many of the outbuildings—kitchens, laundries, and stables—where the slaves usually worked. In these areas Colonial Williamsburg began to implement its Black History Program, which was under the direction of Rex Ellis. Most slaves had lived in the attics of kitchens and stables on their master's property, and their lives had revolved around these parts of the town. The "Other Half Tour" was begun to show visitors the lives of Williamsburg's African American community, which accounted for approximately half of the town's residents, as recorded in the 1776 *Virginia Almanack*. The tour, a rigorous two-hour walk through the town, covered four main topics: the middle passage from Africa, country and town living conditions, religion, and music. Many escaped slaves headed to Williamsburg and the vicinity, which was revealed by the large numbers of ads placed in local newspapers by owners attempting to apprehend these escapees. Overall, the lives of slaves in Williamsburg were probably superior to those on many of the surrounding plantations, because in town there was social pressure to treat slaves with less visible cruelty. The presence of the College of William and Mary also may have created a more enlightened atmosphere than in other areas of the colonies. Ultimately, the challenge of portraying the lives of Williamsburg's black residents, both free and slave, was naturally complex. The commitment of the restoration to illustrate this aspect of the colonial past was an important change, yet there was still much to do to present a more unified vision of the town's past.[13]

As the program in African American interpretation was being developed, the work to reenact the lives of the white working class went forward with the reconstruction of the Anderson Forge. The forge would help to explain the life of a colonial blacksmith, who played an integral role in the growth and development of the town, since he made the nails for building, the shoes for horses, and a variety of iron tools and implements. The research for the reconstruction began in 1980, and the structure was completed in 1986. The construction was performed with tools, techniques, and materials common to the eighteenth century. This structure exemplified the restoration's new commitment to historical reconstruction based on strong research and the use of colonial building techniques. Along with the interpretation of the site by the smiths who worked there, visitors saw the kind of work performed by some of the laboring population, as well as the time and effort needed to produce even a relatively simple nail.[14]

Many of those who worked for the restoration in the trade shops and as interpreters found the work to be stimulating, if not necessarily well paid. They were required to do substantial research to understand the role of the people they were portraying. The increase in the numbers of interpreters demonstrated that the restoration was trying to broaden the presentation of the past and not merely showing off the attributes of the buildings and their

furnishings. Such a transition was essential for the success of the new presentation of the town, which was dependent on getting visitors interested
in the details of eighteenth-century life. Many of the interpreters found a
great deal of personal satisfaction in their work—creating objects that might
be put on display in one of the shops and purchased by a visitor. Those who
represented people from the past such as slaves or shopkeepers based their
interpretations on historical individuals. This work helped to give visitors
a sense of the town's eighteenth-century population, although it was necessarily limited in scope.[15]

Even in the late 1980s, however, the popular view of Colonial Williamsburg tended to concentrate on the quaintness of the restored town. An article in *Travel Weekly* in March 1987 reiterated many of the traditional ideas
that had surrounded the restoration for decades. As the author, Elvira Delany, argued, "Colonial Williamsburg continues calmly to do what it was
meant to do, which is to invite guests within its gates to step back into the
18th century. . . . It involves the visitor in the activities of the butcher, baker
and candlestick maker." Such phrasing was reminiscent of the articles of
the 1930s and 1940s that extolled the town's peacefulness and the charm of
the trade shops. The article made no mention of the restoration's move to
promote African American history, while supporting *The Story of the Patriot*
as an introductory film that "sets the mood." In so doing, Delany was primarily interested in offering Colonial Williamsburg as a showpiece among
the other attractions in the Tidewater area, including Busch Gardens and
Water Country USA. This presentation helped to foster the misinterpreta-
tion of Colonial Williamsburg as yet another theme park set in a pleasant
locale.[16]

While the restoration was working to present the lives of the slaves in
Colonial Williamsburg, it also re-created plantation slave cabins that would
give visitors a glimpse of African American life in the countryside. This reconstruction was created on Colonial Williamsburg's Carter's Grove Plantation, about a quarter of a mile from the large house that had been home
to members of one of Virginia's most prominent families. Archaeological excavations at Carter's Grove found thirteen pits lined with boards that dated
to the eighteenth century. Further investigation revealed that these were
storage pits that likely had slave cabins above them. In rebuilding these
dwellings, Edward A. Chappell, the director of archaeological research for
Colonial Williamsburg, drew on existing slave cabins of the period, notably
one in Clarksville, Virginia, which was a one-room twelve-by-sixteen-foot

clapboard-covered frame building. Archaeological work at other former plantations, such as Monticello's Mulberry Row, a one-thousand-foot-long avenue once lined with seventeen structures, revealed examples of eighteenth-century slave dwellings. Workers salvaged some fifty-three thousand items from Mulberry Row, including toothbrushes and a medicine bottle. Further research revealed that African Americans lived varied and complex lives in colonial times. The earliest slaves had hunted with guns, built their own dwellings, prepared their own meals, and occasionally learned to read and write. All these pieces of information filled in the puzzle that allowed interpreters to present the lives of slaves. For the first time, visitors would finally be able to gain a greater appreciation of the lives of people of African descent who had helped build the colony and the state.[17]

The slave quarter reconstructions at Carter's Grove opened to the public in 1989. These structures were important because they gave interpreters the chance to discuss the lives of plantation slaves, which often differed considerably from the lives of slaves in the town. Colonial Williamsburg became the first major museum to seriously discuss colonial slavery, as opposed to the nineteenth-century version with which most Americans were familiar. As Rex Ellis, the assistant director for African American interpretation at Colonial Williamsburg, commented, "We're going to have to show rebellion, violence and racism in a way we haven't done at Williamsburg; . . . we need to learn from all parts of history, including the uncomfortable parts." Ellis's realization of the need to present a more sophisticated view of colonial life was vital if Colonial Williamsburg was to be an educator in the modern world.[18]

This updated presentation helped to change Americans' understanding of slavery. As the *New York Times* commented in 1988, the "guides no longer speak of servants, but of slaves." In being more forthright about the true situation of the bondsmen in Williamsburg, the restoration was attempting to portray the past more realistically, especially where African Americans were concerned. Aided by a $400,000 grant from AT&T, acquired by Humelsine's successor, Charles Longsworth, the restoration started new black history walking tours and story-telling entertainments. Archaeological digs also helped to expand Colonial Williamsburg's study of African American life. Those digs yielded artifacts that created a more complete picture of how blacks lived in the colonial era. Deeper research into existing artifacts also helped to promote a greater understanding of African American life. There was not a lack of sources, as the restoration had originally claimed,

A reconstructed slave cabin at Carter's Grove, part of Colonial Williamsburg's updated portrayal of colonial slave life (Courtesy of the Colonial Williamsburg Foundation)

but there were instead many avenues of research that modern historians could follow to elicit information about black life under slavery.[19]

Although the restoration had traditionally been a site predominantly for white travelers, geared to showing them a glorified past, with the changes under way, Colonial Williamsburg began to attract more African American visitors who for the first time could learn about the lives of half of the town's residents—individuals who might have been their ancestors. This new interpretation inevitably meant coming to terms with the fifty years of racism and discrimination that had prevented this aspect of the town's life from being portrayed. White visitors also began to ask questions about slave life—a subject that all Americans needed to understand. Finally, a part of Colonial Williamsburg's past that had been ignored for its first half century began to see the light of day.

During its first fifty years, the restoration's traditional presentation had also dealt with women's roles in colonial times in an offhand manner. Although women commonly had worked as hostesses, guides, and interpreters throughout this earlier period, these women generally interpreted male history, focusing more on the illustrious figures of the past than they did on women. The interpretation of women's lives beyond the traditional view of the genteel colonial lady was lacking, as was an interpretation of the status of female slaves beyond the stereotypical "mammy." A conscious attempt to strengthen the interpretation of women's history at Colonial Williamsburg began in 1981 with the three-day conference Women in Early America. Sponsored by the Institute of Early American History and Culture and Colonial Williamsburg, the conference revealed that women's lives in the so-called golden age of the eighteenth century were far from the simplistic and relaxed presentation of colonial women that the restoration had put forth earlier. Although the Revolution aided men in their pursuit of political goals, the same era left women "the unenvied equals of slaves and lunatics." The incorporation of a tour called "According to the Ladies" provided the first chance for visitors to glimpse the varied lives of colonial women. The tour, which compared the situations of women of the various classes, provided a look at the different lives of urban and rural women.[20]

But even this further emphasis on women's affairs left tremendous gaps in Colonial Williamsburg's interpretation program. Both women and blacks served primarily as supporting actors in the drama of Colonial Williamsburg, and the roles they played were not commensurate with their importance in eighteenth-century society. As such, visitors to the restoration failed to grasp the importance of these groups in colonial life because they saw women and blacks primarily as shadowy background figures rather than full-fledged actors on the historical scene. The late arrival of many of these programs was evident since they appeared to be grafted onto existing exhibitions. As a result, visitors inevitably wondered if these programs should be taken as seriously as others that were politically based.

With the implementation of these new programs, the restoration entered its new phase as a social history museum. This transition brought with it a certain level of responsibility, since Colonial Williamsburg proposed to tell a bigger story—one that would return neglected groups to their proper positions in the American historical consciousness. In an article in the Forum section of the winter 1989 issue of *Winterthur Portfolio*, Edward A. Chappell commented on the social responsibility of the American history museum. His argument was "that museums have a responsibility for the broad social implications of what they present, as well as for the accuracy and clarity of the particular subject with which they are dealing." He believed that museums must go beyond simply presenting the facts and have something more to say, "introduc[ing] people to new material and to various ways of perceiving its meaning." As sites such as Colonial Williamsburg strove to reexamine their traditional interpretations of the past, they were forced to integrate modern research techniques and interpretations in their exhibits. But since no museum could be entirely objective, both officials and patrons needed to understand that all types of presentations contained an inherent subjectivity. In demonstrating the responsibility that a museum like Colonial Williamsburg had, Chappell argued that "to venerate fine craftsmanship and elite design while ignoring the lives of those who lacked such amenities . . . is irresponsible."[21]

More recent projects such as Plimoth Plantation had helped to advance the mission of the social history museum, challenging the traditional view that the public was not interested in new interpretations but only in the politically conservative, traditional approach. With the growing popularity of Plimoth Planation, other museums began to follow the lead, ever mindful, however, of their visitor base. As Colonial Williamsburg followed this trend, the revamping of its presentations meant a change not only in interpretation programs but also in new construction, such as the reconstruction of the Public Hospital and the slave quarters at Carter's Grove. Both of these sites dealt with parts of the past that were less comfortable for visitors but that were inherently necessary for understanding the complexity of eighteenth-century life and the treatment of those at the margins of society— African Americans and the mentally ill. Chappell argued, however, that "museums must move on from a history that is simply more democratic, more representative of realities, to depict the systems that everyone dealt with, and that . . . are still likely to affect us today." As the restoration moved into the 1990s, it worked to follow through on Chappell's challenge, yet this process was not necessarily easy. Many visitors were not ready for a more radical step; they had accepted the treatment of previously taboo subjects like slavery and mental illness but were not necessarily prepared for presentations, such as slave auctions, that would force them to deal with major issues that had not been previously portrayed.[22]

A more sophisticated understanding of the restoration's goals had begun to enter the popular press by the end of the 1980s, although this viewpoint was by no means universal. One who recognized the restoration's transition was Bob Vila, whose article entitled "Restoring America" was published in the May 1989 issue of *Popular Mechanics*. Vila realized that one must suspend disbelief in visiting the town, yet he criticized those who felt that Colonial Williamsburg was merely another Disneyland: "[T]o think that Colonial Williamsburg is nothing more than a period theme park is to

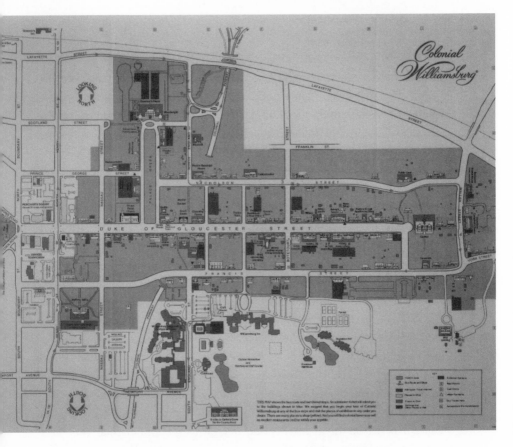

Map of Colonial Williamsburg, ca. 1988 (Courtesy of the Colonial Williamsburg Foundation)

grossly underestimate what goes on there in terms of subtlety, complication and commitment." This realization was the key to the new interpretation. Restoration officials, such as Cary Carson, the vice president for research, indicated that he understood the criticism directed against the restoration, commenting that "to a certain extent, we feel that the classroom we have to teach our history sometimes doesn't live up to what we want to do with it. But we can't literally tear down our predecessor's work." This statement was certainly true; even a modern reconstruction would inevitably have an air of fakeness about it. But the restoration worked to update its presentation, utilizing its researchers who were trained in the fields of architecture, archaeology, and social history. They lent their expertise to the excavation, reconstruction, and interpretation of Colonial Williamsburg's 173 acres.[23]

In truth, the restoration's attempt to portray the eighteenth century was limited, especially since then, as now, people had a wide variety of lifestyles and beliefs. Although many visitors believed that there was a single type of colonial dress, speech, or opinion, life in the eighteenth century was as complex as it is today. As Chappell indicated, "I think our generation is most interested in the differences, the relationships, the intersections between people. . . . There was an incredible range of living and working conditions and intellectual perspectives." The restoration of the Courthouse of 1770 highlighted the complexity of eighteenth-century life and the desire of the restoration to portray that era as vividly as possible. Court cases often illustrated the seedier side of colonial society—public drunkenness, robbery, and the like. By opening the Courthouse to visitors and allowing them to help resolve some cases of the period, the restoration gave the audience a chance to participate and perhaps to gain a deeper understanding. As Carl Lounsbury, the architectural historian in charge of the restoration of the Courthouse, commented, "I don't want visitors to come away thinking that the 18th century was simply a little older and didn't have electricity. I want to stress the differences between the two and how our society . . . evolved and developed."[24]

Although the *New York Times* had presented some of the changes going on at Colonial Williamsburg, these complex issues were not the most important thing for the newspaper in its portrait of the restoration during the Christmas season. In an article published on 16 December 1990, the *Times* focused primarily on the food, festivities, and shopping that were available in the historic area during the winter holiday season. The emphasis on the quaint customs and foods of the eighteenth century demonstrated the traditional perception that those attractions were why one would visit the restoration, namely, to witness "taverns and halls festooned with mountain laurel and white pine roping and boxwood wreaths fashioned from fruits, cones, seed pods and nuts." To whet the appetite, "the tables are laden with . . . Virginia hams and roast beef, barbecued ribs . . . Sally Lunn bread, pickled oysters, plum pudding, sweet potato pie . . . claret punch and foaming mugs of ale." Clearly, such publicity helped the restoration, which suffered a drop in attendance during the holiday season, but was not in accordance with the newly espoused move to present a broader understanding of the lives of all members of colonial society. Obviously, the restoration was reluctant to relinquish its roles as a travel venue and a purveyor of good food and drink, as well as a place where visitors could purchase "romantically packaged jars of violet bath powder" or a "handsome pewter teapot." Even though profits from all of the restoration-run enterprises were plowed back into the research and presentation of the period, tourists were inevitably presented with a conflicting picture of what Colonial Williamsburg was attempting to represent.[25]

Thirteen years after the start of the African American interpretation and presentations program, fifteen black interpreters worked in that department at Colonial Williamsburg. This number fell far short of adequately representing the 52 percent of the town's colonial population that was of African descent, but their presence was a major improvement, considering the many years of neglect in this area. Although only about 5 percent of the restoration's visitors were black, the African American interpretation program attracted people of color who previously had not come to Colonial Williamsburg probably because they thought the lives of their ancestors would not be discussed. In addition, the changes at Colonial Williamsburg were reflected in other historic sites, such as Mount Vernon and Monticello, that had previously spent little or no time covering the lives of slaves. By the early 1990s, most white visitors expected to hear some information about African American life. Although this did not necessarily mean that visitors had a sophisticated understanding of black life before the Civil War, the interest existed, and that aided the development of the restoration's fledgling interpretation programs.[26]

The questions about how far to extend the interpretation of African American life was a difficult one, however. One aspect that the restoration had not previously addressed was particularly problematic: the slave auction. The buying and selling of slaves at public auction were common from the seventeenth century through the Civil War. These auctions were degrading affairs for the slaves, who were pinched, prodded, and examined repeatedly in public view. The reenactment of a slave auction would be a highly controversial, yet important, addition to the work of the restoration. Such a re-creation could not be completely accurate, but even providing a sense of what had occurred would educate visitors about an important part of African American history.

In 1994 Christy S. Coleman, the director of the restoration's African American interpretation department, organized a mock slave auction, arguing that this portrayal was an important ingredient in presenting an accurate view of eighteenth-century black life. "The legacy of slavery in this country is racism . . . [and] until we begin to understand the horrors that took place . . . people will never come to understand what's happening in our society today," Coleman commented. Local African American groups initially expressed dismay at the reenactment in October 1994, but after seeing the event, some accepted that auctions were an important part of the slave experience that needed to be presented to appreciate fully the pain and humiliation that slaves had endured. Jack Gravely, the Virginia political action director for the National Association for the Advancement of Colored People, initially objected strongly to the reenactment, shouting at the auction, "You cannot portray our history in 21 minutes and make it some sideshow." Yet after witnessing the portrayal, Gravely retracted his earlier remarks, commenting that the "presentation was passionate, moving and educational." On the other hand, Curtis Harris of the Southern Christian Leadership Conference felt that the presentation was "nothing more than a show, not an authentic history." Yet such programs were vital if Colonial Williamsburg was to live up to its social responsibility to present the past as accurately as possible and to demonstrate the ways in which past events influenced modern-day issues such as race relations.[27]

Such divisions over the representation of slavery revealed that Colonial Williamsburg would have a difficult time in promoting its desire to re-create the past more accurately. Part of the problem lay in the ignorance of some members of the public, and part in the difficulties left over from decades as an Americanist shrine. Comparisons in the popular press between the restoration and theme parks like Disneyland also lessened the conception that Colonial Williamsburg was pursuing serious history and instead promoted the notion that all the restoration did was put on shows to amuse its visitors. Therefore, Colonial Williamsburg needed to promote a more serious image of itself to ensure that it could carry out its programs effectively. At the root of these issues were the monetary demands of the restoration. The costs of such work were extremely high, and the restoration needed to strike a balance between the price it charged its visitors and the quality of its programs. Visitors also needed to be better informed about the types of presentations that they might see while visiting the historic area, so that they could understand the significance of these portrayals.

Further criticism of Colonial Williamsburg and its operations emerged in 1994 in an article for the *Journal of American History* that was written by anthropologists Eric Gable and Richard Handler, who conducted over two years of ethnographic research at Colonial Williamsburg. Gable and Handler found that a serious gap existed between the work of the restoration's professional historians, who stayed behind the scenes, and those who were responsible for the frontline interpretations of the restoration. "There is a huge gap in pay, in status, and in spatial location within the institution," they argued. The four hundred or so costumed interpreters served as front-line representatives of the restoration who were directly responsible for educating the public. These individuals were divided into four main groups: those who spoke of eighteenth-century life, but not in character; those who portrayed eighteenth-century figures; those who worked in the trade shops; and the African American interpreters, who "used a variety of pedagogical techniques." Ultimately, Gable and Handler found that quite a bit of tension existed between the management, or those in suits, and the frontline interpreters, or those in costumes. Frontline interpreters tended to feel that upper-level management looked down on them and considered them to be less knowledgeable than those historians in suits. Consequently, much of the interpretive work of the restoration was scripted by the managerial historians and merely recited by the interpreters, resulting in a one-dimensional view of the past that mirrored the ideology of the restoration, as opposed to the views of the individual interpreters.[28]

Cary Carson's reply to Gable and Handler's criticisms highlighted the restoration's belief that some type of regulated presentation was necessary to ensure that visitors learned the facts that the restoration thought were important. Carson wrote, "As responsible educators, we believe that some things about the eighteenth century are more worth knowing than others." As a result, certain issues were emphasized, others were given less attention, and interpreters were expected to go along with the restoration's emphasis. But "each [interpreter] is free to be as spontaneous, creative, fresh and original as any imaginative classroom teacher who nevertheless follows a curricular plan." Carson also argued that "the centrality of social history to museum curricula provides another guarantee that interpreters' voices will be heard, no matter what." Presumably he meant that since people were interpreting the lives of other individuals, interpreters would necessarily have a chance to put a human face on their presentations.[29]

The exchange between Gable and Handler on one hand and Carson on the other demonstrated that as Colonial Williamsburg moved to present a more complex view of the past, it inherently opened itself up to criticism from individuals both inside and outside the restoration. Interpreters may not have liked the restoration's corporate culture, as Gable and Handler claimed, but as employees they were obligated to conform to their employer's demands. In this way, the modern Colonial Williamsburg, like its predecessor, had an ideology, but one that emphasized the town's social his-

tory as opposed to its political one. Overall, the restoration retained a portion of its conservative past, even if its interpretive emphasis had been altered to meet the demands of modern social history.

Even through the mid-1990s, Colonial Williamsburg was often presented
in the popular press as a quaint tourist stop rather than as a serious history
museum that was striving to educate its visitors through its interpretation
programs. Articles in both the *New York Times* in 1994 and *Town and Country* in 1995 supported the traditional perceptions of Colonial Williamsburg;
neither one made significant mention of African American interpretation
programs. The *Times* article referred briefly to an interpretation program at
Carter's Grove that discussed the lives of female members of the household, "including a 16th-century American Indian, a 17th-century English
immigrant, an 18th-century plantation housewife and a 19th-century share-
cropper, formerly a slave." Nevertheless, the piece made no mention of the
reconstructed slave cabins or the interpretation program that accompanied
them. The *Town and Country* article focused on the family of Paul Kusserow,
who became the marketing director of Colonial Williamsburg in 1994. Although the author described in detail the surrounding community and life
in the Grissell Hay House, which was on restoration property, she did not
mention the diversity of interpretation programs offered to the public. The
theme of a "trip back in time" permeated the article, which focused on antiques, flowers, and the thrill of living in a restored village. This misrepre-
sentation did not help publicize the new interpretations, since visitors who
might have come to see the presentation of African American life might not
know it existed, nor did the article prepare tourists for the intensity of some
of the new programs.[30]

Financial questions inevitably remained an important issue for the
restoration through the 1990s. Since the town was open to all who wished
to walk through it, the restoration lost thousands of dollars each year from
individuals and groups who viewed only the exteriors of the buildings and
did not purchase tickets to the closed exhibits. Some companies ran tours
focused on the Duke of Gloucester Street or the ghosts of Williamsburg and
gave visitors a short introduction to the historic area, perhaps in some cases
whetting their appetites to purchase the official ticket, but in other cases
driving away the business of those who felt that they had seen enough. Yet
tour operators denied that they seriously cut into potential ticket purchases
from Colonial Williamsburg. In an address to community leaders at the
Williamsburg Lodge in May 1997, the restoration's president, Robert C.

Wilburn, labeled these businesses "parasite tours," arguing that they took away substantially from Colonial Williamsburg's potential proceeds. He indicated that many members of these groups "leave thinking they've seen Williamsburg, getting who-knows-what information about the place. To me it's unconscionable." For visitors who only have a few hours, however, purchasing a $32 basic admission ticket to view more of the restoration would be a waste of money. Ideally, one should be prepared to spend several days viewing the exhibits, but that is not always possible.[31]

By closing off the historic area east of Bruton Parish Church, the restoration would receive a significant amount of new revenues, while allowing unticketed access to the church, the College of William and Mary, and other areas of general historical interest. In addition to boosting revenue, such a closing, which would probably only occur in the summer months, would allow the restoration to create a greater sense of historical verisimilitude within the enclosed area. The other option, if the area was not enclosed, would possibly be cuts in programs to ensure that the restoration remained within its financial limits. Financial exigencies would, therefore, remain an essential ingredient of the restoration's struggle to present the past. The closure plan was not initially popular in the community, and the restoration needed the support of the City Council if it wished to close off city streets. Part of the concern was that the restoration's ticket sales had stagnated at around 940,000 for the previous two years. The cash reserve to help cover any shortfall from admission prices was $15 million, with an annual cost of $14 million to maintain the buildings.[32]

Many of the restoration's critics continued their attacks on the restoration into the late 1990s, arguing that it still represented a false history. In her book *Unreal America*, Ada Louise Huxtable continued to criticize the restoration, claiming that it "pav[ed] the way for the new world order of Walt Disney Enterprises." She argued that "it has been a very short distance down the yellow brick road of fantasy from Williamsburg to Disneyland. Both are quintessentially American inventions." While Huxtable was interested primarily in architecture, and not in the interpretation of American history, her failure to give Colonial Williamsburg credit for attempts to portray the past more accurately appeared one-sided. Naturally, the restoration needed to make compromises in its portrayal, but the reconstruction of earlier buildings, even if flawed, must be considered on a different plane than the creation of Disneyland.[33]

In an attempt to broaden the restoration's appeal, and perhaps to counter

arguments of its theme park qualities, the restoration started the Williamsburg Institute in January 1997. The institute offered courses year-round
varying in length from "a few hours to a few days." These courses provided
hands-on experience in a number of areas, including cooking eighteenth-
century foods in the kitchen of the Governor's Palace, sewing colonial-era
clothing, or working at trades such as coopering, basketry, and carpentry.
One could also plow a field or study garden design and flower arranging.
These programs were offered at different times of the year, with offerings
for adults and children. Such programs encouraged visitors to learn more
about eighteenth-century life through both observation and practice. These
courses highlighted the switch to a social history museum as the focus of
the restoration. They emphasized the work of the skilled craftsperson of
the eighteenth century and what the modern-day visitor could learn from
the colonial-era approach to a variety of trades and practices.[34]

By the end of the 1990s, the press had begun to deal with the restoration's presentation of slavery and the public's reaction to it. As Peter Feuerherd wrote in the journal *Commonweal* in November 1999, "[T]he colonial
town is taking a vigorous, dramatic look at the impact of slavery on eighteenth-century life, and by implication, today's America." Yet not everybody was ready to confront slavery. In his coverage of the public's reaction
to the restoration's program "Enslaving Virginia," Feuerherd noted that
"one discussion of slavery we witnessed included many families, most of
them white. The children were engrossed in the lecture. But a number of
parents quickly wearied of the presentation and moved along to other exhibits." Apparently, not only visitors but also some staff members were not
enthusiastic about the presentations, for Feuerherd noted that "at Carter's
Grove a staff member directed [us] toward the mansion, discouraging us
from spending time at the slave quarters." These issues demonstrated that
presenting a less "safe" interpretation of the past did not always meet with
strong support inside the restoration. As Feuerherd commented, "[T]he
Williamsburg Foundation deserves credit, in any case, for challenging its
visitors and raising questions, thus transcending the Disneyfication of
history."[35]

Another program, entitled "Broken Spirit," was presented at the reconstructed slave cabins at Carter's Grove. This presentation was based on the
lives of the slaves who had lived at the site and was constructed from eighteenth-century plantation and parish records, as well as new research. The
program, written by Christy Matthews, detailed the "breaking" of a newly

arrived African slave named Kofi, who had apparently tried to run away. In reality, he had gone to pray for his god's assistance to help him return to Africa. Yet Kofi's poor English made it difficult for him to communicate with the other slaves on the plantation. "The plot turns on misunderstanding between creole natives and the African newcomer, as well as some tragic personal trade-offs forced by slavery." This portrayal of the complexity of slave life and the master's reaction to disobedience clearly unsettled many of those who witnessed it. As one interpreter, Sheila Arnold, remarked, "[W]hat shocks people so much about this program is that slaves become human. They don't all just think in one way—the way you think they should." These reactions were so powerful that the restoration added a debriefing session so that visitors could ask questions and talk through their reactions to what they had witnessed. Visitors often became passionately involved in the discussions surrounding slavery, debating with each other the causes and effects of the institution. Philip Morgan, a professor of history at the College of William and Mary, commented that "Williamsburg has changed dramatically from a lily white, rather hands off, just watching things [kind of place]. Now they're really engaging people and taking on really significant issues."[36]

Yet many of the African American interpreters were not happy with the way that they were treated by the restoration. Understaffing meant overwork for many of the interpreters, and many were also unhappy about a reorganization of the restoration, which involved dissolving the Department of African American Interpretations and Presentations in 1997. Colonial Williamsburg's management argued that this reorganization improved the presentation for visitors, making it easier for them to navigate the restoration. Three enclosed areas were set up, with a manager for each site. This move and other reorganization efforts made black interpreters feel that they no longer had a collective voice in the presentation of African American history. Although African Americans did assume managerial and supervisory roles, many felt that these opportunities were not made available to them often enough. There were other problems, such as white staff members who used language that deviated from the agreed-upon formulation for reenactments, which, in one case, insulted one of the black female interpreters. In addition, a white restoration employee was accused of referring to African American staff members as "coloreds." In response, the restoration instituted a sensitivity program to deal with the problem and to encourage staff members to be more considerate of their colleagues. Underlying much of the bitterness of African American staffers were the relatively low wages of approximately $7 an hour. Yet the restoration realized that it needed to retain as many interpreters as it could, since these new interpretive programs were important for the future of the project.[37]

The restoration's financial picture began to look more positive as the decade came to a close. The 1998 annual report indicated that Colonial Williamsburg achieved its first surplus since 1990. Overall expenditures increased more slowly than before, because a healthy stock market resulted in a decrease in payroll expenses, primarily in the area of retirement benefits. "Since the markets were strong in 1998, the foundation didn't have to contribute as much to its retirement program." The restoration sold 983,100 admission tickets in 1998, and a larger number of tourists bought more expensive tickets, which allowed them to stay longer and to visit the historic area more often. Revenues from product sales and private donations also increased. Overall, the strong economy was highly beneficial for the restoration, because the value of its portfolio grew, and visitors were willing to stay longer and to purchase more items. Although it is difficult to determine the influence of the restoration's more diverse presentations on ticket sales, the increased publicity that these changes garnered was probably beneficial.[38]

Finally, by the end of the millennium, there was a broader understanding of Colonial Williamsburg as a museum that strove to present a more balanced portrait of the past while at the same time teaching the public a lesson in social issues. In an article in the *New York Times* entitled "Williamsburg Rethinks History," Katherine Ashenburg recounted the changes that had taken place at the restoration since the 1970s, including the refurbishment of the Governor's Palace, the creation of the DeWitt Wallace Decorative Arts Gallery, and the reconstruction of the Public Hospital and the slave quarters at Carter's Grove. These were all significant changes, along with the decision of the restoration to leave the town a bit messy by not cleaning up horse manure in the streets and by not rushing to paint or to fix items as they grew older. According to Ashenburg, visitors wanted more than simply the chance to eat eighteenth-century food or to visit the shops. Her coverage reflected a change from previous articles, which had emphasized these aspects. She wrote, "I went to the Secretary's Office next to the Capitol, where a staff historian . . . discussed the tightening vise of 18th-century slavery laws. The attendance was standing room only, a perspiring room full of whites and blacks, some of them with school-age children."[39]

An article by Alan Solomon in the *Chicago Tribune* also highlighted the

The Fifes and Drums—a Colonial Williamsburg tradition (Courtesy of the Colonial Williamsburg Foundation)

restoration, with particular attention paid to the character interpreters in the town, ranging from George Washington, Thomas Jefferson, and Patrick Henry to an "illegal" gathering of slaves, who discussed the need for change in Williamsburg. The article also pointed out the emphasis on traditional interpretations, such as the Fifes and Drums, whose daily parades had great popular appeal, especially among children. Solomon also mentioned the neighboring sites of Jamestown and Yorktown, thereby emphasizing the historic triangle, much as was done several decades before. Although Solomon's portrayal of the restoration was generally positive, he did point out some inherent flaws in the presentation, such as the presence of George Washington in Williamsburg in the fall of 1775, when he actually was in Boston commanding the Continental Army.[40]

Since the late 1970s, the restoration has made strides in its attempt to present a broader interpretation of the past. Over time, the media have also begun to recognize this trend and the new emphasis of the restoration. Some critics have insisted on promoting the comparison with a theme park, yet clearly the work of the historical researchers, archaeologists, and architectural historians has demonstrated that Colonial Williamsburg is not a fantasy land. The inevitable remnants of the town's previous incarnation, both the buildings and *The Story of a Patriot*, however, mean that the restoration's presentation will be pushed largely toward a political orientation. Even today most visitors probably think of American history largely as a political exercise, with social history as an additional part added on to promote popular interest. Yet Colonial Williamsburg's attempt to portray slavery more accurately, its move to diversify the town's buildings to include places for interpreting the lives of the working class, and the added emphasis on women all indicate a serious attempt to transform the presentation of the past.

Epilogue

Just as it did fifty years ago, Colonial Williamsburg has continued to walk a fine line in its historical presentations, attempting to interpret the past in a way that will meet its educational goals while not alienating its visitors. Although some might be shocked by the restoration's demonstrations of life under slavery, all in all Colonial Williamsburg has sought to present a version of the past that is more geared to attracting visitors than repelling them. Even today, however, not all visitors necessarily want a thorough indoctrination into colonial American social history. Some may come to enjoy the quaintness and charm of an earlier age, to study garden design, or to learn how Christmas was celebrated in the eighteenth century. The restoration will seek to satisfy those individuals as well. Although its modern incarnation no longer promotes to such a large degree the Americanist issues of its founders, Colonial Williamsburg still must work to meet its modern aims of presenting the past effectively and honestly.

Inevitably, critics will charge that Colonial Williamsburg is not all that it should be. This is no doubt true. But the restoration has made major strides in its seventy-five-year history. In its present manifestation, it is no longer the shrine that JDR Jr. would have liked it to be because the focus of the education of today's Colonial Williamsburg is quite different from that of its earlier era. Yet most visitors probably leave knowing more about the colonial period than they did when they arrived. Ultimately, this must be the restoration's goal—to bring a better understanding of the past to its visitors while helping them to realize the diversity and complexity of eighteenth-century life.

Colonial Williamsburg also will continue to promote itself as a tourist destination to attract more visitors who will use its facilities: the hotels, restaurants, conference center, and golf course. Profits from these subsidiaries are plowed back into the restoration for research and the development of interpretation programs. Although these facilities may be eyesores to many purists, ultimately they help to sell Colonial Williamsburg to the consumer. After all, getting people to visit the town must be the restoration's first priority. To attract visitors, the restoration must act as a tourist destination as well as a history museum. The ultimate question is how these qualities should be divided, so that the area's tourist appeal does not overshadow the museum and its efforts. With the dramatic increase in visitors that occurred in the 1950s and 1960s, the restoration became more of a mass marketer of the eighteenth century than merely a purveyor of the quaintness of the past. With the development of the Information Center and the closing of many of the town's streets to automobile traffic, the restoration strove to preserve the experience that visitors had had before World War II. Yet the growth of the town, the diversity of its programs, and the need to compete with other sites has forced the restoration to advertise in ways that would have been unthinkable half a century ago.

Presumably the restoration takes this promotional route today because it thinks such promotion will appeal to a broader range of visitors, especially children, who more and more determine families' travel plans. The restoration's recent financial success appears to support the theory that this type of advertising works. Drawing people to Colonial Williamsburg and keeping them there longer will result in more purchases at the restoration's stores, more meals eaten at the taverns and restaurants, and more money spent on other attractions, such as evening performances and tours, which further utilize the town's sites for dramatic portrayals, dances, and concerts. All these activities make money for the restoration and help to fund its programs. Alliances with other attractions, such as Busch Gardens and Water Country USA, seek to bring in visitors who might otherwise have ignored Colonial Williamsburg. While the restoration is considerably more than just a theme park, it cannot exclude itself from the other recreational sites on the peninsula, because to do so would risk a dramatic drop in revenues.

Today Americans are looking more and more for packaged travel that provides access to a variety of sites in one area, as well as relaxation and entertainment for all members of the family. This trend forces the restoration to make allies of sites that are different from itself. The Revolutionary Fun package, for example, was intended to make it easier for tourists to book a trip to the Hampton Roads area in the southern part of the Tidewater region of Virginia. The package included Colonial Williamsburg, Jamestown Settlement, Water Country USA, Busch Gardens, and the Yorktown Victory Center. Tourists would get unlimited access to all those attractions for one price. The money invested in these types of joint tickets provides large economic rewards to the Williamsburg area, as well as for the restoration itself, with increased visitation as well as purchases in stores and meals in restaurants.[1]

Such alliances are beneficial, since the restoration sees its major competition coming not from other historic sites but from Disneyland and amusement parks such as Six Flags. This competition forces the restoration to use low-brow advertising while at the same time trying to maintain programs that have high integrity and historical accuracy. The Just Partners advertising agency produced five television commercials for Colonial Williamsburg that parodied the "now familiar Super Bowl quarterback or other sports champ plugs for Disney World." In one ad an actor playing Patrick Henry is asked, after he has given his "Give me liberty or give me death" speech, if he is going to a Disney theme park. "No," he replies, "I'm going to [Colonial] Williamsburg." Other ads, such as one showing people dancing the minuet, were discarded, because the Just Partners agency believed the imagery focused too much on tradition and "not enough on fun." Advertisements were also placed in magazines like *Martha Stewart Living, People Weekly*, and *Better Homes and Gardens* that targeted mothers, especially those of young children. Again, this type of advertising sends mixed messages to an audience that may expect a Disneyland experience but is confronted with programs that may be too intense for young children.[2]

Money has been, and probably will remain, the primary point of contention surrounding the restoration. To operate a large, fully developed historical restoration is expensive. Admission fees, private donations, and the Rockefeller trust fund provide Colonial Williamsburg with enough cash to operate but never quite enough to feel secure. As a result, the restoration must inevitably consider carefully what operations it will undertake. The restoration has been fortunate to find contributors since it began seeking outside donations in the late 1970s. In addition to generous gifts from individuals such as DeWitt Wallace, Colonial Williamsburg received more than $1 million from PepsiCo over a ten-year period in exchange for agreeing that the company would be the exclusive supplier of soft drinks for all Colonial Williamsburg properties. The restoration has also sought smaller donations from many of its visitors, urging them to support the restoration's programs with their contributions and providing them with special perks, such as the use of the St. George Tucker House as a hospitality center when they are in Colonial Williamsburg. The broader attempt to court supporters enhances the role that Colonial Williamsburg seeks to play as a nonprofit educational foundation. Much like a university, the restoration desires to promote the image of a serious educational institution that presents the diversity of eighteenth-century life in southeastern Virginia. In the process, it hopes that visitors will be enthralled, or at least interested, and as a result of their visit make a further contribution to the work of the restoration.[3]

As Colonial Williamsburg enters its third decade committed to being a social history museum, it must still confront questions of how to adequately represent the lives of the African Americans, women, and laborers who made up the majority of the town's population. Surrounded by competitors, critics, and opponents, Colonial Williamsburg must work to carve out its niche in spite of these forces. No doubt the restoration could do more to present new and challenging programs that would educate and captivate visitors. Colonial Williamsburg has worked to find suitable individuals to portray important and recognizable figures from the past such as Thomas Jefferson, Patrick Henry, and George Washington. These interpreters maintain their characters and profess no knowledge of modern-day issues or events. Yet many costumed individuals, both black and white, are not "in the eighteenth century." By making all costumed employees people of the colonial period, the restoration could promote the continuity of its interpretations and demonstrate the diversity of townspeople in the eighteenth century. The restoration should also have a greater number of individuals in modern dress who can explain life in the eighteenth century and bridge the gap between past and present.[4]

Colonial Williamsburg's variety of phases have mirrored the American experience over the past seventy-five years. The restoration has brought a changing view of the past to different audiences over this time. Even during its period as a shrine, the restoration's presentation was not static. Rather it pursued different areas of emphasis during the Great Depression, World

War II, and the Cold War. In its last quarter century, the restoration's shift to a social history museum has demonstrated the complexities of historical presentations in the modern age and the difficulties that come from trying to present a more nuanced version of the American colonial experience. The restoration will ultimately be judged on how well it can transcend its origins and present a cohesive examination of the past. Although its critics argue that Colonial Williamsburg has not changed significantly from its days as a shrine, this simply is not the case. Although the restoration's earlier role has not been erased, new research initiatives, broader interpretation programs, and the construction of new interpretive sites have made a difference in the way visitors understand the eighteenth century. The fact that *The Story of a Patriot* now seems so out of place is testimony to the changes that Colonial Williamsburg has undergone in the past two decades. Although the restoration still suffers from a hybridization of its dual incarnations, eventually Colonial Williamsburg may truly live up to its motto "that the future may learn from the past."[5]

Notes

Introduction

1. George H. Yetter, *Williamsburg Before and After: The Rebirth of Virginia's Colonial Capital* (Williamsburg: Colonial Williamsburg Foundation, 1988), 20; Philip Kopper, *Colonial Williamsburg* (New York: Harry N. Abrams, Inc., 1985), 43–46; Carl Bridenbaugh, *Seat of Empire: The Political Role of Eighteenth Century Williamsburg* (Williamsburg: Colonial Williamsburg Foundation, 1950), 1; Rhys Isaac, *The Transformation of Virginia* (Chapel Hill: University of North Carolina Press, 1982), 12–13.

2. Thad W. Tate, *The Negro in Eighteenth-Century Williamsburg* (Williamsburg: Colonial Williamsburg Foundation, 1965; fifth printing, 1990), 26 (page citations are to the fifth printing); Yetter, *Williamsburg Before and After,* 20; Bridenbaugh, *Seat of Empire,* 29.

3. Bridenbaugh, *Seat of Empire,* 43.

4. Ibid., 32.

5. Yetter, *Williamsburg Before and After,* 22.

6. J. A. Osborne, *Williamsburg in Colonial Times* (Port Washington, N.Y.: Kennikat Press, 1936), 1.

7. Kopper, *Colonial Williamsburg,* 115–16.

8. Yetter, *Williamsburg Before and After,* 24–25; Willard Sterne Randall, *Thomas Jefferson: A Life* (New York: Harper Perennial, 1994), 324.

9. John Ensor Harr and Peter J. Johnson, *The Rockefeller Century* (New York: Charles Scribner's Sons, 1988), 153; Paul Fussell, *The Great War and Modern Memory* (New York: Oxford University Press, 1975), 326–27; Robert H. Bremner, *American Philanthropy,* 2nd ed. (Chicago: University of Chicago Press, 1988), 149–50, 225.

10. Yetter, *Williamsburg Before and After,* 49–52; W. A. R. Goodwin, *Bruton Parish Church Restored* (Petersburg, Va.: Franklin Press, 1907), passim; Kopper, *Colonial Williamsburg,* 140–42; James M. Lindgren, *Preserving the Old Dominion: Historic Preservation*

and Virginia Traditionalism (Charlottesville: University Press of Virginia, 1993), 224–25.

11. Charles Hosmer, *Preservation Comes of Age: From Williamsburg to the National Trust, 1926–1949*, 2 vols. (Charlottesville: University Press of Virginia, 1981), 14–15; "[H]istory is bunk . . ." quoted in Peter Collier and David Horowitz, *The Fords: An American Epic* (New York: Summit Books, 1987), 108.

12. Raymond Fosdick, *John D. Rockefeller, Jr.: A Portrait* (New York: Harper and Bros., 1956), 97, 193.

13. Ibid., 17–18, 415.

14. Ibid., 301; A. Edwin Kendrew, Oral History Collection, passim, Colonial Williamsburg Foundation Archives (hereafter cited as CWFA), Williamsburg, Va.

15. Fosdick, *John D. Rockefeller, Jr.*, 300–301; Ron Chernow, *Titan: The Life of John D. Rockefeller, Sr.* (New York: Random House, 1998), 644.

16. Harvey Green, "Looking Backward to the Future: The Colonial Revival and American Culture," in *Creating a Dignified Past*, edited by Geoffrey L. Rossano (Savage, Md.: Rowman and Littlefield, 1989), 1–4; Michael Kammen, *Mystic Chords of Memory: The Transformation of Tradition in American Culture* (New York: Alfred A. Knopf, 1991), 148–49.

17. Kammen, *Mystic Chords of Memory*, 218; Green, "Looking Backward to the Future," 5–8.

18. Green, "Looking Backward to the Future," 13.

19. Kammen, *Mystic Chords of Memory*, 146–52, 261; David Gebhard, "The American Colonial Revival in the 1930s," *Winterthur Portfolio* 22, no. 2–3 (1987): 110.

20. Karal Ann Marling, *George Washington Slept Here: Colonial Revivals and American Culture, 1876–1986* (Cambridge, Mass.: Harvard University Press, 1988), passim.

21. Patricia West, *Domesticating History: The Political Origins of America's House Museums* (Washington, D.C.: Smithsonian Institution Press, 1999), xii–xiii.

22. John Ensor Harr and Peter J. Johnson, *The Rockefeller Conscience* (New York: Charles Scribner's Sons, 1991), 9; Charles B. Hosmer, "Private Philanthropy and Preservation," *Historic Preservation Today* (Charlottesville: University Press of Virginia, 1966), 155–61.

23. Gary Gerstle, *Working-Class Americanism: The Politics of Labor in a Textile City, 1914–1960* (New York: Cambridge University Press, 1989), 8.

24. Kammen, *Mystic Chords of Memory*, passim; John Higham, *Strangers in the Land: Patterns of American Nativism, 1860–1925* (New York: Atheneum, 1969), 9–11.

25. Harr and Johnson, *Rockefeller Century*, 492.

26. Charles Hosmer has done extensive work on the American preservation movement; see *The Presence of the Past: A History of the Preservation Movement in the United States before Williamsburg* (New York: Putnam, 1965) and *Preservation Comes of Age*. See also Lindgren, *Preserving the Old Dominion*, for a history of the preservation movement in Williamsburg before the restoration. For an examination of the architectural aspects of the restoration, see Thomas H. Taylor, "The Williamsburg Restoration and Its Reception by the American Public: 1926–1942" (Ph.D. diss., George Washington University, 1989). John William Turner has written on the

restoration's interpretation of religion; see his dissertation, "Some Historical Factors That Influenced the Interpretation of Religion by the Colonial Williamsburg Foundation" (Ph.D. diss., Virginia Commonwealth University, 1989). Richard Handler and Eric Gable, in *The New History in an Old Museum: Creating the Past at Colonial Williamsburg* (Durham, N.C.: Duke University Press, 1997), provide an ethnographic study of the current interpretative programs at Colonial Williamsburg.

1. The Birth of a Dream

1. Cabell Phillips, "The Town That Stopped the Clock," *American Heritage Magazine* 11 (February 1960): 25; Andrea Kim Foster, "'They're Turning the Town All Upside Down': The Community Identity of Williamsburg, Virginia, before and after the Reconstruction" (Ph.D. diss., George Washington University, 1992), 14–16. Edward L. Ayers, *The Promise of the New South: Life after Reconstruction* (New York: Oxford University Press, 1992), 410. Janet Kimbrough, interview by author, tape recording, Williamsburg, Va., 14 May 1991. Thad W. Tate, interview by author, tape recording, Williamsburg, Va., 17 May 1991. These interviews with Dr. Kimbrough, a long-time resident of Williamsburg, and historian Thad W. Tate confirm the argument that race relations were generally good.

2. James M. Lindgren, "The Association for the Preservation of Virginia Antiquities and the Regeneration of Traditionalism," *Virginia Magazine of History* 97 (January 1989): 48–51; James M. Lindgren, *Preserving the Old Dominion: Historic Preservation and Virginia Traditionalism* (Charlottesville: University Press of Virginia, 1993), 232–33, 247.

3. W. A. R. Goodwin, *Bruton Parish Church Restored and Its Historic Environment* (Petersburg, Va.: Franklin Press, 1907), 14.

4. Charles B. Hosmer, *Preservation Comes of Age: From Williamsburg to the National Trust, 1926–1949*, 2 vols. (Charlottesville: University Press of Virginia, 1981), 12–21; Joseph W. Ernst, ed., *"Dear Father" / "Dear Son": Correspondence of John D. Rockefeller and John D. Rockefeller, Jr.* (New York: Fordham University Press, 1994), 140–41; Lindgren, *Preserving the Old Dominion*, 225, 229.

5. JDR Jr. to W. A. R. Goodwin, 29 November 1926, Record Group (hereafter cited as RG) 3.2E, Box 143, Folder 1251, Rockefeller Family Archives (hereafter cited as RFA), Rockefeller Archive Center, Sleepy Hollow, N.Y.

6. JDR Jr. to Arthur Woods, 30 November 1927, RG 3.2E, Box 170, Folder 1479, RFA; JDR Jr. to Arthur Woods, 31 December 1928, RG 3.2E, Box 170, Folder 1479, RFA; *New York Times*, 12 January 1953.

7. Judge Robert Armistead, interview by author, tape recording, Williamsburg, Va., 16 May 1991.

8. W. A. R. Goodwin to JDR Jr., 12 December 1927, RG 3.2E, Box 159, Folder 1386, RFA.

9. W. A. R. Goodwin to the Business Men of Williamsburg, 12 December 1927, quoted in Elizabeth Hayes, "The Background and Beginnings of the Restoration of Colonial Williamsburg, Virginia," 159, Colonial Williamsburg Foundation Archives (hereafter cited as CWFA), Williamsburg, Va.

10. George Humphrey Yetter, *Williamsburg Before and After: The Rebirth of Virginia's Colonial Capital* (Williamsburg: Colonial Williamsburg Foundation, 1988), 55.
11. Hayes, "The Background and Beginnings," 220; Andrea Kim Foster, "'They're Turning the Town All Upside Down,'" 110.
12. Hayes, "The Background and Beginnings," 220.
13. *Virginia Gazette,* 6 September 1935.
14. Charles O. Heydt to W. A. R. Goodwin, 27 November 1928, RG 3.2E, Box 143, Folder 1251, RFA.
15. Hayes, "The Background and Beginnings," 251–52; A. Edwin Kendrew, Oral History Collection, 574–75, CWFA.
16. Hayes, "The Background and Beginnings," 252–53, 256; Eliza Baker, "Memoirs of Williamsburg Virginia by Eliza Baker," 1933, passim, Oral History Collection, CWFA; Foster, "'They're Turning the Town All Upside Down,'" 166, 182; Kendrew, oral history, 518–19, 525.
17. Elizabeth Lee Henderson, "The Reminiscences of Elizabeth Lee Henderson," 1975, 61, 68, Oral History Collection, CWFA.
18. Ibid., 7, 59.
19. *Virginia Gazette,* 22 August 1930; *Virginia Gazette,* 28 November 1930.
20. Henderson, "The Reminiscences," 7; Hayes, "The Background and Beginnings," 10; Kendrew, oral history, 480.
21. Thomas H. Taylor, "The Williamsburg Restoration and Its Reception by the American Public: 1926–1942" (Ph.D. diss., George Washington University, 1989), 284; Yetter, *Williamsburg Before and After,* 16.
22. W. A. R. Goodwin, "Report and Recommendations," 4 February 1929, RG 3.2E, Box 155, Folder 1354, RFA; Kendrew, oral history, 460.
23. *Virginia Gazette,* 6 June 1930.
24. Kendrew, oral history, 598.
25. W. A. R. Goodwin to Arthur Woods, 9 April 1930, RG 3.2E, Box 155, Folder 1354, RFA.
26. *Virginia Gazette,* 18 April 1930; *Congressional Record,* 71st Cong., 2d sess., 1930, 72, pt. 10:10342–43.
27. *Congressional Record,* 72nd Cong., 1st. sess., 1932, 75, pt. 13:14321; Ernest C. Pollard, "A Triple Shrine of History," *National Republic* 18 (April 1931): 21.
28. Hayes, "The Background and Beginnings," 12; Horace Albright, "Reminiscences of Horace Albright," 1957, 14, Oral History Collection, CWFA.
29. Albright, "Reminiscences," 34, 54, 58.
30. W. E. Carson, *Conserving and Developing Virginia,* State Commission on Conservation and Development, 26 July 1926 to 31 December 1934, 71.
31. *Virginia Gazette,* 3 June 1932.
32. *The Williamsburg Restoration* (Williamsburg: Colonial Williamsburg, 1931), 10.
33. Mrs. George P. Coleman, "The Reminiscences of Mrs. George P. Coleman," 1956, 7, Oral History Collection, CWFA; *Virginia Gazette,* 18 July 1931.
34. *Virginia Gazette,* 1 May 1931.

35. Andrew H. Hepburn, "The Reminiscences of Andrew H. Hepburn," 1956, 40, 44, Oral History Collection, CWFA.

36. Ibid., 51; Mrs. Henry M. Stryker, "The Reminiscences of Mrs. Henry M. Stryker," 1956, 20, Oral History Collection, CWFA.

37. John Ensor Harr and Peter J. Johnson, *The Rockefeller Conscience* (New York: Charles Scribner's Sons, 1991), 355; Raymond Fosdick, *John D. Rockefeller, Jr.: A Portrait* (New York: Harper and Bros., 1956), 272; Baker, "Memoirs," 83.

38. Anne Hard, "Sleeping Beauty Town," *St. Nicholas Magazine* 58 (March 1931): 369–72, 408.

39. Yetter, *Williamsburg Before and After,* 69.

40. Howard M. Canoune to the Williamsburg Holding Corporation, 10 April 1932, Letters of Commendation, General Correspondence Records, CWFA; Charles J. Breck to Williamsburg Holding Corporation, 23 June 1932, Letters of Criticism, General Correspondence Records, CWFA.

41. Henry Breckenridge to W. A. R. Goodwin, 28 September 1932, Letters of Commendation, General Correspondence Records, CWFA.

42. H. J. Eckenrode to W. A. R. Goodwin, 25 January 1933, Letters of Commendation, General Correspondence Records, CWFA.

43. Coleman, "Reminiscences," 7.

44. Ernst, *"Dear Father" / "Dear Son,"* 192–93.

2. *Creating the Faith*

1. Barbara Trigg Brown, "Williamsburg—A Shrine for American Patriots," *American Home* 12 (November 1934): 349, 392.

2. Michael Kammen, *Mystic Chords of Memory: The Transformation of Tradition in American Culture* (New York: Alfred A. Knopf, 1991), 363; Thomas H. Taylor, "The Williamsburg Restoration and Its Reception by the American Public: 1926–1942" (Ph.D. diss., George Washington University, 1989), 193; Philip Kopper, *Colonial Williamsburg* (New York: Harry N. Abrams, Inc., 1986), 201; George Humphrey Yetter, *Williamsburg Before and After: The Rebirth of Virginia's Colonial Capital* (Williamsburg: Colonial Williamsburg Foundation, 1988), 69–71.

3. Thomas G. McCaskey, "The Reminiscences of Thomas G. McCaskey," 1957, 36, 38, Oral History Collection, Colonial Williamsburg Foundation Archives (hereafter cited as CWFA), Williamsburg, Va.

4. Ibid., 136–38; "Mr. Rockefeller's $14,000,000 Idyl," *Fortune* 12 (July 1935): 72; Kenneth Chorley to JDR 3d, memorandum, 24 May 1934, Record Group (hereafter cited as RG) 3.2E, Box 150, Folder 1316, Rockefeller Family Archive (hereafter cited as RFA), Rockefeller Archive Center, Sleepy Hollow, N.Y.

5. McCaskey, "Reminiscences," 135–38.

6. Ibid., 42–43, 77, 116.

7. *Virginia Gazette,* 10 May 1935.

8. *Virginia Gazette,* 24 May 1935.

9. *Virginia Gazette,* 22 June 1934.

10. Ibid.

11. *Virginia Gazette,* 17 April 1936.

12. Elizabeth Pontefrace to Mr. and Mrs. JDR Jr., Thanksgiving Day, 1935, Letters of Commendation, General Correspondence Records, CWFA.

13. W. A. R. Goodwin to JDR 3d, 3 March 1934, RG 3.2E, Box 155, Folder 1353, RFA.

14. Kenneth Chorley to JDR 3d, memorandum, 24 May 1934, RG 3.2E, Box 150, Folder 1316, RFA.

15. Ibid.

16. Peter Collier and David Horowitz, *The Rockefellers: An American Dynasty* (New York, 1976), 145–46, 156; Raymond Fosdick, *John D. Rockefeller, Jr.: A Portrait* (New York: Harper and Bros., 1956), 294–95.

17. Fielding Robinson to JDR Jr., 22 May 1939, Letters of Commendation, General Correspondence Records, CWFA.

18. Kenneth Chorley, "The Williamsburg Restoration—Its Purpose and Objectives," 15 December 1934, Hostess Training 1934, General Correspondence Records, CWFA.

19. Ibid.

20. Mary S. Hazel to Colonial Williamsburg, Inc., 2 February 1939, Letters of Commendation, General Correspondence Records, CWFA.

21. Elizabeth Lee Henderson, "The Reminiscences of Elizabeth Lee Henderson," 1975, 24–25, 32, Oral History Collection, CWFA.

22. See John F. Kasson, *Amusing the Million: Coney Island at the Turn of the Century* (New York: Hill and Wang, 1978), for a study of Coney Island, complete with photographs.

23. *Virginia Gazette,* 22 October 1937.

24. *Virginia Gazette,* 3 July 1936; "Fresh Antiques: Colonial Williamsburg Reproduction Program," *Look* 22 (4 March 1958): 58.

25. *Virginia Gazette,* 3 July 1936.

26. Richardson Wright, "Williamsburg: What It Means to Architecture, to Gardening, to Decoration," *House and Garden* 72 (November 1937): 41, 45–46.

27. Ibid., 51.

28. Ibid., 58–62.

29. Collier and Horowitz, *The Rockefellers,* 145; Fosdick, *John D. Rockefeller, Jr.,* 429; A. Edwin Kendrew, Oral History Collection, 613–14, CWFA.

30. Mrs. Henry M. Stryker, "The Reminiscences of Mrs. Henry M. Stryker," 1956, 28, 103, Oral History Collection, CWFA.

31. McCaskey, "Reminiscences," 92–94.

32. Kenneth Chorley to JDR 3d, 9 March 1936, RG 3.2E, Box 150, Folder 1314, RFA; *Virginia Gazette,* 26 March 1937; Kendrew, oral history, 1598–99, 1602, CWFA.

33. John D. Rockefeller Jr., "The Genesis of the Williamsburg Restoration," *National Geographic* 71 (April 1937): 401.

34. *Virginia Gazette,* 30 April 1937.

35. *New York Times,* 25 February 1937.

36. W. A. R. Goodwin to JDR Jr., 8 July 1937, RG 3.2E, Box 155, Folder 1353, RFA.

37. Ibid.

38. "Suggestions Concerning Admissions to the Exhibition Buildings of Colonial Williamsburg, Inc.," 21 December 1939, RG 3.2E, Box 145, Folder 1274, RFA.
39. Ibid.
40. Francis Bemiss Mason to Kenneth Chorley, 4 April 1939, Letters of Commendation, General Correspondence Records, CWFA; Alice O. Kay to JDR Jr., 27 May 1939, Letters of Commendation, General Correspondence Records, CWFA.
41. Kenneth Chorley to Executive Committee of Colonial Williamsburg, Inc., 11 June 1940, RG 3.2E, Box 159, Folder 1386, RFA; McCaskey, "Reminiscences," 50–52.
42. Raymond T. Rich to Kenneth Chorley, 7 June 1940, RG 3.2E, Box 159, Folder 1386, RFA.
43. Louis Wirth to Emery T. Filbey, 13 November 1940, RG 3.2E, Box 152, Folder 1329, RFA.
44. Ibid.
45. Memorandum on the Educational Possibilities of the Restoration of Williamsburg, Virginia, 13 November 1949, RG 3.2E, Box 152, Folder 1329, RFA.

3. To Preserve a Nation

1. "Radio and Williamsburg," memorandum no. 2, 8 February 1941, Record Group (hereafter cited as RG) 3.2E, Box 152, Folder 1329, Rockefeller Family Archive (hereafter cited as RFA), Rockefeller Archive Center, Sleepy Hollow, N.Y.
2. Ibid.
3. "Draft Statement of Certain Guiding Principles for Colonial Williamsburg, Inc.," memorandum, 8 February 1941, RG 3.2E, Box 152, Folder 1329, RFA.
4. Ibid.
5. Ibid.
6. Ibid.
7. Ibid.
8. Ibid.
9. Ibid.
10. JDR 3d to JDR Jr., 25 March 1941, RG 3.2E, Box 152, Folder 1328, RFA.
11. Dixon Wecter to JDR 3d, 15 January 1942, RG 3.2E, Box 152, Folder 1328, RFA.
12. Harold D. Lasswell to JDR 3d, 26 March 1942, RG 3.2E, Box 152, Folder 1329, RFA.
13. Kenneth Chorley to JDR Jr., 7 April 1942, RG 3.2E, Box 150, Folder 1312, RFA.
14. Donald P. Bean to Harold D. Lasswell, 2 May 1942, RG 3.2E, Box 152, Folder 1329, RFA.
15. Ethel B. Bellsmith to JDR Jr., 15 March 1941, Letters of Commendation, General Correspondence Records, Colonial Williamsburg Foundation Archives (hereafter cited as CWFA), Williamsburg, Va.
16. C. Kenneth Snyder to JDR Jr., 3 February 1942, Letters of Commendation, General Correspondence Records, CWFA.
17. *Virginia Gazette*, 23 January 1942; *Virginia Gazette*, 8 May 1942.
18. JDR 3d to William S. Paley, 17 July 1942, RG 3.2E, Box 152, Folder 1328, RFA; William S. Paley to JDR 3d, 31 July 1942, Box 152, Folder 1328, RFA.

19. "Training Program for Soldiers," 7 May 1942, RG 3.2E, Box 145, Folder 1276, RFA.

20. Donald P. Bean, "This War and Williamsburg," *Publishers Weekly* 142 (22 August 1942): 550.

21. Vernon M. Geddy, "Williamsburg in Wartime," *House and Garden* 82 (September 1942): 17.

22. JDR Jr. to Kenneth Chorley, 23 June 1942, RG 3.2E, Box 145, Folder 1280, RFA; Memo to JDR Jr., 17 April 1945, RG 3.2E, Box 145, Folder 1280, RFA.

23. Art Froehly to JDR Jr., 2 November 1942, RG 3.2E, Box 145, Folder 1276, RFA.

24. Richard Korn to Colonial Williamsburg, 31 August 1944, RG 3.2E, Box 145, Folder 1280, RFA.

25. John F. Sears, *Sacred Places: American Tourist Attractions in the Nineteenth Century* (New York: Oxford University Press, 1989), 4–8.

26. Robert Friedberg to JDR Jr., 18 August 1942, Letters of Commendation, General Correspondence Records, CWFA.

27. *Virginia Gazette,* 16 March 1945.

28. Mary F. McWilliams to JDR Jr., 29 October 1945, RG 3.2E, Box 152, Folder 1331, RFA; A. Edwin Kendrew, Oral History Collection, 2551, CWFA.

29. Kenneth Chorley to JDR Jr., 4 September 1942, RG 3.2E, Box 149, Folder 1310, RFA; Richard Polenberg, *One Nation Divisible: Class, Race, and Ethnicity in the United States since 1938* (New York: Viking Press, 1980), 74; Kendrew, oral history, 2667–68.

30. JDR Jr. to Kenneth Chorley, 5 May 1943, RG 3.2E, Box 144, Folder 1260, RFA.

31. JDR Jr. to Kenneth Chorley, 27 November 1945, RG 3.2E, Box 150, Folder 1312, RFA; Kendrew, oral history, 2633.

32. Kendrew, oral history, 2638.

33. *New York Times,* 14 January 1944; *Virginia Gazette,* 14 January 1944.

34. Arthur Shurcliff to Kenneth Chorley, 11 March 1946, RG 3.2E, Box 150, Folder 1312, RFA.

35. Kenneth Chorley to Messrs. Geddy, Norton, and Green, 23 July 1946, RG 2OMR, Box 3, Folder: Racial Question—Williamsburg 1946–1951, RFA.

36. V. M. Geddy to Kenneth Chorley, 13 September 1946, RG 2OMR, Box 3, Folder: Racial Question—Williamsburg, 1946–1951, RFA.

37. Joanna L. S. Priest to Williamsburg Restoration Committee, 2 December 1946, Letters of Commendation, General Correspondence Records, CWFA.

38. *New York Sun,* 22 November 1946.

4. A Growing Prominence

1. Gerald Horton Bath, "Colonial Williamsburg," *School Arts* 46 (January 1947): 169.

2. D. E. Watkins to Gerald Horton Bath, 28 May 1947, Letters of Commendation, General Correspondence Records, Colonial Williamsburg Foundation Archives (hereafter cited as CWFA), Williamsburg, Va.; John F. Sears, *Sacred Places: American Tourist Attractions in the Nineteenth Century* (New York: Oxford University Press, 1989), 7.

3. Olive A. Knight to JDR Jr., 27 August 1947, Letters of Commendation, General Correspondence Records, CWFA.

4. Richard Gid Powers, *Not Without Honor: The History of American Anticommunism* (New Haven: Yale University Press, 1998), 245–9.

5. Harry F. Byrd to Bela W. Norton, 21 June 1949, Letters of Commendation, General Correspondence Records, CWFA.

6. Richard Handler and Eric Gable, *The New History in an Old Museum: Creating the Past at Colonial Williamsburg* (Durham: Duke University Press, 1997), 18–19; Vanderbilt Webb to Kenneth Chorley, 29 December 1947, Record Group (hereafter cited as RG) 3.2E, Box 145, Folder 1274, Rockefeller Family Archives (hereafter cited as RFA), Rockefeller Archive Center, Sleepy Hollow, N.Y.

7. Thomas G. McCaskey, "The Reminiscences of Thomas G. McCaskey," 1957, 37, Oral History Collection, CWFA.

8. A. Edwin Kendrew, Oral History Collection, 2721–22, 2735, CWFA.

9. Robert Morris to Raymond B. Fosdick, 7 May 1948, Letters of Criticism, General Correspondence Records, CWFA.

10. Beatrice S. Kahn to JDR Jr., 19 May 1948, Letters of Commendation, General Correspondence Records, CWFA.

11. Charles M. Wagoner to Kershaw Burbank, 9 August 1949, Letters of Commendation, General Correspondence Records, CWFA.

12. F. Lloyd Adams to JDR Jr., 15 October 1948, Letters of Commendation, General Correspondence Records, CWFA.

13. Richard B. Sealock to Edward P. Alexander, 7 December 1948, Letters of Commendation, General Correspondence Records, CWFA; *New York Times*, 18 January 1948.

14. *Virginia Gazette*, 17 October 1947.

15. Ibid.

16. *Virginia Gazette*, 9 January 1948.

17. *New York Times*, 3 April 1948.

18. *Virginia Gazette*, 27 August 1948.

19. "A Report to Williamsburg Restoration, Inc., from the Office of Walter Dorwin Teague," 24 November 1948, RG 3.2E, Box 143, Folder 1252, 2, RFA; Colonial Williamsburg and Charitable Contributions, 30 April 1948, RG 3.2E, Box 160, Folder 1393, RFA.

20. Teague report, 3–5.

21. Ibid., 7–11.

22. JDR Jr. to Bela W. Norton, 4 January 1949, RG 3.2E, Box 152, Folder 1331, RFA.

23. Earl Newman to Kenneth Chorley, 25 March 1949, RG 3.2E, Box 164, Folder 1422, RFA; Dorothy Hanson Gillikin to JDR Jr., 30 May 1949, Letters of Commendation, General Correspondence Records, CWFA.

24. JDR Jr. to Henry M. Stryker, 5 April 1949, RG 3.2E, Box 161, Folder 1397, RFA.

25. *Virginia Gazette*, July 1949, special section.

26. John Ensor Harr and Peter J. Johnson, *The Rockefeller Conscience* (New York: Charles Scribner's Sons, 1991), 490–91.

27. Elihu S. Wing to Colonial Williamsburg, 30 November 1950, Letters of Commendation, General Correspondence Records, CWFA.

28. *New York Times*, 12 November 1950.

29. Michael Kammen, *Mystic Chords of Memory: The Transformation of Tradition in American Culture* (New York: Alfred A. Knopf, 1991), 581–86.

30. George E. Cohron to Allston Boyer, 6 March 1950, RG 2OMR, Box 3, Folder: Racial Question—Williamsburg, 1946–1951, RFA.

31. Alonzo G. Moron to Doris F. Statler, RG 2OMR, Box 3, Folder: Racial Question—Williamsburg, 1946–1951, RFA.

32. John D. Green to Kenneth Chorley, 6 April 1950, RG 2OMR, Box 3, Folder: Racial Question—Williamsburg, 1946–1951, RFA.

33. Memorandum of conversation of JDR 3d with John Dickey, 3 May 1950, RG 2OMR, Box 3, Folder: Racial Question—Williamsburg, 1946–1951, RFA.

34. JDR 3d, "A Statement of Policy," Draft 7, 1950, RG 2OMR, Box 3, Folder: Racial Question—Williamsburg, 1946–1951, RFA.

35. Lloyd H. Williams to JDR 3rd, 24 May 1951, RG 2OMR, Box 3, Folder: Racial Question—Williamsburg, 1946–1951, RFA; Kenneth Chorley to JDR 3d, 27 July 1951, RG 2OMR, Box 3, Folder: Racial Question—Williamsburg, 1946–1951, RFA.

36. Earl D. Johnson, Assistant Secretary of the Army, to Chief of Staff, United States Army, 11 October 1950, RG 3.2E, Box 154, Folder 1275, RFA.

37. Harr and Johnson, *The Rockefeller Conscience*, 498–500.

38. Thomas E. Dewey to JDR Jr., 28 June 1950, RG 3.2E, Box 156, Folder 1361, RFA; Coming B. Gibbs to JDR Jr., 14 October 1950, RG 3.2E, Box 156, Folder 1360, RFA.

39. Harr and Johnson, *The Rockefeller Conscience*, 423–24; J. Ronald Oakley, *God's Country: America in the Fifties* (New York: Dembner Books, 1990), passim.

5. For the Greater Good

1. Charles D. Faulkner to JDR Jr., 1 May 1953, Letters of Criticism, General Correspondence Records, Colonial Williamsburg Foudation Archives (hereafter cited as CWFA), Williamsburg, Va.

2. J. L. Underhill to Colonial Williamsburg, Inc., 23 April 1951, Letters of Commendation, General Correspondence Records, CWFA.

3. Allene Veitch to Colonial Williamsburg, August 1952, Letters of Commendation, General Correspondence Records, CWFA; Chester F. Collier to Colonial Williamsburg, November 1952, Letters of Criticism, General Correspondence Records, CWFA.

4. Laurence M. Gould to JDR Jr., 6 December 1951, Letters of Commendation, General Correspondence Records, CWFA.

5. Dean MacCannell, "Staged Authenticity: Arrangements of Social Space in Tourist Settings," *American Journal of Sociology* 79, no. 3 (November 1973): 589.

6. Minutes, Board of Trustees of Colonial Williamsburg, Inc., 18 May 1950, Record Group (hereafter cited as RG) 3.2E, Box 167, Folder 1457, Rockefeller Family

Archives (hereafter cited as RFA), Rockefeller Archive Center, Sleepy Hollow, N.Y.

7. JDR 3d to JDR Jr., N.D., RG 2OMR, Box 3, Folder: Mr. Rockefeller, Jr.—Williamsburg, RFA.

8. Alvin Moscow, *The Rockefeller Inheritance* (Garden City, N.Y.: Doubleday and Co., 1977), 140–46.

9. Interim Report—Special Survey Committee, 3 November 1950, RG 3.2E, Box 162, Folder 1409A, RFA.

10. Ibid.

11. Ibid.

12. Ibid.

13. JDR 3d to James E. Webb, 12 April 1950, RG 3.2E, Box 163, Folder 1416, RFA.

14. Harry S. Truman to JDR 3d, 30 January 1951, RG 3.2E, Box 144, Folder 1265, RFA.

15. Richard M. Fried, *The Russians Are Coming! The Russians Are Coming!: Pageantry and Patriotism in Cold-War America* (New York: Oxford University Press, 1998), 101; Kenneth Chorley to JDR Jr. and JDR 3d, 19 February 1951, RG 3.2E, Box 164, Folder 1422, RFA; *Virginia Gazette*, 11 February 1955; *Virginia Gazette*, 16 November 1956.

16. Notes on Proposed Williamsburg Conferences on International Affairs, RG 3.2E, Box 162, Folder 1409A, RFA; Michael Kammen, *Mystic Chords of Memory: The Transformation of Tradition in American Culture* (New York: Alfred A. Knopf, 1991), 582–84.

17. JDR 3rd to Chief of Naval Personnel, 26 April 1951, RG 3.2E, Box 153, Folder 1332, RFA.

18. Minutes of a Special Meeting of the Staff of Colonial Williamsburg, 18 May 1951, RG 2OMR, Box 3, Folder: Racial Question—Williamsburg, 1946–1951, RFA; John Ensor Harr and Peter J. Johnson, *The Rockefeller Century* (New York: Charles Scribner's Sons, 1989), 498–500.

19. Elizabeth Rapelye to JDR Jr., 9 July 1951, RG 3.2E, Box 156, Folder 1362, RFA.

20. Gladys O. Jaquith to JDR Jr., 21 September 1951, RG 3.2E, Box 156, Folder 1362, RFA.

21. R. C. Boyce to JDR Jr., 16 October 1951, RG 3.2E, Box 156, Folder 1362, RFA.

22. Kate Simpson to JDR Jr., 7 August 1952, RG 3.2E, Box 156, Folder 1362, RFA.

23. *Virginia Gazette*, 16 January 1953.

24. Beverley M. Bowie, "Williamsburg: Its College and Its Cinderella City," *National Geographic* 106, no. 4 (October 1954): 441–78.

25. Kenneth Chorley to JDR Jr., 22 October 1954, RG 3.2E, Box 159, Folder 1384, RFA; Reinhold Niebuhr quoted in H. W. Brands, *The Devil We Knew: Americans and the Cold War* (New York: Oxford University Press, 1993), 34.

26. *Virginia Gazette*, 9 April 1954.

27. Clifford Dowdey, "Williamsburg," *Holiday* 16 (August 1954): 44–45

28. Arthur Goodfriend to JDR 3d, 9 March 1954, RG 3.2E, Box 163, Folder 1416, RFA.

29. *New York Times*, 31 October 1954; *Virginia Gazette*, 17 June 1955.

30. *Richmond Times-Dispatch*, 29 March 1954.

31. Ibid.

32. *Richmond Times-Dispatch*, 30 March 1954.

33. *Richmond Times-Dispatch*, 2 April 1954.

34. *New York Times*, 29 January 1989; John Ensor Harr and Peter J. Johnson, *The Rockefeller Conscience: An American Family in Public and Private* (New York: Charles Scribners' Sons, 1991), 218–20.

35. *Proceedings of the Presentation of the Williamsburg Award to Winston Churchill* (Williamsburg: Colonial Williamsburg, Inc., 1957), 15.

36. Ibid., 15.

37. Harr and Johnson, *The Rockefeller Century*, 498–99.

38. *Proceedings of the Presentation*, 47.

39. *Virginia Gazette*, 25 October 1957.

40. *Virginia Gazette*, 25 May 1956.

41. *Williamsburg—The Story of a Patriot*, Paramount Pictures, 1957; Thad W. Tate, interview by author, tape recording, Williamsburg, Va., 17 May 1991. In "Stepping Outside the Classroom: History and the Outdoor Museum" (*Journal of American Culture* 12 [summer 1989]: 79–85), John Krugler indicated that students in his class who journeyed to Colonial Williamsburg and saw the film noticed little relation between it and the more sociohistorical aspect of the current restoration.

42. A. Edwin Kendrew, Oral History Collection, 2756, 2790, CWFA.

43. Remarks by Winthrop Rockefeller at a Dinner in Connection with the Opening of the New Motor House and the Premier of "Williamsburg—The Story of a Patriot," 30 March 1957, RG 3.2E, Box 150, Folder 1317, RFA; Kammen, *Mystic Chords of Memory*, 551.

44. Remarks by Winthrop Rockefeller.

45. *Virginia Gazette*, 13 May 1955.

46. Thad W. Tate, *The Negro in Eighteenth-Century Williamsburg* (Williamsburg: Colonial Williamsburg Foundation, 1965; fifth printing, 1990), ix–xi (page citations are to the fifth printing).

47. Ibid., 28.

48. Melvin E. Diggs to the Secretary, Colonial Williamsburg, 14 January 1954, Letters of Criticism, General Correspondence Records, CWFA.

49. Marjorie B. Robinson to JDR Jr., 10 May 1954, Letters of Criticism, General Correspondence Records, CWFA.

50. *Virginia Gazette*, 9 April 1955.

51. Kenneth Chorley to Broadus Mitchell, 22 April 1953, Letters of Criticism (reply), General Correspondence Records, CWFA.

52. Carol G. Williams to Kenneth Chorley, 25 October 1954, Letters of Commendation, General Correspondence Records, CWFA; Mrs. Samuel H. Oakley to Alma Lee Rowe, 30 October 1954, Letters of Commendation, General Correspondence Records, CWFA.

53. N. C. Morris to Thomas McCaskey, 7 November 1956, Letters of Criticism, Gen-

eral Correspondence Records, CWFA; C. Russell Doyle to Kenneth Chorley, 30 October 1959, Letters of Criticism, General Correspondence Records, CWFA.

54. *New York Times*, 15 June 1958.
55. *New York Times*, 31 January 1960.
56. Daniel Boorstin, "Past and Present in America: A Historian Visits Colonial Williamsburg," *Commentary* 25 (January 1958): 1.
57. Ibid., 2–5.
58. Ibid., 6.
59. Ibid., 7.

6. Achieving Maturity

1. *New York Times*, 30 May 1965.
2. *New York Times*, 4 March 1962.
3. Jill Allen Mons to Colonial Williamsburg, May 1960, Letters of Commendation, General Correspondence Records, Colonial Williamsburg Foundation Archives (hereafter cited as CWFA), Williamsburg, Va.
4. John H. Eden Jr. to the Williamsburg Restoration, 27 August 1960, Letters of Commendation, General Correspondence Records, CWFA.
5. Mrs. James L. Oliver to Colonial Williamsburg, 21 January 1960, Letters of Commendation, General Correspondence Records, CWFA; Mrs. E. O. Reynolds to Colonial Williamsburg, March 1960, Letters of Commendation, General Correspondence Records, CWFA.
6. Carl A. Albrecht to Management, Colonial Williamsburg, Inc., 26 October 1961, Letters of Commendation, General Correspondence Records, CWFA.
7. T. Jasper Lowe to Winthrop Rockefeller, 15 September 1961, Letters of Commendation, General Correspondence Records, CWFA.
8. Marvin Frankel to Colonial Williamsburg, 18 April 1961, Letters of Criticism, General Correspondence Records, CWFA.
9. *Virginia Gazette*, 27 January 1961.
10. *New York Times*, 22 October 1961.
11. *New York Times*, 9 April 1961.
12. Martin L. Dolan to Thomas B. Schlesinger, 26 October 1962, Letters of Commendation, General Correspondence Records, CWFA; Robert C. Krantz to Nelson Rockefeller, 11 July 1962, Letters of Criticism, General Correspondence Records, CWFA.
13. Aaron W. Berg to Edward P. Alexander, 14 September 1962, Letters of Criticism, General Correspondence Records, CWFA; Edward P. Alexander to Aaron W. Berg, 12 October 1962, Letters of Criticism (reply), General Correspondence Records, CWFA.
14. Anne H. Cutler to Carlisle Humelsine, 9 May 1963, Letters of Criticism, General Correspondence Records, CWFA.
15. Marian G. Hittner to Winthrop Rockefeller, 15 November 1963, Letters of Criticism, General Correspondence Records, CWFA; E. L. Rose to Carlisle Humelsine, February 1964, Letters of Criticism, General Correspondence Records, CWFA.

16. *New York Times*, 22 September 1963; Philip Kopper, *Colonial Williamsburg* (New York: Harry N. Abrams, Inc., 1986), 208.

17. *New York Times*, 13 October 1963.

18. Florence Strand to Colonial Williamsburg, 19 August 1964, Letters of Commendation, General Correspondence Records, CWFA; Winifred B. Clayton to Williamsburg Restoration, 15 August 1964, Letters of Commendation, General Correspondence Records, CWFA.

19. *Virginia Gazette*, 22 February 1963.

20. Ivor Noël Hume, *Martin's Hundred* (New York: Alfred A. Knopf, 1982), 4–21; *New York Times*, 5 April 1964; *New York Times*, 4 January 1970; *Virginia Gazette*, 15 November 1963. See also Alexander O. Boulton, "The House of Many Layers," *American Heritage* 42 (May/June 1992): 82–89.

21. David Gebhard, "The American Colonial Revival in the 1930s," *Winterthur Portfolio* 22, no. 2–3 (1987): 117–19.

22. *New York Times*, 23 February 1962; *New York Times*, 5 April 1964.

23. *New York Times*, 28 May 1962; *New York Times*, 5 April 1964.

24. *Virginia Gazette*, 10 April 1964.

25. Rex M. Ellis, "Presenting the Past: Education, Interpretation, and the Teaching of Black History at Colonial Williamsburg" (Ed.D. diss., College of William and Mary, 1989), 153–55.

26. Ibid., 155–57.

27. *New York Times*, 1 May 1966.

28. *Colonial Williamsburg Official Guidebook and Map* (Williamsburg: Colonial Williamsburg, 1968), vii–viii.

29. Homer L. Pettengill to Colonial Williamsburg, 7 April 1968, Letters of Criticism, General Correspondence Records, CWFA; "Publick Observer," *Virginia Gazette*, May 1967.

30. "Publick Observer," *Virginia Gazette*, July 1968; *New York Times*, 23 June 1968; *New York Times*, 29 September 1968.

31. Mr. and Mrs. T. J. Kent Jr. to Colonial Williamsburg, 18 June 1969, Letters of Criticism, General Correspondence Records, CWFA.

32. Ann Agran to Colonial Williamsburg, May 1969, Letters of Criticism, General Correspondence Records, CWFA.

33. Mr. and Mrs. F. H. Bonaparte to Colonial Williamsburg, 4 December 1971, Letters of Criticism, General Correspondence Records, CWFA.

34. M. K. Walker to Colonial Williamsburg, April 1971, Letters of Criticism, General Correspondence Records, CWFA.

35. S. K. Stevens to Carlisle Humelsine, 11 June 1971, Letters of Criticism, General Correspondence Records, CWFA.

36. Donald H. Parker to Reed W. Edzek, 20 December 1971, General Correspondence Records, Letters of Criticism (reply), CWFA.

37. *Virginia Gazette*, 29 December 1972.

38. *Virginia Gazette*, 25 May 1973; *Virginia Gazette*, 28 December 1973; *Virginia Gazette*, 29 March 1974.

39. Sarah L. Fry to Carlisle Humelsine, 3 July 1971, Letters of Commendation, General Correspondence Records, CWFA; Francis J. Fazzano to Colonial Williamsburg, 24 February 1970, Letters of Commendation, General Correspondence Records, CWFA.

40. *New York Times*, 24 December 1972.

41. *New York Times*, 28 September 1975; Michael Wallace, "Mickey Mouse History: Portraying the Past at Disney World," *Radical History Review* 32 (1985): 34–40.

42. Henry Wiencek, *The Smithsonian Guide to Historic America: Southern New England* (New York: Stewart, Tabori and Chang, 1989), 150–53, 256–58.

43. Rita Jaros to Colonial Williamsburg, 1 November 1972, Letters of Criticism, General Correspondence Records, CWFA.

44. Vincent J. Mara to Colonial Williamsburg, 29 April 1975, Letters of Criticism, General Correspondence Records, CWFA; Mary Mullaney to Mr. Rockefeller, November 1975, Letters of Criticism, General Correspondence Records, CWFA.

45. Sallie Mathews to Colonial Williamsburg, 15 July 1976, Letters of Criticism, General Correspondence Records, CWFA.

46. Mrs. Charles R. Berlucci to City of Williamsburg, 28 April 1976, Letters of Criticism, General Correspondence Records, CWFA; "Publick Observer," *Virginia Gazette*, September 1973. See also Carroll Van West, "Greenfield Village: A Landscape for the Present, the Past . . . and of Mr. Ford," *International Journal of Museum Management and Curatorship* 8 (1989): 263–77.

47. *New York Times*, 1 October 1975.

48. Avrom Fischer to Colonial Williamsburg, 28 August 1976, Letters of Criticism, General Correspondence Records, CWFA.

49. Gladys Vanderbilt to Colonial Williamsburg, 17 August 1976, Letters of Criticism, General Correspondence Records, CWFA.

50. *New York Times*, 29 November 1976.

7. New Challenges

1. *New York Times*, 11 December 1977.

2. Cary Carson, "Teaching History at Colonial Williamsburg" (Williamsburg: Colonial Williamsburg Foundation, 1985), 4–6; Richard Handler and Eric Gable, *The New History in an Old Museum: Creating the Past at Colonial Williamsburg* (Durham, N.C.: Duke University Press, 1997), 67–69.

3. Philip Kopper, *Colonial Williamsburg* (New York: Harry N. Abrams, Inc., 1986), 223; Carson, "Teaching History at Colonial Williamsburg," 8.

4. *New York Times*, 17 June 1979.

5. Handler and Gable, *The New History in an Old Museum*, 69.

6. Rex Ellis, "Re: Living History: Bringing History into Play," *American Visions* 7, no. 6 (November/December 1992): 22–25.

7. *New York Times*, 8 February 1981; Carroll Van West and Mary Hoffschwelle, "'Slumbering on Its Old Foundations': Interpretation at Colonial Williamsburg," *South Atlantic Quarterly* 83 (September 1984): 157–59.

8. West and Hoffschwelle, "'Slumbering on Its Old Foundations,'" 159–60.

9. *New York Times*, 4 July 1982.

10. *New York Times*, 23 May 1983.

11. Ibid.; "Williamsburg: Historic Setting for Vital Talks," *U.S. News and World Report* 94 (30 May 1983): 18.

12. *New York Times*, 9 June 1985.

13. Michael Olmert, "Colonial Williamsburg Corrects the Record," *American Visions* 1, no. 5 (September/October 1986): 45–52.

14. Bob Vila, "Restoring America," *Popular Mechanics* 166 (May 1989): 110.

15. Diane Young, "Back to Their Future at Williamsburg," *Southern Living* 24 (March 1989): 140–44.

16. Elvira Delany, "Colonial Williamsburg: The Charm of Eighteenth Century Colonial Life Can Be Visited in This Quaint Virginia Town," *Travel Weekly* 46 (31 March 1987): 35–37.

17. *New York Times*, 12 September 1988.

18. Rex M. Ellis, "Presenting the Past: Education, Interpretation, and the Teaching of Black History at Colonial Williamsburg" (Ed.D. diss., College of William and Mary, 1989), 279–80, passim; *New York Times*, 12 September 1988.

19. *New York Times*, 11 February 1988.

20. Ellis, "Presenting the Past," 238–39; "the unenvied equals . . .," Cary Carson and Lorena Walsh, "Material Life of the Early American House Wife" (paper presented at the Women in Early America Conference, Williamsburg, Va., November 1981), quoted in Ellis, "Presenting the Past," 239.

21. Edward A. Chappell, "Social Responsibility and the American History Museum," *Winterthur Portfolio* 24, no. 4 (1989): 247–54.

22. Ibid., 254–64.

23. Vila, 107–8.

24. Ibid., 110–11.

25. *New York Times*, 16 December 1990.

26. Michael S. Durham, "The Word is 'Slaves': A Trip into Black History," *American Heritage* 42 (April 1992): 89–92.

27. *New York Times*, 8 October 1994; *New York Times*, 11 October 1994; *Philadelphia Inquirer*, 11 October 1994; Clarence Waldron, "Staged Slave Auction Sparks Debate on Slavery and Racism," *Jet* 86 (31 October 1994): 12–15.

28. Eric Gable and Richard Handler, "The Authority of Documents at Some American History Museums," *Journal of American History* 81 (June 1994): 119–36.

29. Cary Carson, "Lost in the Fun House: A Commentary on Anthropologists' First Contact with History Museums," *Journal of American History* 81 (June 1994): 137–45.

30. *New York Times*, 20 February 1994; Celia Barbor, "Dwelling in the Past," *Town and Country* 149 (November 1995): 184–90.

31. *Daily Press*, 30 May 1997; *Daily Press*, 31 May 1997.

32. *Daily Press*, 29 May 1997; *Daily Press*, 30 May 1997; *Daily Press*, 31 May 1997.

33. Ada Louise Huxtable, *The Unreal America: Architecture and Illusion* (New York: New Press, 1997), 15, 41.

34. *New York Times*, 26 January 1997; JeanMarie Andrews, "The Williamsburg Institute: Apprenticeship to the Past," *Early American Homes* 28 (August 1997): 13.

35. Peter Feuerherd, "Williamsburg: The Past Unchained," *Commonweal* 126 (5 November 1999): 31.

36. *Christian Science Monitor*, 2 September 1999.

37. *Daily Press*, 1 September 1999.

38. *Daily Press*, 2 October 1999.

39. Katherine Ashenburg, "Williamsburg Rethinks History," *New York Times*, 24 September 2000.

40. *Chicago Tribune*, 10 July 2000.

Epilogue

1. *Daily Press*, 27 August 1997.

2. David Kiley, "Shaking Off the Dust," *Brandweek* 38 (1 June 1998): 20.

3. *Daily Press*, 11 March 1996; *Daily Press*, 21 July 1999.

4. *Daily Press*, 23 April 1999; *Daily Press*, 12 May 1999.

5. Eric Gable and Richard Handler, "In Colonial Williamsburg the New History Meets the Old," *Chronicle of Higher Education* 45 (30 October 1998): B10.

Further Reading

These sources were consulted in the course of research but are not cited in the endnotes.

Alexander, Charles C. *Here the Country Lies: Nationalism and the Arts in Twentieth-Century America*. Bloomington: Indiana University Press, 1980.

Alexander, Edward P. *The Interpretation Program of Colonial Williamsburg*. Williamsburg: Colonial Williamsburg Foundation, 1971.

Bellah, Robert N. *The Broken Covenant: American Civil Religion in Time of Trial*. New York: Seabury Press, 1975.

Biles, Roger. *The South and the New Deal*. Lexington: University Press of Kentucky, 1994.

Billings, Warren M., John E. Selby, and Thad W. Tate. *Colonial Virginia: A History*. White Plains, N.Y.: KTO Press, 1986.

Blatti, Jo, ed. *Past Meets Present: Essays about Historical Interpretation and Public Audiences*. Washington, D.C.: Smithsonian Institution Press, 1987.

Blum, John Morton. *V Was for Victory*. New York: Harcourt Brace Jovanovich, 1976.

———. *Years of Discord: American Politics and Society, 1961–1974*. New York: W. W. Norton and Co., 1991.

Bodnar, John, ed. *Bonds of Affection: Americans Define Their Patriotism*. Princeton: Princeton University Press, 1996.

———. *Remaking America: Public Memory and Commemoration in Twentieth Century America*. Princeton: Princeton University Press, 1992.

Boorstin, Daniel J. *Hidden History: Exploring Our Secret Past*. New York: Random House, 1987.

Boyer, Paul. *By the Bomb's Early Light: American Thought and Culture at the Dawn of the Atomic Age*. New York: Pantheon, 1985.

Bridenbaugh, Carl. *Jamestown, 1544–1699*. New York: Oxford University Press, 1980.

Brown, Kathleen M. *Good Wives, Nasty Wenches, and Anxious Patriarchs: Gender, Race, and Power in Colonial Virginia*. Chapel Hill: University of North Carolina Press, 1996.

Brown, Robert E., and B. Katherine Brown. *Virginia 1705–1786: Democracy or Aristocracy?* East Lansing: Michigan State University Press, 1964.

Campbell, Helen J. *Diary of a Williamsburg Hostess*. New York: Putnam, 1946.

Coben, Stanley. *Rebellion against Victorianism: The Impetus for Cultural Change in 1920s America*. New York: Oxford University Press, 1991.

Commager, Henry Steele. *The Empire of Reason: How Europe Imagined and America Realized the Enlightenment*. Garden City, N.Y.: Doubleday, 1977.

Craven, Wesley Frank. *The Legend of the Founding Fathers*. Ithaca, N.Y.: Cornell University Press, 1956.

———. *White, Red, and Black: The Seventeenth Century Virginian*. Charlottesville: University Press of Virginia, 1971.

Cunliffe, Marcus. *George Washington: Man and Monument*. Boston: Little, Brown and Co., 1958.

———. *In Search of America: Transatlantic Essays, 1951–1990*. Westport, Conn.: Greenwood Press, 1991.

Curti, Merle. *The Roots of American Loyalty*. New York: Columbia University Press, 1946.

Dain, Norman. *Disordered Minds: The First Century of Eastern State Hospital in Williamsburg, Virginia, 1766–1866*. Williamsburg: Colonial Williamsburg Foundation, 1971.

Degler, Carl N. *Place over Time: The Continuity of Southern Distinctiveness*. Baton Rouge: Louisiana State University Press, 1977.

Dent, Gary L. "Williamsburg: The Life, Death, and Rebirth of an Early American Town and Capital." D.A. diss., Catholic University of America, 1985.

Dowdy, Clifford. *Virginia Dynasties: The Emergence of "King" Carter and the Golden Age*. Boston: Little, Brown and Co., 1969.

Eaton, Clement. *A History of the Old South*. 2nd ed. New York: Macmillan, 1966.

Fabre, Genevieve, and Robert O'Maelly, eds. *History and Memory in African-American Culture*. New York: Oxford University Press, 1994.

Fischer, David Hackett. *Albion's Seed: Four British Folkways in America*. New York: Oxford University Press, 1989.

Fitch, James Marston. *Historic Preservation: Curatorial Management of the Built World*. Charlottesville: University Press of Virginia, 1990.

Flynn, John T. *God's Gold: The Story of Rockefeller and His Times*. New York: Harcourt, Brace and Co., 1932.

Fosdick, Raymond B. *The Story of the Rockefeller Foundation*. New York: Harper and Row, 1952.

Franceo, Barbara. "The Communication Conundrum: What is the Message? Who is Listening?" *Journal of American History* 81 (June 1994): 151–63.

Franklin, John Hope, and Alfred A. Moss Jr. *From Slavery to Freedom: A History of Negro Americans*. 6th ed. New York: Alfred A. Knopf, 1988.

Fried, Richard M. *Nightmare in Red: The McCarthy Era in Perspective*. New York: Oxford University Press, 1990.

Frisch, Michael. *A Shared Authority: Essays on the Craft and Meaning of Oral and Public History*. Albany: State University of New York Press, 1990.

Gable, Eric, Richard Handler, and Anna Lawson. "On the Uses of Relativism: Fact, Conjecture, and Black and White Histories at Colonial Williamsburg." *American Ethnologist* 19 (November 1992): 791–805.

Glassberg, David. *American Historical Pageantry: The Uses of Tradition in the Early Twentieth Century*. Chapel Hill: University of North Carolina Press, 1990.

Gonzalez, Donald J. *The Rockefellers at Williamsburg*. McLean, Va.: EPM Publications, 1991.

Goodwin, Doris Kearns. *No Ordinary Time—Franklin and Eleanor Roosevelt: The Home Front in World War II*. New York: Simon and Schuster, 1994.

Goodwin, Rutherfoord. *A Brief and True Report Concerning Williamsburg in Virginia*. Richmond: Dietz Press, 1940.

Goodwin, W. A. R. *The Record of Bruton Parish Church*. Richmond: Dietz Press, 1941.

Graebner, William S. *The Age of Doubt: American Thought and Culture in the 1940s*. Boston: Twayne Publishers, 1990.

Green, Harvey. *The Uncertainty of Everyday Life, 1915–1945*. New York: HarperCollins, 1992.

Greene, Jack P. *The Intellectual Construction of America*. Chapel Hill: University of North Carolina Press, 1993.

Halberstam, David. *The Fifties*. New York: Villard Books, 1993.

Halbwachs, Maurice. *On Collective Memory*. Edited by Lewis Coser. Chicago: University of Chicago Press, 1992.

Hawk, David Freeman. *Everyday Life in Early America*. New York: Harper and Row, 1988.

Hawley, Ellis. *The Great War and the Search for a Modern Order: A History of the American People and Their Institutions, 1917–1933*. New York: St. Martin's Press, 1979.

Heinemann, Ronald L. *Depression and the New Deal in Virginia: The Enduring Dominion*. Charlottesville: University Press of Virginia, 1983.

Hofstadter, Richard. *Anti-Intellectualism in American Life*. New York: Alfred A. Knopf, 1963.

Horan, John F., Jr. "Will Carson and the Virginia Conservation Commission, 1926–1934." *Virginia Magazine of History and Biography* 92 (October 1984): 391–415.

Hosmer, Charles B. "Historic Preservation, Tourism, and Leisure." *Monumentum* 13 (1976): 81–92.

Hudson, Kenneth. *Museums of Influence*. New York: Cambridge University Press, 1987.

Jenkins, Edward C. *Philanthropy in America: An Introduction to the Practices and Prospects of Organizations Supported by Gifts and Endowments, 1924–1948*. New York: Association Press, 1950.

Johnson, Gerald W. *Mount Vernon: The Story of a Shrine*. Mount Vernon, Va.: The Mount Vernon Ladies' Association, 1991.

Kammen, Michael. *American Culture, American Tastes: Social Change and the Twentieth Century*. New York: Alfred A. Knopf, 1999.

Karl, Barry. *The Uneasy State: The United States from 1915 to 1945*. Chicago: University of Chicago Press, 1985.

Karnow, Stanley. *Vietnam: A History*. New York: Penguin Books, 1997.

Kennedy, David M. *Freedom from Fear: The American People in Depression and War, 1929–1945.* New York: Oxford University Press, 1999.

Kerber, Linda K. *Women of the Republic: Intellect and Ideology in Revolutionary America.* Chapel Hill: University of North Carolina Press, 1980.

Kert, Bernice. *Abby Aldrich Rockefeller: The Woman in the Family.* New York: Random House, 1993.

Klein, John William. "The Role and Impact of Rockefeller Philanthropy during the Progressive Era." Ph.D. diss., Fordham University, 1980.

Krugler, John D. "Behind the Public Presentations: Research and Scholarship at Living History Museums of Early America." *William and Mary Quarterly* 48, no. 3 (1991): 347–85.

Kulikoff, Allan. *Tobacco and Slaves: The Development of Southern Cultures in the Chesapeake, 1680–1800.* Chapel Hill: University of North Carolina Press, 1986.

Lears, T. J. Jackson. *No Place of Grace: Antimodernism and the Transformation of American Culture, 1880–1920.* New York: Pantheon Books, 1981.

Leuchtenberg, William. *Franklin D. Roosevelt and the New Deal, 1932–1940.* New York: Harper and Row, 1963.

———. *The Perils of Prosperity, 1914–1932.* Chicago: University of Chicago Press, 1958.

Lindgren, James M. *Preserving Historic New England: Preservation, Progressivism, and the Remaking of Memory.* New York: Oxford University Press, 1995.

———. "'Virginia Needs Living Heroes': Historic Preservation in the Progressive Era." *Public Historian* 13 (winter 1991): 9–24.

Longmore, Paul K. *The Invention of George Washington.* Berkeley: University of California Press, 1988.

Lowenthal, David. *The Past Is a Foreign Country.* Cambridge, England: Cambridge University Press, 1985.

Maclean, Nancy. *Behind the Mask of Chivalry: The Making of the Second Ku Klux Klan.* New York: Oxford University Press, 1994.

McCullough, David. *Truman.* New York: Simon and Schuster, 1992.

Middlekauff, Robert. *The Glorious Cause: The American Revolution, 1763–1789.* New York: Oxford University Press, 1982.

Moger, Allen W. *Virginia: Bourbonism to Byrd, 1870–1925.* Charlottesville: University Press of Virginia, 1968.

Morgan, Edmund S. *American Slavery, American Freedom: The Ordeal of Colonial Virginia.* New York: W. W. Norton, 1975.

———. *Inventing the People: The Rise of Popular Sovereignty in England and America.* New York: W. W. Norton, 1988.

Nash, Gary. *Red, White, and Black: The Peoples of Early North America.* 4th ed. Upper Saddle River, N.J.: Prentice Hall, 2000.

Nevins, Allan. *John D. Rockefeller: Industrialist and Philanthropist.* 2 vols. New York: Charles Scribner's Sons, 1953.

Newhall, Nancy. *A Contribution to the Heritage of Every American: The Conservation Activities of John D. Rockefeller, Jr.* New York: Alfred A. Knopf, 1957.

Noël Hume, Ivor. *1775: Another Part of the Field.* New York: Alfred A. Knopf, 1966.

Norton, Mary Beth. *Founding Mothers and Fathers: Gendered Power and the Forming of American Society.* New York: Alfred A. Knopf, 1996.

Odendahl, Teresa. *Charity Begins at Home: Generosity and Self-Interest among the Philanthropic Elite.* New York: Basic Books, Inc., 1990.

Olmert, Michael. *Official Guide to Colonial Williamsburg.* Williamsburg: Colonial Williamsburg Foundation, 1989.

Painter, Nell Irvin. *Standing at Armageddon: The United States, 1877–1919.* New York: W. W. Norton and Co., 1987.

Patterson, James T. *Grand Expectations: The United States, 1945–1974.* New York: Oxford University Press, 1996.

Peterson, Merrill D. *Lincoln in American Memory.* New York: Oxford University Press, 1994.

Phillips, Kevin. *The Cousins' Wars: Religion, Politics, and the Triumph of Anglo-America.* New York: Basic Books, 1999.

Pitcaithley, Dwight T. "Historic Sites: What Can Be Learned from Them?" *History Teacher* 20, no. 2 (1987): 207–19.

Polenberg, Richard. *War and Society: The United States 1941–1945.* Philadelphia: J. B. Lippincott, 1972.

Pulley, Raymond H. *Old Virginia Restored: An Interpretation of the Progressive Impulse, 1870–1930.* Charlottesville: University Press of Virginia, 1968.

Rosenzweig, Roy. *Eight Hours for What We Will: Workers and Leisure in an Industrial City, 1870–1920.* New York: Cambridge University Press, 1983.

———. "Marketing the Past: *American Heritage* and Popular History in the United States." In *Presenting the Past: Essays on History and the Public,* edited by Susan Porter Benson, Steven Brier, and Roy Rosenzweig. Philadelphia: Temple University Press, 1986.

Rouse, Parke, Jr. *The City That Turned Back Time: Colonial Williamsburg's First Twenty-Five Years.* Williamsburg: Colonial Williamsburg Foundation, 1952.

———. *Cows on Campus: Williamsburg in Bygone Days.* Richmond: Dietz Press, 1973.

———. *Remembering Williamsburg: A Sentimental Journey through Three Centuries.* Richmond: Dietz Press, 1989.

Rutman, Darrett B., and Anita H. Rutman. *A Place in Time: Middlesex County, Virginia, 1650–1750.* New York: W. W. Norton and Co., 1984.

Schlereth, Thomas J. *Cultural History and Material Culture: Everyday Life, Landscapes, and Museums.* Ann Arbor, Mich.: UMI Research Press, 1990.

Schwartz, Barry. *George Washington: The Making of an American Symbol.* New York: Free Press, 1987.

Sealander, Judith. *Private Wealth and Public Life: Foundation Philanthropy and the Reshaping of American Social Policy from the Progressive Era to the New Deal.* Baltimore: Johns Hopkins University Press, 1997.

Selby, John E. *The Revolution in Virginia, 1775–1783.* Williamsburg: Colonial Williamsburg, 1989.

Sheehan, Bernard W. *Savagism and Civility: Indians and Englishmen in Colonial Virginia.* New York: Cambridge University Press, 1980.

Shi, David E. *The Simple Life: Plain Living and High Thinking in American Culture.* New York: Oxford University Press, 1985.

Sitkoff, Harvard. *The Struggle for Black Equality, 1954–1992.* New York: Hill and Wang, 1993.

Sobel, Mechal. *The World They Made Together: Black and White Values in Eighteenth-Century Virginia.* Princeton: Princeton University Press, 1987.

Stasz, Clarice. *The Rockefeller Women: Dynasty of Piety, Privacy, and Service.* New York: St. Martin's Press, 1995.

Stover, Kate F. "Is It *Real* History Yet?: An Update on Living History Museums." *Journal of American Culture* 12 (summer 1991): 13–17.

Susman, Warren I. *Culture as History: The Transformation of American Society in the Twentieth Century.* New York: Putnam, 1984.

Taylor, William R. *Cavalier and Yankee: The Old South and American National Character.* Cambridge, Mass.: Harvard University Press, 1979.

Teute, Fredrika J. "A Conversation with Thad Tate." *William and Mary Quarterly* 50, no. 2 (1993): 268–97.

Thelen, David. "Memory and American History." *Journal of American History* 75 (March 1989): 1117–29.

Tindall, George Brown. *The Emergence of the New South, 1913–1945.* Baton Rouge: Louisiana State Press, 1967.

Wallace, Michael. "Visiting the Past: History Museums in the United States." In *Presenting the Past: Essays on History and the Public,* edited by Susan Porter Benson, Steven Brier, and Roy Rosenzweig. Philadelphia: Temple University Press, 1986.

Ward, John L. *The Arkansas Rockefeller.* Baton Rouge: Louisiana State University Press, 1978.

Whitfield, Stephen J. *The Culture of the Cold War.* Baltimore: Johns Hopkins University Press, 1991.

Wolf, Stephanie Grauman. *As Various as Their Land: The Everyday Lives of Eighteenth Century Americans.* New York: HarperCollins, 1993.

Wood, Gordon S. *The Radicalism of the American Revolution.* New York: Alfred A. Knopf, 1992.

Zelinsky, Wilbur. *Nation into State: The Shifting Symbolic Foundations of American Nationalism.* Chapel Hill: University of North Carolina Press, 1988.

Index

Italic page numbers indicate illustrations